Praise for
Palm Beach, Mar-a-Lago, and the Rise of America's Xanadu

"A once-over-brightly jog through the history of Palm Beach . . . Once the enfeebled Flagler meets his maker by falling down marble steps at his Palm Beach mansion, the book takes off. Its richest portion centers on Marjorie Merriweather Post, the cereal heiress and magnate who began planning Mar-a-Lago in 1924 while married to financier E.F. Hutton." —*Wall Street Journal*

"A Florida tale always has unpredictable turns, and Les Standiford has the craftsmanship to guide us through in an utterly engaging way." —Mark Kurlansky

"The author of *Last Train to Paradise* tackles a topic that Palm Beachers know all too well: Mar-a-Lago. Standiford chronicles how the cereal heiress Marjorie Merriweather Post and her husband E.F. Hutton built the Gilded Age mansion that is now dubbed 'The Winter White House.'" —*Palm Beach Post*

"In this charming, zippy history of Palm Beach, Les Standiford charts the destination's fortune from its founding in the 1800s to the modern day." —*Town & Country*

"Delightful . . . Mr. Standiford details every significant residence, club, and hotel; every significant marriage and divorce (first, second, or beyond); and every significant architect and designer. He describes the social calendar, the fads that came and went, the inheritances that kept family names afloat . . . Edifying, energetic, and captivating." —*Florida Weekly*

"When there is a good story to tell, Les Standiford knows how to tell it great." —*FIU News*

"Standiford returns to the Floridian territory of the rich and famous that he chronicled in his biography of Henry Flagler, but this time the author will likely attract even more readers with the newly relevant Mar-a-Lago . . . Recounts the epic struggle of the ultrawealthy to transform what are now known as Palm Beach, Boca Raton, and Key West into a previously unimaginable enclave for conspicuous consumption." —*Kirkus Reviews*

"Mar-a-Lago immediately conjures references to Donald Trump. However, this detailed social history of Palm Beach, Florida, reveals that Mr. Trump is only one of the many celebrities, political figures, and mega-rich entrepreneurs associated with this exclusive enclave . . . This is enjoyable social voyeurism for those who hanker after tales of the rich and famous, past and present." —*Booklist*

"A readable history of the wealthy Americans who developed Florida for their vacationing pleasure . . . This chronicle focuses less on the personalities of the rich and famous and more on land acquisition and building, about which Standiford writes effortlessly . . . Will appeal to those interested in business history." —*Publishers Weekly*

PALM BEACH, MAR-A-LAGO,
AND THE RISE OF AMERICA'S XANADU

Jacket photographs (front): Mar-a-Lago gate, Library of Congress; Henry
Flagler © Alamy; Mrs. Joseph P. Kennedy, Mrs. Merriweather Post, and
Joseph Timilty at the Red Cross "Snow Ball" in Palm Beach, 1965 (State
Archives of Florida/Morgan); Marjorie Post Hutton courtesy of
University of Michigan Library Digital Collections. Bentley Image Bank,
Bentley Historical Library. Item number HS13908 (public domain);
Worth Avenue, Palm Beach, 1941 © Alamy
Jacket photograph (back): Mar-a-Lago, 1967

Published simultaneously in Canada
Printed in Canada

First Grove Atlantic hardcover edition: November 2019
First Grove Atlantic paperback edition: November 2020

ISBN 978-0-8021-5738-6
eISBN 978-0-8021-4645-8

Library of Congress Cataloging-in-Publication data is available for
this title.

Grove Press
an imprint of Grove Atlantic
154 West 14th Street
New York, NY 10011

Distributed by Publishers Group West

groveatlantic.com

20 21 22 23   10 9 8 7 6 5 4 3 2 1

For image credits, see page 319.

PALM BEACH, MAR-A-LAGO,

AND THE

RISE OF AMERICA'S XANADU

Les Standiford

Grove Press

New York

This is for Kimberly and for Jimbo.
I could not have done it without you.

Western facade of Mar-a-Lago as shown in a 1928 issue of American Architect.

In Xanadu did Kubla Khan
A stately pleasure-dome decree: . . .
A savage place! as holy and enchanted
As e'er beneath a waning moon was haunted
By woman wailing for her demon-lover!

—Samuel Taylor Coleridge, 1798

CONTENTS

Contents

AUTHOR'S NOTE

Aside from the White House, there may be no more prominent private residence in the United States than Mar-a-Lago, the nearly eighteen-acre Florida estate spanning southerly Palm Beach island from the Atlantic Ocean on the east to Lake Worth on the west. Mar-a-Lago, designed by Joseph Urban and built between 1924 and 1927 by cereal-empire heiress Marjorie Merriweather Post, contains 115 rooms in its main buildings and covers 62,500 square feet. It cost about $8 million to build, which equates to somewhere between $160 million and upwards of $1.5 billion currently, depending on whose conversion figures are used.*

Admittedly, there are more expansive mansions to be found. The Biltmore Estate, near Asheville, North Carolina, built in 1895 by George Washington Vanderbilt II, is said to be the nation's largest, with well more than twice the square footage of Mar-a-Lago. And perhaps nearly as famed is Hearst Castle, the former home of William Randolph Hearst, completed in 1947 and dominating a mountaintop near San Simeon, California. Hearst Castle comprises 68,500 square feet and ranks seventeenth in size to Mar-a-Lago's twentieth, which is just ahead of the Breakers, the getaway built by Cornelius Vanderbilt in Newport, Rhode Island, and covering 62,482 square feet.

* Conservative measures of comparison employing such indicators as the consumer price index would translate 1920 dollars by a factor of 18 to 20 times. However, a measure devised by Michael Klepper and Robert Gunther in their influential study *The Wealthy 100* makes such translations by comparing the value of an individual's estate relative to the totality of a nation's wealth (the gross national product) at the time. By their calculations, Andrew Carnegie's personal fortune, about $450 million in 1901, was worth $101 billion in present-day dollars. This volume will use the Klepper/Gunther measure primarily.

But size and dollars alone are not what set Mar-a-Lago apart. The others mentioned are known today primarily as museums and tourist attractions, even the Biltmore Estate, which remains in the hands of Vanderbilt descendants. Mar-a-Lago continues its use as a residence. And for all the days of its history, it has held the attention of the public because of those who have lived there, why they have chosen to live there, and what goes on within those formidable walls. Notably, even those who have chosen *not* to take up residence at Mar-a-Lago—and their reasons for turning down the opportunity—have consumed the attention of the nation's citizenry and its media, fomenting debate in both houses of Congress and demanding the attention of several U.S. presidents long before the current lord of the manor arrived.

As it approaches its hundredth anniversary, Mar-a-Lago has assumed a stature in the collective consciousness far larger than its physical bounds. Even on the relatively small island of Palm Beach, eighteen miles long and anywhere from five hundred feet to three-quarters of a mile wide, any number of grand domiciles and structures remain, including the still-standing Whitehall, the meticulously restored seventy-five-room, sixty-thousand-square-foot former home of Palm Beach founder Henry Flagler, as well as still-lived-in homes built for the Kennedys, the Du Ponts, and many other social luminaries. Also standing are the ornate 538-room Breakers Hotel, restyled by Italian craftsmen in 1926 after Rome's Villa Medici; the sprawling other-era Bath and Tennis Club, another Joseph Urban creation; and the fabled Everglades Club, the Paris Singer/Addison Mizner undertaking that sparked the island's emergence as the favored winter retreat for the ultraprivileged.

But none of those comprises the character of Palm Beach to the extent that Mar-a-Lago does. Mentioning Mar-a-Lago to a European, for instance, conveys an immense amount of cultural information instantaneously. This writer has experienced the same phenomenon only once before, during a tour of the Continent in the 1980s. All it took to dissolve cultural and linguistic barriers, even in the most forlorn hamlet, was the mention of Miami. "Ah, Miami," the listener would respond, puzzlement vanished, hand and forefinger quickly forming the universal likeness of a pistol. "Bang-bang! *Miami Vice*, ha ha!"

* * *

Fabulous Mar-a-Lago was from the beginning the perfect centerpiece for the community it anchors, a modern-day Xanadu symbolizing wealth and privilege and exclusivity. Unlike other retreats for the ultrafortunate, Palm Beach has been in existence for a relatively short time, having taken its shape over the course of little more than a century. And, unlike Newport or the Hamptons or Palm Springs, Palm Beach is relatively far-flung, having become what it is in a place where there previously was nothing but sand and sea and sky, located at the time of its founding in literal terra incognita.

Furthermore, what has taken place at Mar-a-Lago and in Palm Beach redefines our very concept of class distinction in the United States. There may have been a time when one demonstrated the blueness of one's blood by tracing the family lineage back to the *Mayflower* or to the Revolutionary War, but at about the same time that the walls were going up around the great estates on the island of Palm Beach, qualifications as to who really mattered here began to change. In the early years of the twentieth century, those who had assembled vast fortunes during the country's Gilded Age began to make their own claims to importance and distinction; and, along with ducal wealth, celebrity also became a new imprimatur of consequence.

Beyond such considerations, however, there is a distinctly human dimension to this story, for the high walls of Mar-a-Lago and other mansions like it were seemingly designed to contain scandal within as much as keep intruders out. Even the likes of Henry Flagler and Mary Lily Kenan Flagler, Marjorie Merriweather Post and E. F. Hutton, Joseph Kennedy and his many heirs, Douglas MacArthur, and on and on were not immune to the lapses common to humankind, even if some residents would prefer it otherwise: "There are certain things that are simply not discussed in public here," explains one longtime Palm Beacher.

This preference not to be in the news goes beyond avoidance of scandal. When Donald Trump, forty-fifth president of the United States, began to refer to Mar-a-Lago as the Winter White House, no chorus of communal pride arose. In the 1950s, Key West residents might have celebrated the visits of Harry Truman to his winter White House, as he proclaimed his quarters on their "Rock," but for many in Palm Beach—and never mind his sometimes simpatico politics—the glare of the spotlight that Trump's presence brought has been as much bane as blessing.

For this writer, what follows is an attempt to trace the record of an improbable dream of wealth and privilege carried from hand to hand, slowly working its way into shape, tempered by the intrigues of jealousy, greed, and the perpetual thirst for control. It is the tale of how an unlikely place was born from nothing and how that place in turn spawned the perfect domicile to represent and nourish it.

FLAGRANTE

When Marjorie Merriweather Post and E. F. Hutton completed the building of their signature Palm Beach mansion in 1927, it was considered a landmark achievement. Even in that otherworldly retreat for the ultraprivileged there had been nothing like exotic Mar-a-Lago, Spanish for "sea-to-lake," since the original mansion on the island, Henry Flagler's Whitehall, was constructed in 1902. But Whitehall was cool, elegant, and patrician, a seventy-five-room model of classical dignity designed by architects Carrère and Hastings in the Beaux-Arts style and meant to remind visitors of traditional bastions of privilege in Newport and other northern retreats. Mar-a-Lago was something of a fever dream: equal parts Mediterranean revival and set-designer fantasy, where architectural dicta gave way often to passion and fancy. Who would have expected otherwise when the architect was Ziegfeld Follies mastermind Joseph Urban?

Passion and fancy might have been the motto emblazoned on the couple's marital crest, in fact, for there was plenty of that trailing like fairy dust in their singular wake. She was heiress to the Postum cereal company fortune and one of the richest women in the world, he the mastermind of one of the largest brokerage houses in the country. Mar-a-Lago was a physical manifestation of their union, an enormous, impossible creation where a simple visit was an exercise in transcending the ordinary. In those times and in that place, there may have seemed no better purpose for their vast fortunes.

Hutton and Merriweather had met at the outset of the Roaring Twenties, he a widower, her first marriage a loveless exercise in escape from adolescence, and for a time theirs had seemed the ideal union: two larger-than-life individuals for whom sparks flew upon the instant of their meeting and who lit up the social scene of New York and Palm Beach in a way that made Scott and Zelda seem ordinary. But a number of things had changed. They had met when she was thirty-three and he a decade older. Now, she was approaching fifty, and Hutton was almost sixty. And while she was trending toward the matronly, he retained his dashing good looks and—so it was said—his eye for an attractive woman.

Marjorie had been made aware of the rumors that she at first dismissed as cattiness, as anyone in her position might well have. As a stout adherent of Christian Science philosophy, she was resolutely patient with Ned Hutton, whom she continued to find handsome, witty, and personable. As Mary Baker Eddy counseled in her *Science and Health*, "Human affection is not poured forth vainly, even though it meet no return . . . for Love supports the struggling heart until it ceases to sigh over the world and begins to unfold its wings for heaven."

Marjorie's own father had left her mother for a much younger woman, a betrayal that she could scarcely comprehend and one that would gnaw at her all her life. She had idolized her father, and he had let her down precipitously. And while she knew what treachery men were capable of, it seemed she could not do without one. Perhaps she thought she could change the leopard's spots by the sheer force of her will, which was considerable. Or perhaps she felt secretly unworthy, preordained to relive her punishment time and time again.

On the way down the aisle during her first marriage, to a man seemingly above her station, she had heard a dismissive remark from a member of the groom's family—*Sweet enough, given where she comes from,* was the gist of it—and she vowed then and there to make the speaker eat those words, however long it might take. But whatever the reasons, the defenses she erected to shield herself from Ned Hutton's infidelities would finally crumble.

Mrs. Eddy counseled, "The nuptial vow should never be annulled, so long as its moral obligations are kept intact." But ultimately Marjorie determined that her husband's unwillingness to "forsake all others" did in fact demand dissolution of their union. She would divorce him, but given that they were residents of New York, there could be no other grounds: she would need proof of his adultery.

Suspecting he was dallying with a newly hired French maid, Marjorie tied threads across the threshold of a doorway separating the maid's chambers from Hutton's bedroom. When that plan failed, she hit on a scheme that her gadget-inclined father might have approved: a set of lead plates and pulleys rigged to Hutton's bed and designed to ring a bell if the weight of two bodies was pressing vigorously on his mattress. But the clang of the bell never came.

Another woman might have decided to let well enough alone, but Marjorie was not one to waver. During their stay at Mar-a-Lago for the season of 1935, Marjorie took her husband's valet aside one morning and asked that he give the silk sheets of the master's bed a good dusting with talcum powder when the room was made up. Then, for good measure, she again went to fix a pair of slender threads across the threshold that divided the maid's room from her husband's.

That afternoon, when Ned Hutton seemed nowhere to be found, and the attractive young maid could not be summoned for a "Oui, oui, madame," Marjorie made her way to her husband's chambers and pulled open the door.

As to what she saw when the door swung open, court records detailing Ned Hutton's fierce denial of Marjorie's accusations remain sealed to this day. If she in fact found what she wished for—those threshold threads sundered, ghostly pairs of powdered footprints at his bedside, or something more salacious—we will never know.

All we can be sure of is that on September 7, 1935, following a shuttered hearing in a judge's chambers on Long Island, Marjorie's complaint was upheld. She was granted her request for divorce from E. F. Hutton on the grounds of adultery. She was freed, and a meteoric era in Palm Beach had come to an end.

- 1 -

NOUVEAU RICHE

On May 25, 1914, about two weeks after its writer had dressed himself in his Sunday finest, laid himself down in the master bedroom of his Santa Barbara mansion, and blown off the top of his head with a hunting rifle, the will of cereal magnate C. W. Post was filed for probate in Washington, D.C. On the following day, the *New York Times* reported details, noting that Post's widow and second wife, Leila, would receive something less than half of the $20 million estate, with the lion's share going to his daughter, Marjorie Post Close. Post's first wife, Ella, whom he divorced in 1904, had died in 1912.

That bequest might have seemed bounteous enough for Mrs. Close, then twenty-seven, but a follow-up *Times* story painted an even rosier picture. The estate had in actuality been found to be worth $33 million, the *Times* reported, and the second Mrs. Post, a former plant employee whom Post had married shortly after his divorce, had agreed to a $6 million settlement for her share, ceding daughter Marjorie the remaining $27 million and total control of the Post cereal empire.

"There is no trouble between Mrs. Close and myself," Leila Post told reporters. "I think too much of my late husband to have any differences with his daughter." No doubt, $6 million to a former factory secretary had a way of smoothing over any differences, but in any event, the settlement made Marjorie Merriweather Close—née Post—one of America's most wealthy and influential women on the instant, vaulting her into a prominence and a place of significance traditionally reserved for balding muttonchoppers in the waning years of the republic's Gilded Age.

In truth, however, Marjorie Post was neither an ordinary daughter of privilege nor a typical child of her time. As the only offspring of the eccentric C. W. Post, who had morphed a struggling Battle Creek, Michigan, health spa into a leviathan food company purveying the coffee substitute Postum and the breakfast cereal Post Toasties, she in essence became a substitute for the son he never had. From her preteen years, he included her in board meetings and furthermore encouraged her to voice her opinions on matters of importance, often quizzing her on various business decisions to be made.

Biographer William Wright recounts the story of a tearful Marjorie coming home one day to tell her father that a local tough had pushed her down as she crossed a vacant lot. "Well, we will see about that," the elder Post replied, dragging his daughter out the door. If Marjorie thought they were headed for a confrontation with the boy's parents, however, she was wrong. C. W. took her to the local gym where he told a trainer what had happened. "She needs boxing lessons," the cereal magnate said and left his daughter to the task. The next time the tough threatened Marjorie, she delivered a fabled uppercut that put an end to those depredations.

She and her father went hunting, shopped, and traveled the world together, and when Post lost his final battle with the recurring depression that had sent him to a Battle Creek sanatorium in the first place, Marjorie Post Close, at thirty-three, was well prepared to take over what was one of the country's most successful business enterprises.

Though steel barons or manufacturers of automobiles might turn up their noses at the idea of "cereal" as a product of substance, Post's millions spent just as nicely as theirs, and the

C.W. Post and daughter Marjorie, ca. 1889.

prospect of minding an empire tending to the physical well-being and gustatory pleasures of the republic would prove a natural fit for the outgoing, other-oriented Marjorie. Post had also left another valuable legacy to his daughter, one that would be the perfect complement to her business acumen. Money was made to be spent, according to C. W., and in doing so, she should trust no one's advice but her own. In order to achieve wise counsel, then, she would have to acquire the necessary knowledge herself. It was advice that stayed with Marjorie all her life, leading to an autodidact's approach to art history, shipbuilding, jewelry making, antiques, and much more. C. W., however, did not extend his warnings to cover her choices in men.

* * *

At the time when Marjorie began to transform from a precocious preteen into an attractive young woman, things had begun to change in the Posts' Battle Creek household. In 1901, as Marjorie was turning fourteen, C. W. had begun to look for ways to extend the reach of his business empire and lead his adopted city into prominence. That year saw him open the six-story, 135-room Post Tavern, billed as "the finest hotel between Chicago and Detroit," and soon afterward he added an office building and a theater to his downtown complex. Young Marjorie was pressed into service as a hostess at the Post Theatre's grand opening, delivering a rose to each lady seated in the boxes. Gossip had it that there was something more than a professional relationship between C. W. and his opening-night headliner, comic actress Maxine Elliott, but whatever the truth about that relationship, it was widely known that Marjorie's mother, Ella, was spending more and more time away from home, "traveling for her health," according to the newspapers.

Though Marjorie's Aunt Mollie, married to C. W.'s brother, Carroll, had stepped in as a surrogate mother, her father remained at the center of her world. And yet for all his doting, as a man of his day, C. W. Post was scarcely fit to discuss matters of the heart with an impressionable teenager, especially when his own marriage was considerably strained. The matter came to a head when, during one of his wife's tours of Europe, C. W. began an affair with Leila Young, a twenty-two-year-old secretary working at his company, whom he promptly installed as a paid companion to young Marjorie. Compounding the awkwardness, C. W. in 1902 pulled up stakes in Battle Creek to take up residence in Washington, D.C., where he installed Marjorie in a private boarding school while he stepped up his work lobbying on behalf of anti-labor legislation and other business ventures. Though Marjorie's mother would follow, she would set up a separate residence in the city.

According to biographer Nancy Rubin (*American Empress*), C. W. was not above putting his daughter in the middle of the difficulties between him and his wife, often complaining that he had no idea where Ella might be found and beseeching Marjorie to pass along mail and messages to her mother. At the same time, he began work on the construction of a new home in Greenwich, Connecticut, to be known as the Boulders, which would serve as a suitably magnificent domicile for an American business titan and his daughter.

Though the Boulders would not be completed until 1905, C. W. grew weary of his drear relationship with Ella and in 1904 filed for divorce. In a rather remarkable speech delivered to his Battle Creek employees at a testimonial dinner shortly after his remarriage in November of that year, C. W. spoke openly about the dissolution: "When scarcely out of our teens, the first Mrs. Post and I were married, and in less than a year found a childish mistake had been made." Post announced this to the gathering, then went on to say that the couple soon after their marriage decided to live apart for much of the time though they would keep up appearances in public. His wife's absences and the demands of his own business meant that young Marjorie would have to spend too much time alone, however, and for that reason, Post said, he sought out a companion for his daughter.

"Not a housekeeper," Post said, "but a companion that would see that she was warm, comfortable, and contented." The search for such a person led him to Leila Young, Post explained, and though she was originally employed some five years previously to come daily at noon and stay through the dinner hour, it soon became convenient for him to promote her to a position as his assistant, tending to correspondence, the preparation of his speeches, travel arrangements, and the like.

Leila became a virtual member of the family, Post said, before adding: "During those days, my friends, I caught glimpses of what a peaceful, contented home might be, if nature happened to supply the members of the home circle with temperaments that harmonized." Five years of such glimpses had led him to dissolve a loveless bond, Post declared, adding that he had settled a trust fund on his first wife "the income for life being enough yearly to keep a dozen families, and sufficient to indulge her desire for travel to any limit.

"She is happy and contented and we have had no occasions for the usual acrimonious contentions customary in separation," Post asserted. "On the contrary, I frequently hear of the kind expressions from her, and I have a steady and profound regard for the many sterling qualities of her character."

Unexpected as it had to have been, Post's address to his employees would end on an even more astonishing note. "The public generally seems to think a man of means should marry a wealthy society woman, and the so-called society paper that criticized me rather sneered at the fact that I married a new wife that was a poor girl and earned a living as my secretary and the fact that she ever worked seems to trouble it," he said, before finishing with a flourish. "I can't imagine what use I would have for a society pet that would drag an old work horse around nights to social functions and make him listen to the drool about the latest kind of necktie, cut of riding pants, and all the tiresome stuff the dudes feed on."

Though Post might have hoped this remarkable public confession would absolve him in the eyes of the world, and whatever its effects in that quarter, subsequent events suggest that it did not have an entirely salutary effect on his daughter. Previously, and owing to the lack of any real relationship between her father and her mother—not to mention the absence of any troublesome brothers—Marjorie had enjoyed the full attention of her larger-than-life and highly accomplished father. Now—at seventeen, and despite any assurances to the contrary—she found herself with a rival, if not an actual replacement.

* * *

As work on the Boulders progressed during this period, C. W. and Marjorie made regular inspection trips, often staying over at a Greenwich hotel. On one night in the summer of 1903, a by-then voluptuous, attractive, and elegantly dressed sixteen-year-old Marjorie found herself approached during a dance at the inn by a twenty-one-year-old Columbia Law School student named Edward Bennett Close. Somewhat plump and awkward, Close was no one's idea of a dreamboat, but his pedigree—his father a descendant of the original settlers of Greenwich, his mother a member of the Knickerbocker Brevoorts—was flawless. Within four days of their meeting, Close had proposed, and though Marjorie was hardly ready for such a prospect, the gears had been set in motion.

As Close persisted, Marjorie's frustration at her father's infatuation with Leila grew apace: "This creature who was only ten years older than I was," she would later exclaim. When her father remarried, C. W. was fifty, Leila twenty-seven. In an interview she granted nearly sixty years later, Marjorie well remembered her state of mind: "Did I have a mess on my hands after that. I was furious . . . I had twenty-seven boils that year. I was wild."

By the following spring, Close was graduated from Columbia and again proposed to Marjorie, who, as evidence of her father's betrayal, was sporting a newly appeared vivid streak of white in her hair. At this point, she was eighteen, graduated from the Mount Vernon School, and primed to begin a life of her own, with $2 million or more of trust funds already in the bank.

Edward Close might be no dashing man-about-town, but he was devoted and comfortably fixed. Furthermore, Marjorie had seen a father she thought she knew and could depend on transform himself virtually without warning into a Lothario. Close, on the other hand, had been described by one of his fellow Connecticut preppies as exactly the sort of man she would have been yearning for at the time: "A very nice fellow but the type of man who, unless you met him several times, you wouldn't remember him at all . . . He was not a dynamic man but a very kindly man."

In late August 1905, Close presented Marjorie with a stunner of a diamond from Tiffany, and on December 5, the two were wed in Manhattan's Grace Church in a smallish ceremony nevertheless hailed in the nation's society pages as one of the most important unions of the year. Though Marjorie's mother—perhaps put out at the speed with which she had been replaced—threatened a boycott of the wedding if C. W. brought his new wife along, she ultimately agreed to attend, promising to behave herself.

Close's father was deceased and his mother was incapacitated from a stroke, further reducing the size of the wedding, which went on without a reception, followed only by a photographer's session and the couple's departure by train for a honeymoon in Hot Springs, Virginia. Still, if there were not so many members in the Close entourage, one pair of matrons who did show up did their best to put the bride in her proper place. Marjorie later recounted to her son-in-law, the actor Cliff Robertson, that as she stepped down the aisle during the rehearsal, she heard the fateful words of one of the dowagers proclaiming to her friend in a voice loud enough to carry through the room: "Well, she's a cute little thing considering who she is and where she's from."

Such words might have done in a more vulnerable eighteen-year-old, but they had just the opposite effect on young Marjorie. She was hurt, she would tell Robertson during their conversation in the mid-1960s, but she was also equally infuriated. "I told myself, I'll show those sons of bitches if it takes me sixty years," she said. And then she leaned in toward her son-in-law and smiled. "And you know, Cliff, it *has* taken me sixty years."

On the train to Hot Springs, Marjorie showed her new husband a letter from her father, notifying her that he had purchased a hundred thousand dollars of bonds in her name as a wedding gift, and next, from another package, a set of keys dropped. Those keys would fit the lock on the door of the newly completed Boulders in Greenwich, now to be the wedded couple's home, a gift from Post. There also was a note from C. W. to Close admonishing him to take good care of his daughter and also a letter to Marjorie addressing the change of status in their relationship, which read in part: "It naturally brings a tinge of sadness to realize the little girl of the past with whom I had so many good times, has faded into the past, but I am more than comforted with the splendid young woman grown from my small pal of years ago . . . I feel very sure you are going to be happily married . . . Always remember that Daddy is somewhere around . . . and that he loves you."

The pair had enjoyed only a few days of their honeymoon, however, when another hiccup arose that was a portent of things to come: Close announced that it had been troubling him that Marjorie was (as was her father) a devotee of Christian Science, a rather suspect version of religion in the eyes of the Greenwich establishment. He would much prefer it if Marjorie would put all that nonsense behind her and join him in the practice of Episcopalianism. Once again, young Marjorie must have felt tremors in the very ground beneath her, but she stood up to her new husband. He might prefer "traditional religion," as he called it, and she was willing to attend Episcopal services with him, but as for herself, she was a Christian Scientist and that was that. He knew it before they married, she reminded him, and it would do him no good to quarrel about it now.

The moment passed, but in truth, Close never stopped pressuring Marjorie over what he perceived as a basic lack of sophistication, badgering her over such matters as her midwestern twang and her propensity to spend money on things he considered ostentatious. The birth of two daughters—Adelaide in 1908 and Eleanor in 1910—distracted the couple somewhat from their essential differences, and C. W. immediately set up substantial trust funds for the pair, often visiting the Boulders and injecting a bit of the old Post bravura into Marjorie's increasingly conventional existence.

C. W. and Leila had become inveterate world travelers when the magnate wasn't consumed with the affairs of Post City, a Texas model town he had developed, or badgering the houses of Congress over various excesses and fixes for the economic system. While the two divided their "downtime" between apartments in Washington, Battle Creek, the Blackstone Hotel in Chicago, and their newly discovered playground of Santa Barbara, Marjorie was becoming more and more the typical suburban housewife, tending to her two round-faced little girls and listening to her husband proclaim the virtues of the simple, comfortable life.

There is no telling how long the situation might have continued, but in December 1913, just as he was about to appear before a group in Philadelphia to deliver a speech excoriating Woodrow

Wilson and the impending new income tax legislation, C. W. Post was flattened by a severe outbreak of his chronic stomach troubles, the same issues that had sent him off to Battle Creek as an ailing, undistinguished salesman at thirty-seven, nearly a quarter of a century earlier. He and Leila went by train to Santa Barbara, where C. W. endured further bouts of stomach trouble that began to debilitate his spirit as well as his body.

Post had always lived in fear that his body would betray him and was soon proclaiming his own dire self-diagnosis. Nothing was going to help him out of this crisis, he assured Leila, for he was certain he had stomach cancer and the writing was clearly on the wall. As for C. W.'s doctors, they were not so sure about the cancer. He was in fact suffering from appendicitis, they told him, and he needed to be operated on immediately.

C. W.'s opposition to surgery had less to do with his status as a Christian Scientist than with his fear of being cut open by doctors, whom he scarcely trusted, but finally he was beaten into submission. In early March 1914, he agreed to travel by train to the Mayo Clinic in Rochester, Minnesota, there to be operated on by the famed Mayo brothers, William and Charles, the only members of the profession he regarded with the slightest confidence. The president of the Santa Fe Railway, a crony of his, sent a scout train ahead to clear the tracks for the engine pulling Post's private Pullman car, and newspapers across the country breathlessly covered the MILLIONAIRE'S RACE AGAINST DEATH.

Indeed, Post's train from Los Angeles arrived in record time and the Mayos removed his inflamed appendix, with both Leila and Marjorie in attendance. The doctors proclaimed the operation a success and told reporters Post would enjoy a speedy recovery. (Marjorie would later confide that the Mayos had shown her the inflamed organ, some sixteen inches long and "the worst thing you've ever seen.")

What could not be excised, however, was Post's long-dormant tendency toward depression. It is tempting to speculate from this position in time that despair was the very engine of his corresponding bursts of manic energy and euphoria that catapulted him to success. Still, if effectively treating bipolar disorder (as Post's problem might now be diagnosed) seems a monumental task today, it was a virtual impossibility at the time. The doctors at the Mayo Clinic sent Post home to Santa Barbara in mid-April 1914 with a warning to Leila and his caregivers: the mercurial entrepreneur was not to be left alone, and certainly he was not to be allowed access to any weapons.

For a time, relieved of his physical symptoms, Post seemed a changed man. He wrote to Charles Mayo that he was in the "very best of spirits" and felt on the road to a complete recovery. But within days, he had unaccountably descended again into a despair that seemed beyond his power to combat.

On the morning of May 9, Post called Leila to his room to discuss some details of their financial situation, then sent her downstairs to take care of some correspondence for him. When Leila left the house for the post office, Post asked his nurse, a woman named Ella Brown, if she mightn't leave the room while he tried to get some sleep. "My mind is perfectly clear," he told her. "But I cannot control my nerves."

With the nurse absent, Post sat down to compose a short letter to the women closest to him, the last part of which referenced a son stillborn to him and his first wife, Ella Letitia Merriweather, in December 1883, after eight years of marriage and some four years prior to Marjorie's birth:

> Forgive me dear Leila and Marjorie if any
> sentiment I have expressed is not in harmony with
> your own convictions.

I had to give vent to pent up feelings—
So I talked with our dear son—he seemed so near,
and perhaps suggested or helped me.
Oh! Happy soul!
So free from earth's
Grandeur and suffering.

Post next dressed himself in suit and tie and went to the closet where he had hidden a hunting rifle in circumvention of his doctors' orders. And then this man of great accomplishment, having lavished love and gifts of untold scope on many and having enjoyed a more than generous portion of the bounty that the world has to give, took the weapon to his bed, lay down, put the barrel in his mouth, and, as he could not manage it otherwise, pulled the trigger with a toe. In this way, and though the coroner ruled that the incident constituted "a fit of temporary insanity," he perpetuated one of the great riddles of our kind.

- 2 -

FINDING XANADU

Following her father's death, it would take more than six years for Marjorie to work her way out of her ill-advised first marriage to Edward Close and into a second such entanglement with legendary and libidinous stockbroker E. F. Hutton in 1920. And she could scarcely have foreseen herself turning into a virtual house detective into the bargain, just as she could never have imagined herself becoming the whispered-about grande dame of Palm Beach, Florida, if for no other reason than the fact that Palm Beach scarcely existed prior to the turn of the twentieth century.

The town was not incorporated until 1911 and had until the last decade of the nineteenth century existed as a nearly uninhabited adjunct of Lake Worth, the mainland community abutting its namesake body of water just to the south and west of Palm Beach. That "lake" was itself named after General William J. Worth, commander of U.S. forces during the latter part of the Second Seminole War, 1835–1842. The lake—officially designated as Lake Worth Lagoon—was once a body of fresh water fed by seepage from the Everglades and separated from the Atlantic by the barrier island on which Palm Beach is located, but man-made cuts to the north at the port of Palm Beach and about twenty miles farther south at Boynton Beach have turned the lagoon into a body of salt water that now forms a leg of the Atlantic Intracoastal Waterway, a protected course for watercraft that runs all the way from Boston to Brownsville, Texas.

The early white settlers in the Palm Beach area were drawn there after General Worth finally subdued the Seminoles in the region and Florida was designated the twenty-seventh state in 1845, eight years after Michigan and about eight months before Texas. The principal lure for those first Europeans was the Homestead Act of 1862, which offered 160 acres of public land free to anyone twenty-one years of age who had never taken up arms against the United States, including women and immigrants who had applied for citizenship. Blacks were not included until the Southern Homestead Act of 1866. All that was required was the willingness to build a home, cultivate the land, and live on the site for five years.

In the case of Palm Beach, it may be hard for the modern-day visitor to fathom that natural beauty had little to do with attracting settlers, for at that time, the area on the eighteen-mile-long barrier island separating Lake Worth Lagoon and the ocean was essentially nothing but a swamp. The earliest homesteaders, many of them budding tomato and pineapple farmers, built shelters on the shores of the lagoon side of the island and crossed over to the ocean—for fishing and bathing—on pathways fashioned from planks, anywhere from five hundred feet long at the island's narrowest to three-quarters of a mile at its widest, trails that threaded precariously through a tangle of Florida holly, mangrove, and thorny brush and vines, where alligators and mosquitoes (said to number "millions to the square inch") awaited. One oft-repeated story featured the unfortunate end of an unwary mule that walked into a cloud of mosquitoes that enveloped the poor creature like a million tiny bats, sucking at his juices until he keeled over into the muck, never to rise again.

A Confederate army deserter and former keeper of the Jupiter Lighthouse, Augustus Lang, is said to be the first white settler in Palm Beach, circa 1863. However, Lang never filed a claim on his land, and the palmetto shack in which he lived (framed from live oak and roofed and clad by the fronds of the low-growing palm) was taken over by a drifter come up from the shores of Biscayne Bay (Miami would not be incorporated until 1896) named Charlie Moore. Moore took up permanent residence in 1872, availing himself not only of the digs but of the lush gardens left behind by Lang, whose checkered background may or may not have included a stint as a gardener to the king of Prussia.

Lang, Moore, and the other Europeans who wandered into the area in the middle of the nineteenth century should not be regarded as its original settlers, however, for Native Americans had lived there from about 1000 BC. Based on analysis of artifacts recovered at a number of Native American burial mounds on the Florida mainland near Boynton Beach, the actual original settlers have been identified as a part of the Jeaga tribe, some two thousand of whom were scattered across what is now Palm Beach County, with Ais tribesmen living to the north and Tequesta occupying the south where Fort Lauderdale and Miami now sit.

Archaeologists contend that there were native tribesmen living in northern Florida as early as eleven thousand years ago—mastodon remains have been found in campsites in the Florida Panhandle—but they also speculate that tribes were probably as reluctant to combat the heat, the alligators, and the mosquitoes in

The lighthouse at Jupiter Inlet, about twenty miles north of Palm Beach, giving an idea of the landscape that Flagler encountered in the 1890s.

South Florida as were latter-day Europeans. We do know that the original name for Lake Worth Lagoon was Hypoluxo, a native term that translates to "water all around, no get out," a reference to the original landlocked character of the lake. Turtle shell and marine and other vertebrate remnants found in the Jeaga mounds suggest that they were a hunting and gathering tribe that practiced little agriculture.

The Jeagas lived in South Florida well into the eighteenth century, and the *Journal* of Dutch merchant Jonathan Dickinson contains a fascinating account of his party being shipwrecked and held captive by a band of Jeagas in 1696 near the present-day town of Hobe Sound. "We rejoiced at this our preservation from the raging sea," Dickinson wrote of learning his ship had run aground, "but at the same instant feared the sad consequences that followed." Dickinson and his party were well treated, though, passed along by the Jeagas to the Ais and eventually delivered to St. Augustine, where the Spanish took them in and arranged for their passage back to Philadelphia.

Would that the treatment of the Jeagas and other native tribes by the Spanish and other Europeans had been as benevolent, however. The beginning of the end for Florida's indigenous tribesmen came in 1513, with the Spaniard Ponce de León's arrival, which included stops near present-day St. Augustine, Cape Canaveral, and the Dry Tortugas. Though legend has it that the explorer was searching for a fountain of youth, it is just as likely that he was searching for gold and other objects of trade and commerce. His relations with the natives were relatively benign, but any number of far more zealous mercenaries followed in his footsteps, intent on deceptive trade, theft, murder, and outright enslavement of the local population, often introducing European diseases, including smallpox, which swept through the native camps with devastating effect. While there were said to be about twenty thousand Ais,

Jeagas, Calusa, Mayaimi, Tequesta, and other natives living in South Florida at the time of Ponce de León's first landfall in 1513, only two hundred to three hundred are believed to have remained by 1763, when Spain ceded control of Florida to England. Most of those still there at the time are said to have left for Cuba aboard boats manned by the Spanish.

Those original Native Americans were not the last to occupy Florida, for by 1750 other tribesmen from Georgia and Alabama were fleeing to the wilds of Florida in the face of similar assaults at the hands of European settlers. These Creeks, as Europeans referred to them, became known in their new Florida habitat as the Seminoles and Miccosukees and were gradually pushed down the Florida isthmus as European settlers tamed the state from north to south. The three wars waged by the U.S. government against the Seminoles between 1818 and 1858 reduced the tribe to about three hundred residents left hiding in the swamps by the end of those "Indian campaigns."*

Against this backdrop, development in South Florida began in earnest during the final decade of the nineteenth century, when northerner Henry Flagler—former partner of John D. Rockefeller and one of the great accumulators during the nation's Gilded Age—arrived in Palm Beach for a look-see. As for the place Flagler was seeking, what had been called vaguely the lake district had at least acquired a name since the days of Lang and Moore. On January 9, 1878, the good ship *Providencia*—bound from Trinidad to Cádiz, Spain, and carrying some twenty thousand coconuts—ran ashore on the barrier island where only a few settlers had yet followed their hardy predecessors.

Those hoping to avail themselves of salvagers' rights to the ship's cargo hurried down to the shore to find the ship intact but the

---

* Census figures today show that the tribe has recovered to more than two thousand members, living on six reservations comprising about ninety thousand acres of land with various enterprises, including the well-known Hard Rock Casinos generating more than a billion dollars in revenues annually.

captain and crew resigned to the need to off-load their cargo if the ship was to be saved, and soon pioneers Will Lanehart and H. F. Hammon had secured the rights to the jettisoned coconuts, which they peddled as best they could at two and a half cents apiece. While some of the fruit was actually sold, just as much of it was tossed aside.

As it turns out, coconuts require almost nothing by way of tending to sprout in the subtropics and soon the formerly scrub-covered barrier island between Lake Worth and the Atlantic was studded with a forest of fast-growing coconut palms. Nearly a decade later, in 1887, there were sufficient settlers in the "lake district" to allow for the installation of a post office, which petitioners hoped to designate as Palm City. When they discovered that the name had already been taken by another developing hamlet thirty or so miles to the north, the pioneers settled on their next best suggestion: Palm Beach.

* * *

That a titan of Flagler's stature came to inspect such a far-flung destination was a decision that would not only change Florida but also redirect the attention of the nation itself. Flagler was no draft dodger or soldier of fortune skittering about the fringes of civilization in search of a safe haven or a foothold, but rather one of the nation's most successful businessmen, a major ally of John D. Rockefeller in the formation of Standard Oil during the last half of the nineteenth century, or "the brains" behind the outfit, as Rockefeller said of him.

In the late 1860s, Rockefeller, then a young grain and kerosene merchant in Cleveland, Ohio, was looking for a partner to join him on a venture into the burgeoning new business of petroleum spirits, a substance most were hailing at the time not as a motor fuel or a lubricant but as a replacement for a worsening shortage of whale oil, which in that preelectrical age was the preferred fuel for lamps. He found his man in Henry Flagler, a detail-oriented thinker who was the perfect counterpart to the other-oriented natural sales-man Rockefeller. For his part, Flagler, the son of an impoverished minister from rural New York, was an up-by-his-own-bootstraps entrepreneur, who had met and befriended Rockefeller while marketing corn from a merchant relative's silos near Toledo.

At the outset of the Civil War, Flagler cobbled together $50,000 of his own and convinced friends and relatives to lend him an equal amount, this to be invested in a salt-mining enterprise in Michigan. Flagler's intention was to make a fortune by selling salt to the Union army for the purposes of preserving its food, disregarding the fact that he knew nothing of the business of salt mining. When the enterprise unsurprisingly failed, Flagler found himself back in northwestern Ohio after the war ended, broke and dispirited and thinking he might look up Rockefeller—with whom he had become close during their grain-bartering days—for advice on what to try next.

What Rockefeller had to suggest would forever change the world. The two soon became a matchless business team, and within a few short months they had begun a process of consolidation among the mom-and-pop refineries of northern Ohio that would one day become the most powerful business enterprise ever assembled: Standard Oil.

By Rockefeller's own accounts Flagler's "vim and push" were responsible for the company's rise. "He invariably wanted to go ahead and accomplish great projects of all kinds . . . and to his wonderful energy is due much of the rapid progress of the company in the early days," Rockefeller wrote. Although one producer's oil was pretty much equal in quality to another's while sitting in tanks near the wellhead, Flagler came up with the idea of negotiating favorable terms with rail lines whose tankers would transport their raw product to refineries and from thence to market, and his ideas on the strategy of incorporating what was the same business entity in separate states—Standard Oil of Ohio, of Pennsylvania, and so on—proved another invaluable aid to the leviathan's rise.

When the original Standard Oil Company went public in 1870, it was capitalized at $1 million with ten thousand shares offered. Rockefeller took about twenty-six hundred of those and Flagler about half that. By 1882, the company's net worth had grown to more than $82 million, meaning that Flagler's original $130,000 had grown to nearly $11 million. With most of the competition squeezed out, Flagler and Rockefeller's undertaking had outstripped its Cleveland roots and the two moved their offices and their homes to New York, the nexus of the new American commerce where other such moguls had set up shop, including railroader Cornelius Vanderbilt, financier John Jacob Astor, and department store chieftain Alexander T. Stewart, who made about $2 million a year from his famed Iron Palace and other retail undertakings.

Despite his spectacular business success, Flagler's true introduction to the grand style of living came in the early 1880s when his first wife, Mary, died of complications from tuberculosis. With his eleven-year-old son, Harry, still living at home, Flagler determined that a Manhattan apartment, no matter how luxurious, was not the proper place for child rearing. After some research, he settled on the purchase of a vast forty-two-room wooden home called Lawn Beach, part of a thirty-two-acre estate at Satan's Toe in Mamaroneck, New York, on the north shore of Long Island Sound.

There, at age fifty-two, Flagler threw himself into nest building in earnest, leading a complete renovation of the estate, picking out interior fixtures, building a two-hundred-foot breakwater, and trucking in sand for a private beach along the shore, turning it into a destination that friends and business associates delighted in visiting. For the first time, Flagler was experiencing just how practically his vast fortune might change the quality of his life and was taking pleasure in an undertaking that did not have anything to do with work.

At about the same time, public pressure was mounting against the high-handed business tactics that Flagler and Rockefeller, steel baron Andrew Carnegie, and other moguls had used to construct virtual monopolies within their respective arenas. Flagler was being summoned regularly to defend Standard Oil before Senate antitrust committees, where one attorney called him out personally as a thief and a robber. Whole political parties were being formed on antitrust platforms—including the Greenback, Labor, and Prohibition parties—and industrialized states that had once welcomed the development spawned by oil, steel, and railroading were now pushing anti-monopoly slates through their legislatures.

With the worth of Standard Oil soon to reach $150 million and his own holdings hovering in the neighborhood of $20 million, Flagler determined that there was little reason to subject himself to scorn on a regular basis, and he did something that few men whose lives are defined by such highly successful business careers have done: he simply stepped out of harness.

There is no agreement on just how they met: Flagler's first biographer, Sidney Walter Martin, insists Ida Alice Shourds was a practical nurse who provided care for Mary during her illness, while Flagler's son Harry Harkness suggests she was an aspiring actress and that there was a more salacious beginning to the relationship. But it is undisputed that shortly after his wife's death, Flagler became seriously involved with Ida Alice, a woman twenty years his junior. She was described by contemporaries as an outgoing, full-figured redhead with piercing blue eyes and a hard-to-dismiss personality. And just as the rough-about-the-edges Ida Alice had the same sort of humble beginnings as the unlikely companion with whom C. W. Post would take up, Flagler was similarly unconcerned with the opinions of his friends and associates. In June 1883—Flagler at fifty-three and Shourds at thirty-five—the two were married.

His business interests dictated a delay in the couple's extended honeymoon until December, but Flagler had an idea all along of the perfect destination. He would take his new bride back to Jacksonville, Florida, where in the 1870s he and Mary had enjoyed the occasional pleasant respite in weather that was conducive to her health and salubrious for Flagler, a midwesterner through and through who until that time had never seen a beach or a palm tree. Located just below the Georgia border on the Atlantic, Jacksonville was about as far southward as one could easily travel by rail at the time. While there, though, Flagler and Ida Alice took a sailboat ride about forty miles farther down the St. Johns River to visit St. Augustine, which, continuously inhabited since the days of the Spanish explorers in 1565, constitutes the oldest European city in the United States.

The Flaglers lingered in Jacksonville until March 1884 and were so taken with the area that they returned to vacation there the following winter. However, if Flagler was finally learning how to enjoy himself, he still had not shed all his old instincts, for he had learned in the interim since his last visit that a new hotel, the 275-room San Marco, was going up on the waterfront in St. Augustine, a development that would lead Flagler to formulate some ideas of his own.

In 1885, the population of Jacksonville had not yet reached 17,000 and, just to the south, the whole of St. Johns County, of which St. Augustine was the seat, contained just 5,714 citizens, with the principal occupation of those being the growing of citrus fruit and vegetables. The layout of St. Johns County is not unlike that of Palm Beach: it rests on a narrow peninsula bounded by the St. Johns River on the west and the Atlantic Ocean on the east, with arable land bordering the river, giving way to pinelands a few hundred yards inland and turning to palmetto scrub from thence to the ocean. A census report of the time of Flagler's initial visits states: "Much of the land is, and probably must remain, worthless."

On their second trip to the area, the Flaglers traveled in his newly acquired private Pullman car from New York to Jacksonville, a two-day rail journey at the time. That luxurious car would have to stay on a siding in Jacksonville, though, for the newly constructed Jacksonville, St. Augustine and Halifax River Railway—which would take them the next thirty or so miles of their journey—consisted of narrow-gauge track incompatible with the standard rigging of Flagler's car. Thus, the couple were ferried across the St. Johns from Jacksonville to South Jacksonville to board the new train, which chugged down to a depot in north St. Augustine. Including the carriage rides to and from their hotels, the forty-mile trip took an entire day.

Still the Flaglers enjoyed their stay, especially the San Marco, which with its presumptions toward "resort" status was a decided upgrade over the small, utilitarian hotels they had found in St. Augustine previously. The couple extended their time there so they could attend a festival in early March celebrating the landing of Ponce de León, and before long Flagler was scouting the area for a likely site where he might build a hotel of his own, reasoning that if he enjoyed St. Augustine, others of means would as well if there were a destination worth the trouble of reaching the place.

Given his prodigious means, it is generally agreed that Flagler was motivated less by visions of profit than by his own remarks that he simply wished to share the pleasures of the area with others, as well as to spend some of his money creating opportunity for the area. In any case, before his return to New York in April, he had purchased a marshy, underperforming section of orange groves from pioneering physician Dr. Andrew Anderson, and by the summer of 1885 he had commissioned the enterprising young architects John M. Carrère and Thomas Hastings to work on a grand design for what would become the 450-room Hotel Ponce de Leon. (That pair would go on from what was their first significant commission to design the New York Public Library, the Henry Clay Frick House, and many more buildings.)

Asked by an acquaintance why he was undertaking such a project, Flagler responded by telling a joke about a teetotaling parishioner questioned by his pastor as to why he had gone on an uncharacteristic drinking spree. "I've been giving all my days to the Lord up to this point," the man said. "And now I'm taking one for myself." Flagler was claiming the same privilege, he explained. "For about 14 or 15 years, I have devoted my time exclusively to business, and now I am pleasing myself."

For all that, and while Flagler was never one to turn down a business deal that made sense to him, his interest in railroading was primarily limited to the use he could make of the lines in expanding a hotel empire. The opulent Ponce de Leon, with twenty-four-karat gold trim, the largest incandescent lighting system extant, and seventy-nine stained glass windows by Tiffany, opened to great acclaim in 1888, establishing Flagler's unbreakable bond with Florida (he would build a home he called Kirkside nearby, in 1893).

He would also add the somewhat more modest Alcazar Hotel, a seventy-five-room establishment that opened in 1889, and in that same year he bought out a budding competitor, the Casa Monica, which had opened its doors the year before. A story that makes the rounds to this day has it that the Casa

Monica was doomed from the time of its grand opening, a ceremony that had to be rescheduled owing to a mysterious delay in the delivery of the new establishment's furnishings. Somehow, it seems, those furnishings were mislaid by the carrier, an entity known as the Jacksonville, St. Augustine and Halifax Railway, H. M. Flagler, proprietor.

Whether or not Flagler would stoop to blocking delivery of a competitor's bedframes is a matter of conjecture, but anyone thinking of going up directly against the man who was seen as the modern-day equivalent of Ponce de León would have had to give the matter serious thought. Another oft-told tale concerning a Florida settlement with pretentions to success suggests what a formidable opponent he could be. In 1893, Flagler's line had been extended as far south as Rockledge, located across the Indian River Lagoon from Cape Canaveral, about eighty miles south of Daytona Beach. Though the main line was located on higher ground just west of the settlement, Flagler had agreed to build a spur that ran directly to the middle of town and a depot located between the four-hundred-room Indian River Hotel and the three-hundred-room Plaza, built by developers inspired by Flagler's success.

Though the arrival of the railroad made local developers giddy (and made such edifices as the Indian River and Plaza viable entities), relations between the town and Flagler would eventually sour. Some accounts have it that the town withheld payments due Flagler for freight being hauled on the spur, part of an effort to negotiate more favorable carriage rates from the mogul. Others say that Flagler was piqued by the refusal of his offer to buy the desirable Plaza Hotel as an addition to his portfolio. If the cause is uncertain, there is no disputing what finally happened. In the middle of one night in 1908, a work car arrived at the end of the spur in Rockledge and a great racket ensued, waking a number of guests in the hotels bracketing the depot. Though it was too dark to see exactly what was going on, with daybreak came the answer. The work car had left, having literally rolled up the rails of the spur in its wake. The Rockledge spur had vanished overnight and never would return, leaving the once vibrant resort to languish until the 1960s, when it would enjoy a rebirth as a bedroom community for the burgeoning space center at Cape Canaveral.

Many such stories—in keeping with Flagler's record as a hard bargainer for Standard Oil and his own interests—still circulate, and the tales make for undeniably good copy, even if they are as much legend as fact. One might wonder just how much time he had to give over to vengeful activities in the midst of an

Work crews encounter the watery right-of-way for
Flagler's Oversea Railway, ca. 1909.

ever-burgeoning expansion of his holdings. But in this instance, court records are indisputable, and Flagler's seeming impetuousness in this case cost him. In 1909, the Florida East Coast Railway, as Flagler's enterprise had become known, agreed to pay the owners of the former Rockledge spur right-of-way $15,000 for abrogating their agreement to run trains from the main line to the downtown Rockledge depot.

* * *

If Flagler was destined never to operate a hotel in Rockledge, however, this was no bar to his expansion elsewhere. In 1890, the year after he bought out the Casa Monica, he extended his hotel empire southward from St. Augustine to Ormond, about fifty miles south of the ancient city and just north of Daytona Beach, where his rail line ended at the time. The Ormond Hotel had been built by a trio of northerners who had also invested in orange groves in the then remote area. The seventy-five-room hotel was an unimposing, homey-looking wooden structure on land bordered by the Halifax River on the west and the Atlantic on the east and had struggled since its opening in 1888. Flagler took it off the hands of the more than willing developers and expanded the building and its facilities, adding an eighteen-hole golf course. Though Flagler had never picked up a club, he understood the growing popularity of the sport among the leisured set and thus made the Ormond one of the first in a long line of Florida golf resorts. Flagler's old partner, John D. Rockefeller, enjoyed the Ormond Hotel so much that he eventually purchased a house nearby, where he wintered until his death in 1937.

In 1892, Flagler, who had begun to embrace his role as a developer, went so far as to obtain a charter from the state to extend his railroad south along the Indian River all the way to Biscayne Bay. Though he had little intention of going as far south as that remote outpost, there was no reason not to lock up any future possibilities. Additionally, a land grant act passed by the Florida legislature in 1889 promised developers up to eight thousand acres per mile of track laid (Flagler would ultimately acquire some 2 million acres of land in this manner). With such inducements in mind, Flagler determined to at least have a look at the possibilities as far south as Lake Worth. And in the meantime, he would set his sights on a terminus in the Rockledge area about halfway to Lake Worth.

His rails south toward Rockledge were the first he had built on undeveloped lands, reaching New Smyrna* by late 1892, Titusville in early 1893, and Cocoa and Rockledge less than a month later in late February 1893. Flagler's railroad, including modernized and brand-new routes, now extended nearly halfway down the state. By January 1894, he had reached Fort Pierce, some 230 miles south of Jacksonville, having laid about 140 miles of virgin track. Only seventy miles separated Flagler's line from Lake Worth, where Flagler was resolved to stop. In his mind, Lake Worth and Palm Beach would constitute the boundary of what the reformed oilman had come to call "my domain."

To understand the impact of the arrival of the railroad in Palm Beach, one needs only to consider the account of Ella Geer Dimick, wife of one of the original settlers, E. N. Dimick. In a 1962 interview, she described what it entailed to travel in the 1880s from Jacksonville to her settlement. Unless one were to travel solely by sea, she said, one would take a small steamer down the St. Johns River and debark at the flyspeck town of Salt Lake.

---

* New Smyrna began its existence in 1768, founded by Scots physician Andrew Turnbull, who recruited several hundred Greeks in and around his wife's birthplace, Smyrna (Izmir), to create a hemp, sugar, and indigo plantation in the New World. About half of the 1,300 colonists fell victim to disease and the predations of the Seminoles before lighting out for a better life in St. Augustine, about seventy miles north, where descendants remain today. There were about 150 hardy souls in the area when Flagler's railroad reached New Smyrna in 1892. "Beach" was added to its name in 1947, when the city annexed a tract adjoining the Atlantic. It was a practice repeated by a number of Florida settlements hoping to entice settlers and tourists, including Ormand, which became Ormand Beach in 1950; and Dania, which did not transform to Dania Beach until 1998.

Then by a wagon drawn by sturdy mules over
eight miles of palmetto roots, and through deep
sand, to Titusville. Then by small sailboats
[about 120 miles, along the Indian River Lagoon]
to Jupiter, which with reverse winds and bad
weather, often consumed two weeks. From Jupiter
one could take his choice, either out of Jupiter
Inlet a distance of ten miles at sea, or through the
sawgrass route a distance of eight miles, rowing or
poling, as it was impossible to sail through owing
to the narrowness of the channel. It was so very
winding and indistinct that an experienced pilot
was required. This was a hard day's work, getting
through to the "haulover"; here several men were
needed to drag the boat across to Lake Worth,
a distance of 250 yards. Difficult as it was, our
freight and supplies were often carried through
this way.

Even with his trains already in Melbourne, about halfway
down the Indian River, the trip would have been arduous for
Flagler as he made his way to Palm Beach, a trek that would have
taken a number of days at least. But it was well known to Flagler
that Robert McCormick, of the Chicago harvesting-machine family, had purchased large tracts of land in the Palm Beach area in
the late 1870s and had built a winter home of note on the east
shore of Lake Worth, where the tropical gardens he planted were
flourishing. Flagler, by now interested in all things Florida, was
eager to inspect the area for himself.

What he saw in April 1893 was unprepossessing enough,
there being no more than a dozen or so houses in addition
to McCormick's scattered about, but Flagler had developed

something of an insight as to what might draw others to an exotic place. Intrigued by the balmy climate, the waving palms, and the sight of eighteen miles of isolated Palm Beach island bracketed by a placid lake and a turquoise sea, he determined to stake his claim there. Using surrogates to keep his interest quiet and prices down, he bought up some two hundred acres of land—including McCormick's pleasing, if modest, homestead for $75,000—and announced that he would build a grand hotel on the site, with his railroad to arrive in the area as soon as he could make it happen. It was a stunning development for settlers there. Land on the island, which had been declared "worthless and likely to stay that way," was suddenly being priced at anywhere from $150 to $1,000 an acre, and hand-to-mouth homesteaders had become rich overnight.

The speed with which Flagler's new Palm Beach hotel project unfolded was a reflection of his enthusiasm for the place. Two work camps—one for white workers south of the building site and another for blacks, the Styx, just north of today's Royal Poinciana Way—were quickly established. Ground was broken on the first of May, with a thousand men at work on the project, most of them earning between $1.25 and $2.25 per day. Though the logistics of transporting materials and men to this far-flung place were the same as what the early settlers faced, the 1,150-room, six-story Royal Poinciana Hotel—billed as the largest wooden structure in the world—was completed in an astonishing nine months, opening its doors on February 11, 1894.

Given that the railroad would not reach its depot on the mainland across Lake Worth until March 22, only seventeen guests were registered at the opening, paying nightly rates of anywhere from $6 to $100 to wander the hotel's three miles of corridors, take dinner in a hall that could accommodate sixteen hundred, receive the attention of a prodigious staff (fourteen hundred at full strength), play a round of golf on one of two courses, or perhaps stroll down to the shores of Lake Worth for a view of the sunset from a spot close to where Flagler would one day build his mighty mansion, Whitehall.

Yet as pampered as those seventeen guests must have felt, some of them might have also wondered what had possessed a man with Flagler's matchless record of success to create such a monumentally extravagant establishment in the middle of nowhere. They might well have gazed about those lovingly manicured but nearly vacant grounds and asked themselves what could possibly make him think such a venture would pay off.

From Flagler's point of view, there was no mystery. He had found the secluded island of Palm Beach beautiful and pleasing and assumed that others would be eager to take the same pleasures. After all, visitors had flocked to the fabulous Ponce de Leon in St. Augustine. Why would they doubt advertisements that promised a nirvana-like experience in one of the largest hotels in the world situated in the middle of a tropical paradise?

In later years, journalists would plead with Flagler to answer such questions, as if his answers might unlock some secret to rival those of the Rosicrucians. After spending several days in Flagler's company in 1910, magazine writer Edwin Lefèvre, baffled by Flagler's impenetrable nature, decided that it all came down to this: at fifty-five, this little-traveled businessman who had never been to Europe or indeed as far as California came to Florida and: "He saw what you and I saw when we went to Pompeii or first gazed on the Pyramids! He saw palms—*palms!*—this man who had grown up in Ohio amid the wheat."

* * *

If any of those fortunate seventeen opening-night guests did worry about the outcome of Flagler's gamble, they need not have. Given its unmatched amenities—it had elevators, steam heat, indoor plumbing, and electric lights, and was surrounded by lush landscaping and fastidiously furnished and splendid in every way—word of the hotel's splendor spread rapidly among the Northeast's social elite and those who wished to rub elbows with them.

The Royal Poinciana was soon dubbed the Newport of the South and was drawing thousands of visitors each winter season, from December to April, when the heat and the absence of the yet-to-be-invented air-conditioning sent most northerners fleeing home. In fact, the allure of the island resort was so great that many former devotees of the Ponce de Leon, the Alcazar, and the Cordova were staying in St. Augustine only "on the one-day plan," hopping aboard Flagler's train for Palm Beach as soon as a room opened up at the ever-booked-up Royal Poinciana.

*Aerial view of the original Breakers hotel with
the Royal Poinciana hotel at the right.*

The Poinciana was such an immediate hit that in the summer of 1895 Flagler set about building a satellite sister hotel—originally known as the Wayside and later the Palm Beach Inn—located directly east of the Royal Poinciana on the ocean, opening for the 1896 season. Because many of Flagler's guests were soon asking to be placed at the "one over by the breakers," following a 1901 renovation the hotel received the name it still bears: the Breakers.

Though the Breakers originally appealed to a slightly less swanky crowd, with its rates beginning at $4, Flagler also built cottage communities on the dunes to the north and south of the new oceanfront establishment. These "cottages"—more properly described as multibedroom, two-story homes—became the favorites of many notables including the Vanderbilts, playwright Eugene O'Neill, and Mr. and Mrs. Edward T. Stotesbury, a couple who would one day soon mentor a young Marjorie Merriweather Post in the ways of the Palm Beach gentry. Many of the cottages, in one of which Flagler would spend his last weeks, exist to this day.

With the Royal Poinciana added to the Ormond Hotel and the Ponce de Leon, Alcazar, and Casa Monica in St. Augustine, Flagler had succeeded in creating a winter playground that captured the imagination of the nation's most privileged where virtually nothing had existed less than fifteen years before. The Atlantic Coast Line's New York and Florida Special was running multiple trains each day to Jacksonville during the height of the tourist season, trying to keep up with the demand, and land values all along the rail line from Jacksonville to West Palm Beach were skyrocketing. Truly, Flagler's intuition that he was a very good judge of what other wealthy people would enjoy seemed to have been incontrovertibly confirmed. While Ponce de León may have discovered Florida, Henry Flagler had finally found a use for it.

- 3 -

MADNESS

Though the business future would have seemed very bright for Flagler in 1894 (he turned sixty-four on January 2), problems were brewing in his personal life. Flagler had concerns about his son, Harry, who had dropped out of Columbia in 1892 at the age of twenty-one and come to St. Augustine somewhat reluctantly to work with his father in the hotel and railroading business. Harry found such work unsatisfactory, and by 1894—inside two years—had moved back to New York, where he reenrolled at Columbia and soon married Anne Louise Lamont, daughter of noted banker Charles Lamont, on April 24 of that year. Though Flagler and Ida Alice attended the ceremony, Flagler, whose first child, Jennie Louise (born in 1855), had died of complications following childbirth in 1889, would later confide in his friend Dr. Anderson that his son had, in leaving St. Augustine and his burgeoning business, deserted him.

Nor was his relationship with Ida Alice going smoothly. While many acknowledged that his second wife constituted a handful, her striking good looks and provocative dress along with her forceful personality made her at the very least interesting, both in the public eye and surely for Flagler himself.

Indulging her whims for luxury and prestige, Flagler early on purchased a 160-foot yacht called the *Alicia* on which Ida Alice became fond of entertaining. During one cruise off Mamaroneck in 1885, while she was entertaining a group of society matrons, a storm blew up, carrying gale-force winds. When the captain announced his intention to rush them back to shore, Ida Alice countermanded him. A yachting party she had announced and a yachting party they would have. The craft pitched and heaved through the rest of the day, returning to the dock eight hours overdue, delivering its pale and shaken guests safe if not quite sound. Flummoxed by his wife's lack of common sense, Flagler thought enough of the incident to lament it in a letter to his St. Augustine partner, Dr. Andrew Anderson.

Though the following years passed with no incidents of such magnitude, Flagler was forced keep a watchful eye out. In 1893, Ida Alice came into possession of a Ouija, a type of parlor game board patented by businessman Elijah Bond in 1890, upon which a participant places a hand on a planchette that glides around a printed alphabet, supposedly without the operator's willful guidance, "spelling out" messages. The devices were popular with spiritualists, who claimed that users could communicate with the dead.

Florida developer Henry Morrison Flagler in his late seventies, during the construction of the "railway across the ocean."

The second Mrs. Flagler soon became obsessed with the device, consulting on a regular basis with occultists of one stripe and another and spending hours alone, convinced that she was in communication with astral spirits who were advising that she murder her husband, for, as they informed her, he was engaged in a number of salacious affairs. Furthermore, she breathlessly assured friends, the czar of Russia had been in contact with her via the Ouija: the czar proclaimed that he had fallen in love with her and promised that the two of them would be wed the moment Flagler was out of the way. Ida went so far as to commission from Tiffany the design of a $2,000 diamond ring, which she ordered sent to her new suitor. The shipment was intercepted before it was sent to Russia, but Flagler was little comforted.

On one occasion in 1894, Flagler arranged with George C. Shelton, a well-known Manhattan physician and friend, to come out to Satan's Toe to surreptitiously examine his wife. Initially, Ida Alice seemed excited by Shelton's arrival and told him she had some secrets to share. The moment the two were presumably out of earshot of other guests, Ida Alice began to recount the details of a headline-gathering divorce case involving a prominent New York City couple. Soon she was vividly describing sex orgies in which the warring couple, as well as other prominent New Yorkers, had taken part, interspersing accounts of various episodes of abuse perpetrated on her by Flagler. Shelton was flabbergasted, trying to get her to lower her voice, casting nervous glances over his shoulder at the shocked and spellbound guests.

At that point, Ida Alice grasped him by the arm and pulled him to her bedroom where she produced three pebbles from a jewelry case. She handed Shelton the stones and asked what he thought of the markings on them. To Shelton these appeared to be common, unblemished pebbles someone might pick randomly off the ground, and he made the mistake of saying as much.

His response sent Ida Alice into a fury. "Of course you cannot see them; there are only three people in the world who can, and only members of a secret society possess them and the power to interpret them." After checking to see that no interlopers had gathered near her door to eavesdrop, she continued.

"This one," she said, holding the first up in her fingers, "has cured many forms of paralysis." Then she showed him the next.

"And this one will produce pregnancy in a woman if she carries it with her for a month." Shelton nodded. Just several months earlier he had explained to a tearful Ida Alice that she would never be able to bear children.

Ida Alice reached for his hand and pressed the two pebbles into it. "I want you to take good care of them for me, George." Then she held up the third between them and giggled. "Now, this one I am going to send to the Czar."

When Shelton shared this experience with Flagler, the latter was saddened if not surprised. The two agreed that it might be best if the couple moved back to their Fifth Avenue home where Dr. Shelton could visit regularly. Flagler complied, but despite the move Ida Alice's symptoms did not materially improve. She might call the doctor complaining of a splitting headache and begging him to come examine her, but Shelton would arrive to find her modeling a new hat or ready to regale him with lurid tales of her husband's infidelity, any memory of a headache vanished. On a separate occasion she handed a check for $1,000 to her manicurist, as a gratuity. When the manicurist reported the matter to Dr. Shelton, Ida Alice waved away the good doctor's concerns. It was nothing, she assured Shelton, only a speck of the vast fortune that was hers.

Shelton was also alarmed by Ida Alice's frequent matter-of-fact assurances that she would have to murder Flagler, and he urged Flagler to start sleeping in a separate bedroom that he could lock, but Flagler would not agree. Such a change might shock Ida Alice to the point of no return, he told Shelton. He would trust in a higher power for his safety.

Finally, on October 24, 1895, after convincing Flagler that there was no other course to take, Shelton called in a pair of physicians specializing in mental disorders. When Ida Alice heard of the visit, she locked herself in her bedroom and refused to come out. One of the consulting physicians, Dr. Frederick Peterson, the president of the New York Lunacy Commission, sent the others away and sat down to wait Mrs. Flagler out.

Before long, a maid emerged from the bedroom to tell Peterson that Mrs. Flagler wanted her to call a detective for help. Peterson nodded. "Tell her that a detective is on the way," he said.

After a few minutes, Peterson made a show of arriving at the home, then tapped on Mrs. Flagler's door to identify himself as a detective from the central office. A grateful Mrs. Flagler admitted Peterson to her room, where she quickly began to describe her home as being filled with Russian spies bent on keeping her from uniting with the czar. She showed Peterson the Ouija with which she and the czar were able to communicate and repeated her certainty that she would have to kill Flagler before he poisoned her.

After calming her down, Peterson left her room to reconvene with Dr. Shelton and his colleague Dr. Allan Starr, and the three agreed on what would happen next. Peterson had already drawn up the papers for the commitment of Ida Alice to Choate House, a sanatorium in Pleasantville, New York. She was diagnosed with "delusionary insanity," another name for paranoid psychosis, and was to be taken there immediately.

Peterson returned to the door of Ida Alice's bedroom and gave the signal they had arranged earlier: three soft taps and the door swung inward. Ida Alice might have been smiling with relief when she saw Peterson, but when the orderlies piled in after him, she was already screaming. Ida Alice was carried by force downstairs to a waiting carriage, then taken to the station where a special railroad car had been prepared to take her the thirty miles or so up the Hudson to Choate's. Distraught by the situation, Flagler was sent off to St. Augustine by his doctor in hopes that he might try to settle his mind, though before he left he implored Shelton to visit her regularly at Choate's. The visits, however, seemed only to agitate Ida Alice, who blamed Shelton for imprisoning her in what she called a hole.

Still, her symptoms began to abate, and in March 1896, Dr. Starr went to Pleasantville to visit and was delighted with what he saw. Ida Alice was able to speak to him candidly about her delusions almost as if they were the afflictions of a third party, and she asked Starr to pass along to Flagler that she loved him very much and that she had regained full possession of her right mind. Starr thought that Mrs. Flagler was well enough to return home, though he counseled careful vigilance on Flagler's part, cautioning him that a relapse could occur without warning. Certainly, the Ouija board should be hidden away.

Flagler was delighted at the news and had the Mamaroneck home, about twenty miles to the southeast of Pleasantville, prepared for their arrival on June 5, twelve years to the day after they were wed. Dr. Choate himself told Flagler that he regarded Ida Alice as "entirely cured," and Flagler was unable to detect even the slightest suggestion of her former agitation. On June 8, he wrote to his friend Dr. Anderson in St. Augustine: "I am surprised and need not say delighted at the outcome—it seems too good to be true."

Those turned out to be fateful words. On July 1, a favored niece of Flagler's, Elizabeth Ashley, arrived for a stay at Satan's Toe with her husband, an accomplished attorney whose company Flagler enjoyed. He thought that the couple would be good company for his wife and help to divert her from troubling thoughts. However, almost immediately after the Ashleys' arrival, Ida Alice was asking again for her Ouija. She repeated to Mrs. Ashley the tales that Flagler was cheating on her regularly and confided that she had fallen in love with the czar of Russia. When Flagler was present, Ida Alice acted as if nothing were the matter, but she resumed her raving the moment she and Mrs. Ashley were left alone.

Flagler was of course disturbed to hear this news and wrote to Anderson in St. Augustine that Dr. Starr's timetable for a relapse seemed to have come eerily true. He asked Anderson to share the word with a friend in common: "Mr. MacGonigle writes me occasionally expressing his joy over my happiness. You may tell him about Alice's relapse, for I don't believe I can bear to receive any more congratulations, but don't say anything to others yet."

Flagler walked cautiously for the next several months, carrying on a continuing consultation with an array of physicians uncertain as to the ultimate outcome, consorting with a wife who seemed utterly pleasant and devoted to him during the day, and going to bed each night wondering if he would awake to find her about to plunge a knife into his chest.

Matters reached a head on October 10, when Ida Alice managed to obtain a Ouija from a neighbor's wife. Almost immediately she withdrew into her room, absorbed in communications with those on the other side. In desperation, Flagler turned to his old friend Dr. Shelton, who had been away in Europe for several months.

Shelton advised Flagler to return to Manhattan at once. Ida Alice would be confined at Satan's Toe, watched over by four attendants who were to be supervised by another doctor experienced in mental disorders, Dr. Roland du Jardins, who would take up residence with his wife. Flagler responded glumly to the suggestions of his old friend Dr. Anderson that he stop worrying and resign himself to the fact that Ida Alice was incurably ill.

"I know that all you say is true," Flagler wrote back, "that having done everything for my poor wife that human skill can devise, my duty to myself and the enterprises upon which the welfare of so many depends, is to make the best of it—this I shall try to do."

Making the best of it proved to be nearly impossible, however. Ida Alice's rages became more intense and more frequent, leading Du Jardins to hide all the knives and silverware in the kitchen. Ida Alice, however, found a pair of kitchen shears left behind and slipped them into her pocket. The next time Du Jardins came into her room, she fell upon him, slashing at him with her scissors. By the time he was able to throw her off and run from the room, Du Jardins's face was bruised, and his hand was pouring blood.

On March 23, 1897, Ida Alice was committed once again to the sanatorium, insisting during this second intake that her name was Princess Ida Alice von Schotten Tech. She explained that yes, she *had* been married to Henry Flagler, but he was now dead and she was at present engaged to marry the czar of Russia on a date soon to be announced.

Modern psychotropic drugs can help alleviate symptoms of delusional psychosis and assist those afflicted in controlling recurrent episodes, but at the outset of the twentieth century, physicians were reduced to bafflement and prescriptions of rest and confinement. Said Dr. Carlos F. MacDonald (who assumed the directorship of Choate's on the death of its founder), chronic delusional insanity "invariably occurs in persons having what is known as a nervous or insane temperament, whether through heredity or inherited predisposition or whether acquired in early life. Such cases do not recover." MacDonald conjectured that Ida Alice, predisposed to the condition since her humble birth, had these tendencies triggered by her marriage to Flagler. The stress of her attempts to measure up to the standards of the grand existence he had suddenly bestowed on her were simply too much for her to bear, and her mind gave way.

Whatever the causes, Ida Alice would never again emerge from that sanatorium, where it was reported that she spent considerable time sitting at a window through which she apparently saw and spoke to unseen visitors. According to Dr. MacDonald she began to paint her cheeks with red dye she extracted from yarn, blacken her eyebrows with burned cork, and use the cream brought to her with her coffee as a conditioner for her hair.

For several years, her life passed in this fashion, with her brother, Charles, visiting from time to time to hear of her continuing affair with the czar and the many devious surgeries performed on her by the sanatorium staff in secret. She filled notebooks with indecipherable scrawls that she called poetry and song lyrics and collected and bagged thousands of mystically powered pebbles.

Gradually she began to enter what MacDonald called the third state, her memory fading, her powers of concentration lessening, her previously volatile emotions calming toward torpor. In 1899, Flagler petitioned the Supreme Court of the State of New York to declare Ida Alice insane and incompetent and set up a trust in her name funded by Standard Oil stock valued at more than $1 million, providing an annual income well beyond what it took to keep her at the sanatorium. She spent her days in a private cottage with her own maids and car, enjoying the occasional outing for lunch or a drive with Dr. MacDonald or other members of the staff.

In fact she would outlive Henry Flagler himself by nearly thirty years, dying of a cerebral hemorrhage at the sanatorium in July 1930. MRS. FLAGLER DEAD—DECLARED INSANE IN 1899, the headlines read. She was then eighty-two and her estate, though diminished by regular dispensations to various relatives who had petitioned the trustees for her support, had grown to more than $15 million, which was ultimately divided between two nephews and a grandniece.

* * *

Evidence that seemingly supported at least a portion of Ida Alice's contentions that Flagler had been unfaithful would come along on May 10, 1901, when headlines in the *New York Times* reported that Henry Flagler had been sued as a corespondent in a divorce action. The story reported that a man named Clarence W. Foote had brought a suit for $100,000 against one John Malden, alleging that the latter had alienated the affections of his wife, Helen Long, in dalliances that took place from January to November 1896. Also named was Mr. Flagler, who, Foote alleged, met with his wife "together at an apartment house" from December 1896 to June 1897. According to Foote, Flagler and his wife also spent time aboard the yacht *Alicia* in June and July 1897 and following that were keeping company in a house on East Fifty-Seventh Street in Manhattan. Foote claimed that Mr. Flagler had given his wife that house as a present, along with some $400,000 in Standard Oil securities.

In response, Flagler's attorney told reporters that the action was nothing more than a blatant attempt at blackmail, Helen Long being the daughter of a business associate who had traveled aboard the *Alicia* from time to time and someone for whom Flagler had occasionally acted as financial adviser. An August 8, 1897, issue of the *New-York Tribune* reported that the *Alicia* had put in at eastern Long Island's exclusive Prospect House with a "Miss Long" as one of the passengers. But also aboard were Helen's mother; her younger sister, Irene; and Mr. Long's business associate J. H. Clary and his wife.

Flagler's attorney insisted that there was nothing to the allegations, noting that Flagler had already appeared to answer the charges in a court in White Plains, where the complaint was dismissed and a judgment entered against the plaintiff for costs. Flagler made no further public statement regarding the matter and Helen Long seems to have made no subsequent intrusion into his life, though biographer Thomas Graham provides some suggestion as to how the matter was actually resolved: New York City real estate records show that on October 20, 1897, a transfer of a four-story brownstone at 27 East Fifty-Seventh Street did take place, from one Jasper C. Salter to one Helen Long. It scarcely seems coincidence that the address was located just three blocks north of Flagler's Fifth Avenue home nor that Jasper C. Salter was Flagler's personal secretary at the time.

* * *

Whatever the exact nature of the relationship between Flagler and Helen Long, it is well documented that he did not want for company during the long period of Ida Alice's decline. As early as 1891, when he and Ida Alice were guests—along with his niece Elizabeth Ashley—aboard a yacht owned by North Carolinians Mr. and Mrs. Pembroke Jones, Flagler made the acquaintance of a twenty-three-year-old schoolmate of Elizabeth Ashley's, Mary Lily Kenan, herself descended from a prominent North Carolina family. Whether or not sparks flew at any point during that cruise, the two would meet again soon, for shortly afterward, Flagler had his private railcar sent to Wilmington to bring the Joneses, Elizabeth Ashley, and Mary Lily Kenan down to the Ponce de Leon in St. Augustine, where on one evening a ball was held in the opulent, Tiffany-shaded grand dining hall and the debonair sixty-one-year-old Flagler swept young Miss Kenan about the floor.

Opinions differ as to what shape the relationship took in the ensuing years, with some insisting that Flagler's initial interest in a woman thirty-eight years his junior was nothing more than fatherly and others insisting far more was going on. As for Miss Kenan, she was not exactly inexperienced, having had an on-again, off-again relationship with Robert Bingham of Louisville, begun in 1890 during their college days at the University of North Carolina and said to have gone well beyond the platonic. Though Bingham soon left North Carolina to enroll at the University of Virginia, the relationship continued at long distance. Meantime, Elizabeth Ashley and Mary Lily traveled together often with Flagler, and in 1894 Mary Lily's brother—William Rand Kenan, a talented chemical engineer—came to work with Flagler on his Florida projects.

By this time, Ida Alice's behavior had become more of a concern, and whether or not Flagler had begun a full-blown affair with Mary Lily or was simply diverting his mind from his troubles by showing his niece and her friend a good time, the gossip had begun. During the season of 1897, while Ida Alice was in seclusion at Satan's Toe, Elizabeth Ashley and her new husband were invited to spend the season in one of the beach cottages at the Breakers, and the Ashleys asked Mary Lily to come along.

On more than one evening Flagler, still consumed by the situation with Ida Alice, joined the three for dinner, and he often asked the musically talented Mary Lily to sing one or another of his favorite songs. While everyone who witnessed such an episode agreed that Mary Lily's youthful exuberance and musical talents could lift Flagler visibly out of his dour spirits, there was soon general agreement on another count among gossiping cognoscenti in Palm Beach, St. Augustine, and elsewhere: sixty-seven-year-old Henry Flagler and then thirty-year-old Mary Lily Kenan had become an item.

Flagler was never to lay eyes on Ida Alice after she was carried off to Pleasantville for the second time on March 23, 1897, and it seems safe to say that his emotional attentions from that point forward were directed toward Mary Lily, whose infatuation with the highly successful and attractive Flagler seems unquestionable from the start. If his business operations in Florida had only redoubled following his supposed ending of the line in Palm Beach, he was now equally occupied with a more personal matter: the necessity of a divorce from Ida Alice.

- 4 -

BUYING A LEGISLATURE

On April 23, 1899, in a story published in the *Florida Times-Union*, a Jacksonville newspaper that had become part of his empire, Flagler made the somewhat surprising announcement that he intended to give up his New York residence and become a citizen of Florida. His burgeoning business affairs in the area demanded the change, and it was also pointed out that he would escape the inheritance tax burdening wealthy New Yorkers.

The reasoning certainly made good business sense, but other factors were at work. There was no longer any hiding the fact that he and Mary Lily Kenan were romantically involved and while Flagler had stated privately that he intended to marry her, the knotty problem of his present marriage to Ida Alice stood in the way.

For a resolute individual such as Flagler, this was but a momentary blockade. In June 1899 he petitioned the Supreme Court of the State of New York that his wife, Ida Alice Flagler, be declared legally insane. There being little doubt of the matter, the court granted the petition. The ruling might have seemed to have little bearing on Flagler's quandary, since New York's laws did not countenance insanity as grounds for divorce, but securing the decree was crucial to Flagler's larger plan.

Neither did Florida law allow for mental instability as grounds for divorce, but in his new "domain," Henry Flagler was a far bigger fish than he had been in New York, where the Astors and the Vanderbilts and the Rockefellers were just a few of those who eclipsed him in wealth and power. While only provable adultery provided sufficient grounds for divorce in Florida up until that time, a bill was introduced in the state's legislature on April 9, 1901, described as an act making "incurable insanity a ground for divorce for husband and wife, and regulating proceedings in such cases."

Prior to the introduction of the legislation, lawmakers had heard Flagler's name mentioned only in relation to a gift of $10,000 to the state's fledgling agricultural college, which would become the University of Florida in 1903. No public mention of his name in connection with the divorce bill was made, however; nor had a single gossip item been printed regarding the whispered-about relationship of Flagler and Mary Lily Kenan. The new divorce bill sailed through the state's senate on April 17 and passed its house of representatives two days later by a vote of 42 to 19. Governor William S. Jennings signed it into law on April 25.

What would eventually become known as the Flagler Divorce Law provided that the "insanity" of the afflicted partner had to have existed for four years prior to the petition, that the lack of competency was required to be adjudged by a competent court, that a guardian for the insane party would be appointed, and that where the afflicted party was a wife, she would be well provided for by her husband.

By June 3, Flagler had filed for divorce from Ida Alice, and on August 12, 1901, his attorney—George P. Raney, the Florida legislator who had guided the divorce bill through the state's house and senate just weeks before—was in a Miami courtroom to make the case. On hand to testify as to the hopelessness of Ida Alice's prospects were the good doctors MacDonald and Shelton from New York. Flagler's New York attorney stipulated that in fact the New York supreme court had found Mrs. Flagler hopelessly insane, and attorney Eugene Ashley, husband to favored niece Elizabeth, presented himself as Ida Alice's financial guardian, already certified so by the state of New York. For his part, Flagler showed the court documentation of the trust fund that he had established for Ida Alice, now grown in excess of $2 million, and with that the matter was settled. On the following day, Judge Minor S. Jones issued his decree dissolving the marriage of Henry Morrison and Ida Alice Shourds Flagler.

On August 23, Flagler made an honest woman of Mary Lily, marrying her at the Kenan family homestead in Kenansville, North Carolina, before a small wedding party that included a few family members and friends on the Kenan side and only Eugene Ashley on his. Flagler was seventy-one, Mary Lily thirty-four.

Flagler with his third wife, Mary Lily Kenan, of North Carolina.
When they wed in 1901, he was seventy-one, she thirty-four.

As reporters and the public gleaned what had taken place, a fair amount of outrage was splashed across the pages of such publications as the *Ocala Banner,* the *Palmetto News,* and the *Pensacola Journal,* with editorials lambasting the apparent buying and selling of the legislature by an arrogant elitist. Though the $10,000 Flagler donated to the college seemed like an outright bribe to some, no evidence of wrongdoing was ever uncovered. Flagler did pay former governor Francis P. Fleming $15,000 and Raney $14,500 for their services as his divorce attorneys, but once again it would have to be left up to coincidence that those two were the principal lobbyists for the passage of the divorce bill through the legislature. Though the Flagler Divorce Law would be repealed by indignant lawmakers in 1905, it seemed to have encouraged Flagler to believe that money might actually influence legislation. In 1903, he would write to his manager for the railroad—now having become the Florida East Coast Railway or FEC—that perhaps they might think about spreading some money around in hopes that a pending anti-monopoly measure being considered by the state legislature could be scuttled "if it can be done at a moderate expense."

Following their wedding, Flagler and Mary Lily traveled in his private railcar to his estate in Mamaroneck, which he had transferred to the FEC to simplify his change of residence. In short order, the FEC would deed Lawn Beach to Mary Lily as a kind of wedding gift, although Flagler had something far grander than that in mind as a token for his new bride.

There was predictably a certain amount of disagreeable gossip for the newlyweds to deal with. Typical arch commentary came from Laura Rockefeller, wife of Flagler's former partner, John D. Rockefeller, who wrote to her husband overestimating the ages of the parties by a bit: "We have the announcement of Mr. Flagler's marriage to a Miss Kenan, of N. Carolina. She is thirty-six, he, seventy-two."

The *Atlanta Journal* finally broke the media silence on the scandalous aspect of the relationship in a story published the day before the ceremony: "The announcement caused no surprise, because the affair has been talked about and gossiped over for the past two years."

Yet for all the clamor over the divorce bill, the divorce, and the May-September nature of the Kenan-Flagler union, the two were actually well suited, according to Sidney Martin, Flagler's first biographer. "There was much to say in Mary Lily's behalf. She was Flagler's equal socially and intellectually. She was a good wife to him. She was socially inclined and loved excitement and a good time. Such was afforded her whenever she desired it."

No greater evidence of Flagler's own affection for his new bride might be offered than the magnanimous wedding present he was to bestow on her. In 1899, in part to reassure the Kenan family of his intentions, he had already presented Mary Lily with some rather extravagant engagement presents, including one thousand shares of Standard Oil stock worth about half a million dollars, as well as a diamond bracelet and a diamond-studded strand of pearls, one said to be "as big as a Parrott's egg." But those were just the warm-up to a gesture that was not only sufficient to surpass any ordinary bride's dreams but a prize that would become the still-standing foundation for as exotic and enduring an enclave for the privileged as might have been imagined.

According to biographer Martin, "If lavished wealth was what she craved, Mary Lily Flagler had reason to be happy. She had always wanted a marble palace, so Flagler built her a mansion in Palm Beach which she called Whitehall." Flagler had purchased the property on which the home is situated in 1893, at the same time that he was building the Royal Poinciana. Known as Brelsford's Point, the site was a spacious tract fronting Lake Worth, just south and west of the hotel. Though he first envisioned an upscale domicile in the Cuban fashion, his tendencies toward grandeur obliterated anything so ordinary.

Early in 1900, even before he and Mary Lily were wed, Flagler commissioned architects John Carrère and Thomas Hastings, who had executed the much-acclaimed Ponce de Leon Hotel in St. Augustine, to design Whitehall, a seventy-five-room mansion in the Beaux-Arts style, with a marble-columned facade and a stunning marble entrance hall, 110 feet wide and 40 feet deep, with a double marble staircase worthy of Versailles leading to the upper floors.

On the ground floor, the architects included a sizable central courtyard—the only vestige of the Cuban theme—a vast ballroom, ninety-one by thirty-seven feet; a music room of sixty-four

Aerial view of Whitehall, with Lake Worth to the west, shortly after its completion in 1902.

by twenty-four feet; a dining room of forty-four by twenty-three, a billiard parlor, ladies' parlor, pantry, and kitchen; and offices for Flagler, with furnishings and details by the noted design firm and furniture makers Pottier and Stymus, who had made pieces for the likes of Ulysses S. Grant, railroad titan Leland Stanford, and Thomas Edison. On the second floor was the meticulously crafted, oak-detailed master suite with a bathroom seventeen by eleven feet that included an alcove for a needle shower. Fourteen bedroom suites were available for guests, and in the attic were servants' rooms and storage. There was also a sizable basement, something of a rarity for soggy South Florida. Agents were dispatched to search across France and Italy for furnishings, rugs, tapestries, and rare paintings (Flagler, with little formal education, had good taste but only a passing knowledge of art).

Whitehall is said to have cost $2.5 million in all, making it a grand wedding gift by any standard. A conservative comparison with present-day costs, one based on changes in the consumer price index since 1901, suggests that it would have taken $20 million or so to build Whitehall today. Using the Klepper/Gunther formula, however, one might peg the current-day cost of Whitehall at $500 million or so.

* * *

Typical of the projects in which Flagler had a personal interest, and despite its elaborate nature, the construction of Whitehall was a whirlwind enterprise, beginning a few months before the couple were married in August 1901 and concluding in time for them to begin entertaining there in late January 1902. A *New York Herald* story on March 30 of that year described the finished product, Whitehall, as "more wonderful than any palace in Europe, grander and more magnificent than any other private dwelling in the world."*

* The structure still exists, carefully restored as the Henry Morrison Flagler Museum.

Joining in for the first grand dinner at Whitehall—during which world-famous organist Clarence Eddy provided entertainment— were Flagler's guests for the season, Admiral of the Navy George Dewey and his wife, Mr. and Mrs. Frederick Vanderbilt, Flagler's old friend Dr. Andrew Anderson from St. Augustine, and original Standard Oil partner Samuel Andrews and his wife. The ensuing months of that season would see Mary Lily warming to her role of hostess, with the likes of John Jacob Astor squiring her about the dance floor and Frederick Townsend Martin, prominent among the New York Four Hundred, sitting in on rounds of the fabulously popular new card game known as "bridge."

Martin would later write of his admiration for Flagler, saying, "When I first met Henry Flagler he was a white-haired old man whose every gesture and every word spoke of tremendous will power and force of character." In his memoir *Things I Remember*, Martin lauded Flagler's legacy in creating so many successful businesses in his later career, thus giving work to and providing opportunity for thousands.

Flagler's grand mansion of Whitehall was to become a beacon for society's upper echelon over the ensuing decade, with Mary Lily proving herself a charming hostess and an accomplished entertainer when called upon to sing. The couple's regular summer residence at Satan's Toe provided a natural bridge that brought a regular flow of privileged northerners down to experience the delights of Florida. And before long, while the blue northers were howling back home, others in their social swirl were strolling about Palm Beach and gawking at Whitehall and thinking, "Why wait for an invitation from the Flaglers? We can build our own place in paradise." And so a fabled place was born.

- 5 -

END OF THE LINE

Despite having finally ensconced himself in a comfortable marriage and having built a home of which there seemed to be no earthly equal, Flagler would not be content to fritter away his time at balls and bridge parties. If she had hoped otherwise, Mary Lily was deceiving herself, for even during their long courtship, fraught with its many concerns, Flagler was pushing ahead to extend his domain. Though he vowed that the West Palm Beach station would be the final stop for the FEC, he had already reneged on that promise well before his third marriage was consummated and the building of Whitehall even begun.

Even as his railroad was inching its way down the peninsula along Lake Worth, a pioneer by the name of Julia Tuttle was pressing Flagler to extend the line to the very tip of the state's peninsula, on the shores of Biscayne Bay, where in 1890 she had purchased 640 acres of land on the north bank at the mouth of the Miami River. She had also purchased the long-abandoned army outpost after which the settlement of Fort Dallas had taken its name and turned it into a rooming house and was now seeking ways to stimulate development in what she considered the perfect place.

Before Tuttle, a land syndicate had been active in and around Fort Dallas, buying up sizable plots of land for the creation of a banana plantation along the river. Cuban bananas sold for about $1 a bunch at the time and those had to be freighted to and about the United States at considerable cost. The idea of a fortune to be made in domestic bananas was necessarily abandoned, however, when it was discovered that while bananas would in fact grow in the region, they simply wouldn't grow much bigger than a sizable thumb.

In 1893, Tuttle had met with Flagler and offered him half of her property for a hotel and depot site on the north bank of the Miami River and convinced fellow Fort Dallas pioneer Charles Brickell to offer a similar parcel for development on the south bank. But Flagler, not yet fully committed to Palm Beach at the time, declined the offer.

Late in 1894, however, fate intervened. A hard freeze rolled into Florida just before Christmas, lowering temperatures in the newly established citrus groves in the central part of the state into the teens. Though the citrus trees and field crops sustained significant damage, growers thought they might salvage enough of a crop to survive. But then, on February 6, another front rolled in to freeze crops and kill citrus trees and coconut palms all the way south to Palm Beach. It was a devastating blow to many of the hardy pioneers who had followed in the wake of Flagler's trailblazing down the state, and it sent hundreds of homesteaders fleeing back north.

The freeze that wreaked havoc elsewhere in Florida also provided the occasion for the persistent Julia Tuttle to send word to Flagler that the citrus trees in Fort Dallas remained in full flower. If ever a place could be considered "frostproof," Fort Dallas was it, she contended.

It was enough for Flagler to dispatch one of his lieutenants, James Ingraham, down to have a look. When Ingraham returned with confirmation of the homesteader's claims (legend has it that he was carrying a bouquet of fragrant orange blossoms pressed upon him as proof by Tuttle), Flagler decided to have a look for himself.

The inspection team, which included Flagler, Ingraham, and railway superintendent Joseph Parrott, traveled from Palm Beach to Fort Lauderdale by boat, then were carried by mule-drawn wagons the final thirty or so rugged miles to Fort Dallas. At the time, mail passed once a week along that same sixty-eight-mile passage, which was called the barefoot route, owing to the propensity of carriers to shed their shoes when walking on stretches of hard-packed beach sand along the way.

The party soon comprehended what a transformation a rail route would make for the area, and once Flagler arrived on the shores of Biscayne Bay, he found himself staring out over the same sort of paradisiacal setting that he had encountered in St. Augustine and Palm Beach. A splendid bay, west of which lay uncountable acres well suited for farming and development; a barrier island to the east, between the bay and the Atlantic; and, in this case, someone willing to give him several hundred acres for a hotel and railyard terminus. On June 12, 1895, he signed an agreement to bring his railroad to Fort Dallas, where he would also build yet another grand hotel—the six-story, 350-room Royal Palm—along with a terminal and a municipal waterworks.

It might be mentioned that Flagler's chief pleasure in his Florida development came from his hotels. It simply pleased him to provide accommodations of unparalleled quality in a place that he thought exotic and had come to love, and he was of course gratified that the hotels were on the whole profitable. As far as railroading went, he took pride in pushing back the Florida frontier and in making it possible for many to homestead, farm, and otherwise make a living in his domain. The railroads themselves were only marginally profitable. The chief income from his Florida operations came from property sales, leasing, and management of lands he acquired as incentives from a legislature anxious to see the entire state made available to development.

Work on laying the track to Fort Dallas commenced in September, with stations built at previously undeveloped stops along the way, including Delray, Deerfield, Fort Lauderdale, and Dania. On April 15, 1896, the railroad at last reached Fort Dallas, 363 miles south of the Jacksonville station. Overjoyed citizens celebrated the city's incorporation on July 28, and while many wished to change the name of the place to Flagler City in recognition of the boon they had received, the never-a-grandstander Flagler was opposed to the notion. They should call the place Miami, after the Indian name for the river where his hotel would stand, he said, and the 502-strong citizenry went along.

Though Flagler was spending most of his Florida time in St. Augustine and Palm Beach, he would become far more involved in Miami's development than he ever had in theirs. He saw to the cutting of a deep channel into Biscayne Bay and to platting and paving streets and building a power plant, schools, and churches; and he donated land for public buildings and a market. He also founded a newspaper, the *Miami Metropolis*, which would eventually become the *Miami Daily News*.

By 1902, the year Whitehall was unveiled as the new apex of social aspiration, Miami had become a bustling center with a population of more than five thousand, and while Flagler never maintained a home there, he was widely regarded as the city's founder and its chief patron: it was no stretch to add "city builder" to his résumé. Yet Flagler was still well short of reaching the end of the state of Florida with his railroad.

At the time, the most populous and important city in the state was not only its southernmost settlement but the nation's southernmost as well. Key West was a settlement perched on a rocky island of one mile by five, situated 156 miles south by southwest from Miami and reachable only by boat. Yet it was a strategically situated military post and fishing port with a population of nearly twenty thousand, lying isolated in the Straits of Florida just ninety miles north of Havana. Not only was it an important coaling station for navy vessels patrolling the waters between the United States and Central and South America, but it was also a cigar-making center; a bustling fishing, shrimping, and turtling port; and the only significant population center of the continent unattached to the mainland.

The editor of the *Key West Gazette* had actually called for the building of a railroad down to the city as early as 1831, at a time when less than one hundred miles of track had been laid in the entire country, but experts dismissed the feasibility of the project, labeling it more daunting engineering-wise than the construction of the hundred-mile-long Suez Canal (1859–69). Realistic estimates for the 153-mile Key West Extension—much of which would traverse open water—ran anywhere from $30 million to $50 million, considered an impossible sum to recoup by railroading.

But from the moment Flagler had brought his railroad to Miami, speculation began to grow that he would be the man to do the impossible. And in 1905, when a U.S.-supported revolution had resulted in the secession of Panama from Columbia and the new government's authorization of an agreement for the building of a canal across the isthmus, Flagler had his justification for going to Key West.

The work itself was exhausting, and every mile the line progressed south of Miami meant that much more trouble in moving men and supplies to the fore. In addition to the rigors of the work itself was the danger posed by hurricanes. The Florida Keys are actually not islands at all but remnants of an ancient underwater reef, most measuring under half a mile in width. The highest point above sea level south of the Florida mainland is found on Windley Key at eighteen feet, but most of the landmass measures well under the height of a Greyhound tour bus, which is capped at thirteen feet, six inches. When even a minimal hurricane approaches land, it pushes a tidal surge—or tidal wave—ahead of it, four to eight feet high at the mildest. Four such storms did sweep over the Keys during the span of the road's life, and each time the cost was high.

The first storm, in 1906, took workers entirely by surprise. One quarters boat, a kind of floating dormitory, was ripped loose from its moorings and swept out to sea with 140 men aboard. One man saved himself by climbing into an empty water tank he unbolted from the craft. The tank was discovered floating in the waters off Nassau days later; those who chanced upon it were astonished to find a man inside—Jonah-like, delirious but still alive. Another man, named Mullin, was the sole occupant of a cement barge that was torn from anchor during the storm and pulled out to a reef that was still in sight of shore. Witnesses reported that Mullin kept the barge's boiler stoked and its lights ablaze for nearly an hour until the craft was finally swallowed by the surge. His body was never found.

The workers suffered greatly, and even Flagler's trusted project managers were not immune to the rigors. Original project engineer J. C. Meredith died in 1909, his diabetes exacerbated by the demands placed on him; and even his replacement, William J. Krome, described by biographer Martin as a "muscular giant," was forced off the job for several months by exhaustion.

Even Flagler, "the Chief" himself, proved vulnerable. In 1908, the project received what looked like a fatal blow. The financial justification for the extension had been based on the building of a deepwater port in the southernmost city, to accommodate the vast amount of oceangoing steamship traffic on its way to and from the Panama Canal. But as progress reached the halfway point down the chain of the Florida Keys, word came that the U.S. Navy refused permission to dredge the waters of Key West harbor, claiming that such work would interfere with naval operations. Shortly thereafter, the seventy-eight-year-old Flagler was himself stricken with exhaustion. Gleeful muckraking journalists reported that his "illness" was in fact a nervous collapse brought on by the project's disintegration; one newspaper went so far as to prepare a lengthy obituary on Flagler, further declaring that "work [on the Key West railroad] has been abandoned."

As to Flagler's demise, the writers were, as the saying has it, "misinformed." Part of what revived Flagler's determination was his conviction that his old foe Theodore Roosevelt was behind the navy's refusal to permit the dredging in Key West. It had usually been Flagler who'd appeared in court to contest Roosevelt's trust-busting activities directed at Standard Oil, and he was sure that this was Roosevelt's way of continuing the anti-big-business campaign. Whatever the factors, Flagler rallied. He directed that the work resume, and toward the end, in 1911, the pace increased greatly, fueled in part by a concern that Flagler live to see his "impossible" project become reality. As William Krome put it, "There isn't a man working on this project who wouldn't give a year or two of his own life to get Mr. Flagler's railroad to Key West."

Finally, on January 22, 1912, the first train—with Flagler and his entourage aboard—pulled into the station at the end of the American line, to be greeted by ten thousand or more enthusiastic citizens. And in the aftermath, booking agents could hardly keep up with the demand from passengers wishing to travel on "the railway across the sea." Flagler, a savvy businessman to be sure, had publicly stated that he wanted to "go to Key West" to collect freight traffic. But along with the navy's denial of the dredging permits had come the development of new technology in the shipping industry. Steamships were being retrofitted to use oil instead of coal for fuel, thus making it possible to sail from Panama to any number of mainland U.S. ports without a stop.

In the end, the principal effect of what became known as the Oversea Railway was to transform Key West, which had always been a workingman's town, into a tourist destination. Passengers on the Havana Special (one could board a Pullman car in Penn Station that would be ferried within a few days across the Florida Straits to Cuba) delighted in the breathtaking views across the shallow, variegated waters, and they wrote of watching schools of dolphins leaping from the currents beneath the bridges along the route. Others described schools of sharks cruising along in the shadows cast by the cars crossing the bridges, like a set of exotic pacerfish.

* * *

"Now I can die happy," a visibly moved Flagler told the assembled crowd during the arrival celebration, which included a children's choir brought to serenade him. Later, as he was being led from the reviewing stand, Flagler turned to Joe Parrott to remark, "I can hear the children, but I can't see them."

Indeed, the drive to "ride his own iron" to Key West appeared to be the last thing sustaining Flagler. Though Whitehall had continued to serve as a center of society under Mary Lily's attention during the construction of the Key West Extension, Flagler had begun to slip away from social occasions earlier and earlier. He was seventy-five when the project began in 1905, and as if the strain of overseeing the engineering project of an era were not enough, being painted as a slave-driver in federal court in 1908 and witnessing the breakup of the Standard Oil Company by Supreme Court decree in 1911 could only have compounded matters.

Flagler and Mary Lily returned to Whitehall for some quiet weeks following the celebration of the railroad's arrival at Key West, and after a stay in St. Augustine they returned to Satan's Toe for the summer of 1912. Still, he went to his offices in the city several times a week by train. An assistant would meet him on the platform at Grand Central Terminal and escort him to the offices at 26 Broadway, where one day the elevators failed. Though the company offices were on the eighteenth floor, Flagler announced that he would take the stairs.

"We tried to stop him," recalled his secretary, Warren Smith. "Even sent a chair to one of the landings, where he could rest, but he persisted in coming the rest of the way immediately by foot, and arrived none the worse for wear, apparently." All of it was evidence of a remarkable constitution and force of will.

On the morning of March 4, 1913, not long after the celebration of his eighty-third birthday, Flagler found himself alone on the main floor of Whitehall and in need of the use of the facilities, a bathroom tucked under the south wing of the grand staircase in the main foyer. He had always been enamored of things that he considered clever inventions, and among those high in his estimation was the pneumatic door closer, which he had ordered installed in a number of rooms at Whitehall, including the foyer bathroom.

One enters this room to stand on an elevated platform and must search about for the light switch on the wall to the right. Several steps lead down somewhat precipitously from the platform to the facilities, and if one has not quite cleared the door frame and is standing somewhat unsteadily to begin with, then the closing of the door, propelled by a mechanism about the size and weight of a blacksmith's anvil, might well come with sufficient force to propel a person forward and off the platform into free fall and onto the hard tiles below.

However it happened, Flagler fell, and some time passed before the eighty-three-year-old—dazed, his hip broken—was found by servants and carried to his room. Though his recovery seemed to progress well enough at first, a move to Nautilus

Cottage, on the grounds of the Breakers, where the breezes were cooler seemed to bring on a relapse, and on April 1, Andrew Anderson, Joe Parrott, James Ingraham, and other FEC officials hurried down from St. Augustine to be at his side. Reports have it that a frantic Mary Lily, addled by exhaustion and fear (others attributed her state to the effects of alcohol and laudanum), at first refused the men entry to Flagler's bedroom, but she soon relented. Inside, the group found Flagler conscious but pitifully weakened, a state in which he remained until the middle of May, when he lapsed into a coma from which he would not awake. He died on the twentieth of May.

- 6 -

NO SECOND ACTS

If there had never been a Flagler born to become a developer tycoon with a second life in Florida, then undoubtedly the very existence of a paradisiacal Palm Beach island would have called a substitute discoverer down to make it flower. Sooner or later, someone surely would have come along to see the possibilities. But just how long that might have taken or exactly in what direction the development of the place might have gone is open to debate.

One of the most significant decisions Henry Flagler made in the early days had to do with the relocation of laborers imported for the building of the Royal Poinciana Hotel in the 1890s. Given the close quarters on the island, the tent-dotted shantytowns that had sprung up to house white and black laborers clearly could not continue to exist within the sightlines of well-to-do guests paying daily rates in excess of a month's wages for those workers. Furthermore, those temporary camps were occupying real estate that had acquired immense value in the wake of Flagler's developments.

The solution was a simple one: Flagler would develop a community on the west shore of Lake Worth where the principal depot of the FEC line was located and from whence the service workers who were needed to complete and maintain the island properties could be ferried back and forth. Thus were planted the seeds of today's West Palm Beach, which though hardly unappealing, is still very much the stepchild to the enclave that begat it.

Such a development might seem inevitable, though a Machiavellian legend surfaces from time to time concerning the relocation of the Styx, as the settlement for black workers came to be called. As one version of this story goes, in January 1894, shortly before the Royal Poinciana was to open, Flagler announced to the residents of the Styx that he had arranged for a grand carnival to be set up on the west shore of Lake Worth as a reward for their Herculean efforts, with food and circus entertainment free for their families as well. Tickets were distributed, and excited workers, wives, and children were escorted to boats while Flagler stood waving in the shadows of the Royal Poinciana to see them off. The moment the boats were out of sight, so goes this story, Flagler turned to give the high sign to a group of heavies.

Crews rushed into the tents and shanties of the Styx, collecting bedclothes and belongings that were brought down to the docks and loaded onto barges. Once the dwellings were cleared, others doused the structures with gasoline and the whole settlement was set ablaze. When stunned workers rushed out of the circus tents to view their homes going up in flames across the lake, Flagler was there to reassure them. His men had saved their belongings, he is supposed to have said, indicating the loaded barges, and though the Styx was no longer inhabitable, he pointed benevolently to the grounds adjoining the circus tents, where he would gladly make new homesites available at rock-bottom prices to any workers wishing to buy them. Flagler then proceeded to develop the land, profiting mightily on both ends of the deal.

The tale persists in the Palm Beach area as urban legend and is sometimes repeated in print by columnists and tabloid writers despite the lack of any credible support. Though the attempt to disprove a myth is generally an exercise in futility, T. T. Reese, Jr., a surviving member of a pioneering Palm Beach family, in 1994 wrote a letter to the *Palm Beach Post* in an effort to clarify the matter once and for all. According to Reese, the land on which the Styx was situated remained populated by service workers well after the Royal Poinciana opened.

In 1910, Reese said, Colonel E. R. Bradley, owner of the infamous Beach Club casino, a wide-open establishment that Flagler frowned upon, bought up thirty acres of property a few blocks north of the Royal Poinciana, including the land where the Styx was located, platting 230 building lots there. Bradley gave Styx residents, many of whom had paid no rent for years, two weeks to move out and hired Reese's father to see that everyone complied. The younger Reese, who died in 1997, wrote that he remembered watching residents walk across the bridge to the mainland, hauling their belongings, and that following the residents' departure, he helped his father clear the land, pile up the trash, and burn it.

Newspaper clippings of the time support this version of the events, including a piece from February 1904 describing one landowner's proposal to clear his portion of the Styx of shanties and urging other landowners to follow suit. Additionally, the recollections of Inez Peppers Lovett, herself a Styx resident, support the essence of Reese's account.

"My father came here in the 1800s," recalled Ms. Lovett. "We lived in the Styx, which was just shacks—no running water, no outside toilets, no electric lights . . . The black families built the homes and paid rent on the land. My father collected the $3 a month rent for the owner . . . I moved out of the Styx in my teens. They just told us, 'We want our land.' Then after we all moved out, they cleaned it out." While the image of a sizable number of marginalized workers being evicted from their dwellings is miserable, Flagler had little to do with the episode.

Flagler's building of the Royal Poinciana in the 1890s certainly put a theretofore unknown place on the map, but it was at the time just one more in a series of such undertakings that he justified collectively. "It occurred to me very strongly that someone with sufficient means ought to provide accommodations for that class of people who are not sick, but who come here to enjoy the climate, have plenty of money, but could find no satisfactory way of spending it," he once told reporters.

What developed in Palm Beach, however, was singular. The building of the Royal Poinciana and the Breakers, grand as they were, might be seen as simply the repetition of a series. And even the construction of the imposing Whitehall might be seen as St. Augustine redux, for Flagler had followed up the princely Ponce de Leon there by constructing a fine residence called Kirkside. But Palm Beach was an island—a palm-studded island with a subtropical climate, contained unto itself—and Flagler's establishment thereupon of his hotels, and what was seen as one of the most glamorous private homes in the nation, created a special allure. And even if it took some doing to get to Palm Beach, its far-flung location was yet another aspect of its allure and its insulation, much as would later prove to be true of destinations such as Las Vegas and Palm Springs.

Even if Flagler's demise would prove no lasting impediment to the rise of Palm Beach as a destination for the privileged, it meant a diminution of social activities at Whitehall. Following a memorial service at the chapel at the Royal Poinciana, his remains were transferred by train to St. Augustine where the open casket was placed in the rotunda of the Ponce de Leon. On May 23, 1913, he was laid to rest in the mausoleum of Memorial Presbyterian Church alongside his first wife, Mary, and his daughter Jennie Louise.

Flagler's will gave five thousand shares of Standard Oil stock to his estranged son, Harry, with another eight thousand shares to be divided among Harry's three daughters. There were also various bequests to associates, including FEC superintendent

Joseph Parrott ($100,000); engineer Ingraham ($20,000); and the managers of the hotels in St. Augustine, Palm Beach, and Miami ($10,000 each). But the bulk of the estate, valued in the neighborhood of $100 million, was bequeathed to Mary Lily. A codicil in the will stipulated that the estate holdings, including the FEC, the hotels, and the land development company, were to be operated by a trust for five years, with Mary Lily to receive annual payments of $100,000 during that time, thus allowing for an orderly business transition. Following that period, she would be able to dispose of those properties as she pleased.

Mary Lily, forty-five at the time, also received title to Whitehall in Palm Beach as well as Flagler's real estate holdings in Manhattan (she had previously been deeded Lawn Beach in Mamaroneck), thus becoming one of the wealthiest women in the nation. She would not take as easily to the position as Marjorie Merriweather Post would just a scant year later, however, for nothing in her relationship with Flagler had prepared her for such a transformation. She may have been an accomplished hostess and a fine singer, but those were hardly the skills requisite for managing a mammoth business portfolio.

Shortly after the funeral, Mary Lily closed Whitehall (the 1913 season had already run its course) and returned to New York City to stay for a while with her friends the Pembroke Joneses, eventually dividing her time between an apartment at the Plaza, Satan's Toe, and an occasional residence closer to her family in Asheville, North Carolina. By all accounts the period following Flagler's death was trying and lonely for Mary Lily. And it was scarcely enhanced by the outbreak of World War I and such events as the sinking of the *Lusitania*, which carried as one of its passengers her physician first cousin, Owen Hill Kenan. He survived, but nearly twelve hundred did not, and his description of the demise of Alfred Vanderbilt in the tragedy was the stuff of dramatic headlines in the aftermath: THEY'VE GOT US, SAYS VAN-DERBILT; AMERICAN MILLIONAIRE GREETS FRIEND AS LUSITANIA GOES DOWN.

Newspapers of the time were also understandably on the alert for word of any possible dalliance on the part of the world's wealthiest widow, and later in 1915 headlines across the country featured the exploits of one Zora Emma Johnson, an attractive fifty-one-year-old con woman posing as Mary Lily Flagler in order to bilk a number of impressionable young men out of their savings by promising them future employment once she received her inheritance. Following her conviction on one of the charges, the irrepressible Johnson was overheard proclaiming to her attorney as she was being hauled out of court: "I'll prove that I am Mrs. Flagler yet."

A number of Mary Lily's former friends and family members distanced themselves from her for various reasons, leading her to find some solace in the companionship of her niece Louise Wise (the daughter of her sister Jessie), though Louise was nearly thirty years younger. Also in 1915, matters involving Mary Lily took a turn that would eventually reverberate well into the twenty-first century, when she received some surprising news out of her own past. Her former college sweetheart and lover, Robert Bingham, forty-four, an attorney, judge, and sometime politician living in Louisville, had been widowed in 1913 when his wife was struck and killed by a trolley car. The bereaved Robert wrote out of the blue to Mary Lily in 1915 to let her know that he was planning a trip to Asheville that summer, suggesting that perhaps they might arrange to meet. Some inkling of how this news might have struck Mary Lily is contained in the remarks of a former classmate regarding Bingham: "He was the handsomest man I ever saw. All the women loved him and all the men admired him. He was the social lion of our day."

The circumstances surrounding that meeting in Asheville would turn out to be the stuff of considerable intrigue, matters fueled by family acrimony among Bingham descendants. In 1987, less than a month before the planned publication of a Bingham family biography, *The Binghams of Louisville*, Macmillan Publishers created something of a stir when it announced that it was canceling publication of the book, citing "serious substantive disagreements" that had arisen between the author and members of the Bingham family regarding the interpretation of facts unearthed during his research. The author in question was David Leon Chandler, who had completed the book with the help of his wife, Mary Voelz Chandler, shortly after his 1986 publication of another not-so-flattering biography, *Henry Flagler*, with the subtitle: *The Astonishing Life and Times of the Visionary Robber Baron Who Founded Florida.*

In the new book, bolstered by extensive interviews with Bingham's son Barry and granddaughter Sallie (herself an actor and author), as well as with Kenan family historian Tom Kenan III, Chandler found Robert Bingham something less than a model figure. According to Chandler, Bingham, who would eventually found the powerful publishing empire anchored by the *Louisville Courier-Journal* and the *Louisville Times*, was decidedly down on his luck at the time that he revived his relationship with Mary Lily Kenan in 1915, about $1 million in debt from various political campaign expenses and recently rebuffed in attempts to access the trust fund left by his well-to-do deceased wife for the maintenance of their children. Chandler quotes Sallie Bingham as saying that it was Bingham's bankers who came up with the idea of his traveling to Asheville during that fateful summer, to see "if Mary Lily could help him out."

Tom Kenan suggests in the book, however, that Mary Lily, "utterly lonely," was likely the one who forced the play when

Bingham arrived in Asheville, for as he puts it, "She was a powerhouse." In any case, Bingham was soon a guest in Mary Lily's apartment at the Plaza in New York and at Satan's Toe, and society columnists reported seeing them together at White Sulphur Springs and Louisville as well. According to Tom Kenan's account, Mary Lily was thoroughly reinvigorated by the affair, telling her brother and sisters and niece: "I wouldn't trade places with anyone in the world right now."

She was so transformed that she announced she would reopen Whitehall for the season of 1916, news that was breathlessly reported in *Palm Beach Life*, the society supplement to the *Palm Beach Post*: "The great showplace of Palm Beach has been closed for nearly three years since the death of Mr. Flagler, and it is a genuine pleasure for her many friends to have Mrs. Flagler back in her accustomed place . . . this modest, unassuming little woman, so small of stature but so big of heart. It is a pleasure for everyone to see the big iron gates of Whitehall swung open once more, for we now feel that Mrs. Flagler is really here to stay."

By the fall of 1916 the reunited couple announced their engagement, and though concerned Flagler trustees and Kenan family members expressed fears to Mary Lily that Bingham was nothing more than a fortune hunter, she was having none of it, telling a reporter for the *New York Evening World*: "I know Judge Bingham; he's a most estimable gentleman." For his part, Chandler notes, Bingham agreed to sign a prenuptial agreement forgoing all interests in Mary Lily's vast fortune.

On the afternoon of November 15, the two—he just turned forty-five, she forty-nine—were wed at the home of the Pembroke Joneses on East Sixty-Fourth Street in Manhattan, with the ceremony conducted by the Reverend George Ward, who had also presided over the late Mr. Flagler's funeral service at the Royal Poinciana Chapel in Palm Beach. Despite those

Robert Worth Bingham during his four-year stint as U.S. ambassador to Great Britain, entering the office of Secretary of State Cordell Hull in August 1937.

aforementioned murmurings of unease, the ceremony was attended by several members of the Kenan family as well as by the Binghams. Maid of honor for the new Mrs. Bingham was Louise Wise.

A *New York Times* story on the wedding reminded readers of the size of the estate Flagler had left his widow and included the announcement by Mary Lily that she had drawn up a new will leaving the majority of her holdings to her niece Louise. While this might be viewed as an unusual comment for a bride to make for a story regarding her wedding, it might be supposed

Mary Lily was attempting to allay the concerns of her family. Although there were smaller bequests announced in her will—to Reverend George Ward and to the University of North Carolina, endowing a fund for notable professors—a final clause warned that if any named beneficiary attempted to contest the will, the document should be carried out as if that person were not named in it.

The *Times* piece also carried a summary of Bingham's career, noting that the father of three had served one appointed term as mayor of Louisville and had served briefly as an elected circuit judge before resigning to return to the private practice of law in 1911. The story said that following a honeymoon in the South the two planned to divide their time between Louisville, Whitehall, and New York, where the newlyweds planned to build a home on a block-length parcel of land Mary Lily had acquired on Fifth Avenue between Ninety-Sixth and Ninety-Seventh Streets.

Hardly had the wedding vows been exchanged, however, when notes of discord arose in the midst of what once might have seemed a fairy-tale operetta. According to Chandler, there was no "honeymoon in the South" but rather an immediate return to Louisville where Bingham immersed himself in business and political pursuits. He set the two of them up in a suite of rooms in a less than glamorous Louisville businessman's hotel, the Seelbach, leaving Mary Lily alone most of the time to deal rather unpropitiously with his three resentful children. Chandler reports that seventeen-year-old Henrietta had soon run to her father to complain that Mary Lily was abusing drugs.

Most of those who have written about the brief and disheartening union of Robert Bingham and Mary Lily Kenan agree that the new bride soon found herself in less than ideal circumstances, beset by ill health and troubling premonitions as she witnessed her fabulous new prospects quickly dissolving like so much gossamer.

Bingham had signed that waiver of his dower rights, but he had scarcely gone unrewarded, according to Chandler. Not only had Mary Lily presented her new husband with a wedding gift of $50,000 in cash and paid off the $1 million debt that some said had sent him to her doorstep to begin with, but she also established for him a trust fund composed primarily of Standard Oil stock that provided an annual income of more than $50,000, which, according to the Klepper/Gunther formula, might be worth as much as $10 million in today's currency.

Yet there were few reciprocal signs of bliss or devotion from Bingham. By January 1917, in fact, he had issued orders that work on the proposed new mansion in New York be halted, making it clear that he would not be content to flitter about from one pleasure palace to another on the arm of a wealthy dowager. Mary Lily had found a country estate near Louisville that he was willing to let and renovate, but that would have to do. He needed a base for important business on his home turf, for, as he announced later that month, he would be running for the office of Jefferson County commissioner come fall.

As if to absent herself from the prospect of preparing for that auspicious campaign, Mary Lily ordered up her private railcar and left on a vacation trip to New York, where she treated herself to a shopping spree that included a stop at Tiffany. There, says Chandler, she bought herself a strand of pearls for $228,000.

Upon her return to Louisville, her spirits somewhat emboldened, she announced that she would not be content to endure the remainder of the winter in such bleak environs. Orders were relayed to Palm Beach. Whitehall was to reopen for the 1917 season, she said, and she and her new husband would be there through the Easter holidays. On February 21, *Palm Beach Life* trumpeted the news with the same fervor Mary Lily's return the year before had occasioned, noting that the Pembroke Joneses would join the triumphant return. "Though no plans have been laid for any large functions, Judge and Mrs. Bingham will have a large number of house guests from time to time and will entertain their large circle of friends informally," the magazine assured its readers.

In his account, Chandler notes that shortly after the newly-weds' arrival in Palm Beach that early spring, Mary Lily consulted with her attorneys to make another change to the will that she had filed in December. It was a minor bit of business, upping the amount set for Flagler Hospital in St. Augustine from the high five figures into the low sixes, but the fact that she had called in her own attorneys for the work and again made no mention of any change as regarded the standing of her new husband would soon prove to be significant.

The plans to spend another splendid season in paradise did not proceed as scripted. Though the newlyweds made it through February and well into March without serious incident, the approach of Easter proved to be a disaster. His children were refusing to join the couple at Whitehall for the holiday, Bingham announced to his new bride, and he was going back to Louisville to join them, either in the spittoon-studded Seelbach hotel or in the partially renovated rental estate, Lincliffe.

However disappointed she might have been by Bingham's declaration, Mary Lily gave in. Whitehall was closed, all social engagements were canceled, and the former Mrs. Flagler decamped north with her new husband. An announcement in the *Louisville Courier-Journal* of April 5, 1917, provided the punctuation mark: "Judge Robert Worth Bingham and Mrs. Bingham, who spent the winter at their home at Palm Beach, have returned and are at their apartment at the Seelbach."

By early May, renovations had been completed at Lincliffe, and Bingham and Mary Lily finally had a home to call their own.

A housewarming celebration in early June was covered by the Louisville press in glowing terms, though Chandler writes in his book that Kenan family members conveyed a different story: by that time, Mary Lily was a physical wreck. She spent the evening of the housewarming drunk and virtually incapacitated, barely able to drag herself about the spacious grounds of the estate overlooking the Ohio River, her presence scarcely noticed in press accounts of the affair.

She was by that time under the care of an old friend of Bingham's, Dr. Michael Ravitch, a dermatologist. Most puzzling about the choice of Ravitch was the fact that Mary Lily had been diagnosed with heart disease. And while Louisville might not have had a reputation as the Lourdes of the medical establishment at the time, any number of qualified heart specialists were available to be consulted in that city. Nonetheless, Mary Lily was to remain steadfastly a patient of Dr. Ravitch, even though any progress she made seemed to consist of the sudden though temporary relief from her chest pains following injections of an unknown substance that he provided for her regularly in his offices.

Though temperatures soared as Louisville's June turned into July, the couple did not decamp to Mamaroneck or Asheville or to any other more temperate place. Instead they stayed on at Lincliffe, where on the afternoon of July 12, the high would reach 102 degrees. While accounts are consistent as to the day's resolution, they do differ in the details. One has it that on that day Mary Lily found she was unable to lift herself from her bed. Other sources say that seeking relief from the heat, she drew herself a cold bath, directed a maid to bring up a pitcher of mint julep before she took down a bottle of laudanum pills from her medicine cabinet, and lowered herself into the comforting water. As this account would have it, an hour later the maid returned to the bathroom to find Mary Lily unconscious, her body halfway in and out of the tub.

What seems certain is that on that day, Mary Lily was diagnosed by Dr. Ravitch as having suffered a heart attack. Yet, rather than being taken to a hospital she was instead confined to her bed, where for the next two weeks Ravitch continued to inject her with what nurses said were substantial doses of morphine, ostensibly to ease her chest pains. On July 26, 1917, Bingham passed along to a reporter for the *Courier-Journal* the disquieting news that his wife was suffering from myocarditis and that she had lapsed into a coma. On the following day, while receiving oxygen, she fell into a series of convulsive fits that soon ended in her death. She was fifty-one.

All of this this might be viewed as the lamentable end of an almost preternaturally privileged individual who found herself ultimately incapacitated while dealing with her burdens, real or imagined. Mary Lily Kenan would not be the first or the last of the extraordinarily endowed or talented to ride a hot rod to oblivion. And that may have been exactly what happened. But Chandler's interpretation of the facts of Mary Lily's demise, as well the interpretation of others close to her, differs markedly from the philosophical, and that is what led to the contretemps that erupted in 1987 prior to the planned publication of his book. Chandler's startling contention is that Mary Lily did not die from heart disease—or that if she was suffering from such an affliction, she died of willful maltreatment of that condition as a result of malevolent collusion between Robert Bingham, Dr. Ravitch, and others.

Bingham may not have set out to murder his new wife, Chandler says, but in his book he is certain of one thing: Robert Bingham was intent on moving a portion of his second wife's vast fortune into his own hands, and it is a contention based primarily on one simple fact. Shortly after Mary Lily's death, a previously unknown codicil to her will was discovered, bequeathing the amount of $5 million to none other than Robert

Bingham of Louisville. This secret codicil, it seems, had been prepared by an attorney friend of Bingham's and signed in a shaky hand by Mary Lily in the offices of Dr. Ravitch following one of her treatments. According to David Davies, the attorney who drafted the codicil, it was perfectly reasonable: Mrs. Bingham simply wished to provide a suitable bequest for her new husband because he deserved it, acting so honorably when he forswore any claim to her vast fortune.

When Flagler trustees and Kenan family members learned of this codicil, however, they were outraged. They ordered an exhumation of Mary Lily's remains and an autopsy performed to ascertain with some certainty the cause of her death. The examiners found "enormous" quantities of morphine in Mary Lily's organs, along with the presence of heavy metals such as arsenic and mercury, and had tissue samples sent to labs in New York for further analysis. The Kenan family contested the will containing the $5 million codicil that was filed, and though the Louisville courts decided in Bingham's favor, the Kenans appealed, awaiting final word from the autopsy.

And then, suddenly, inexplicably, the appeal was dropped. Bingham (who would go on to create his newspaper empire and even serve as ambassador to Great Britain in the 1930s) collected the $5 million from Mary Lily's estate, the whole of it said to have grown to somewhere between $130 million and $160 million by that time, and there the matter rested, along with Mary Lily's remains, until Chandler began his research in the 1980s. Perhaps most troubling to both Bingham and Kenan descendants was the ultimate conclusion that Chandler's research led him to: Mary Lily was ill, all right, but she did not have heart disease. She was suffering from tertiary syphilis, Chandler contended, a disease that she had likely contracted from Bingham, perhaps as early as the 1890s during their college affair.

To Chandler, this explains why Dr. Ravitch was called in as a caregiver for Mary Lily in the first place. In those times, dermatologists were in fact the physicians of choice for those who suffered from syphilis. Ravitch had treated Bingham for the disease, Chandler theorizes, and when Mary Lily somewhat late in life began to exhibit symptoms, it was only natural that Ravitch was summoned. Furthermore, Chandler contends, his theory also explains why the Kenans dropped their opposition to Bingham's shenanigans with the will and let him have the paltry $5 million rather than reveal such a shameful secret to the world. Chandler points out that the final autopsy findings remain sealed in the family's vaults to this day.

No member of the Kenan family who has seen the autopsy findings has come forward in support of Chandler's suspicions, though Sallie Bingham and other members of that family have sided with him. Bingham's son, Barry, who took over the newspaper empire following his father's death, was initially cooperative with Chandler, but when, at eighty-two, he discovered the writer's troubling conclusions, he threatened Macmillan with a lawsuit if they were to publish the book, claiming copyright over his comments to Chandler as well as over the family documents that he had made available to the author.

Though the objection based on copyright was dubious, Barry Bingham had resources that were a formidable match for Macmillan, and with a lengthy and expensive court battle looming, the latter entity was the first to blink. In the end, Macmillan announced that it was declining to publish Chandler's book, incurring the wrath of Sallie Bingham, other authors, and free-speech advocates everywhere. Ultimately, Crown Publishers stepped up to issue Chandler's book and no lawsuits ensued.

In 2008, twenty-one years after the publication of *The Binghams of Louisville*, forensic pathologist Thomas K. Resk and professor of political science and law enforcement James A. Bailey collaborated on an article for the journal *Forensic Science, Medicine, and Pathology* in which they made an assessment—albeit at some distance in space and time—of the extant evidence, in an attempt to assign a cause of death for Mary Lily Kenan Flagler Bingham. In their article "The Mysterious Death of America's Richest Woman in 1917," they speculate that the "final" autopsy was likely unable to come to a definitive conclusion owing to various limitations of the science available in that era, as well as the amount of time elapsed between death and exhumation. The authors' own best guess, based on the anecdotal evidence available, is that Mary Lily in fact died of a heart attack. If they are correct, this would provide another possible reason why the Kenan family decided not to further contest the codicil naming Bingham as an heir. If those autopsy records showed nothing conclusive, then the grounds on which to base an appeal might have seemed insufficient.

- 7 -

THE BATON PASSES

The abdication and the death of Mary Lily Kenan were a blow even to those who scarcely knew her, for to many the Flagler name and the grand mansion of Whitehall were inextricably connected with the almost otherworldly lure of Palm Beach. But just as the aura of the legendary Roman nobles' retreat at Herculaneum was far more substantial than that of any emperor whose robes trailed along its seaside cobbles, the metaphorical and physical weight of the town of Palm Beach had come to surpass that of any mere mortal by the time Henry and Ida Alice had died. As one commentator has put it, "Flagler's opening of the east coast [of Florida] to rail travel and his resort hotels in Palm Beach and Miami marked the establishment of Florida's greatest industries . . . No depressions or freezes, however damaging or painful, could destroy them, and in the following decades they would become as identified with the state as palm trees and alligators."

In the beginning, Flagler had made Palm Beach. Now Palm Beach was making people. The insulated town riding the crest of the narrow barrier island between Lake Worth and the Atlantic had come to make manifest the words of Robert Barnwell Roosevelt, who wrote as early as 1884: "To the rough, practical northern mind, Florida is a land of dreams, a strange country full of surprises, an intangible sort of place, where at first nothing is believed to be real and where finally everything is considered possible."

By the time of Mary Lily Kenan Flagler Bingham's death, Palm Beach had become a beacon for the privileged where they might find themselves well insulated from any annoyances of modern existence, including class struggle, labor unrest, and world war. As historian Mark Derr describes it, even at the time of the Flaglers, "few places were more 'sporting' than Palm Beach with its beaches, its heated pools, casino, yachts, polo club, golf course, tennis courts, excursions into the wilds of Florida, gossip, and games of musical beds between mates and lovers."

When Flagler began his efforts in Palm Beach in 1894, the area was still part of Dade County, which stretched all the way from the tip of the state's peninsula in the south to the St. Lucie River in the north, a distance of some 170 miles. West Palm Beach, incorporated as a town in 1894, became a city in 1900, and by 1909 local leaders—disgruntled by the fact that the northern part of Dade County was paying more than 60 percent of the taxes while receiving far less than its fair share of services—were successful in carving out Palm Beach County from the parent. And in 1911, Palm Beach was incorporated as a town, one that would burgeon to as many as 1,135 citizens for the census of 1920.

Though such distinctions as town, city, and county had their practical advantages, it is not as if would-be citizens were waiting for formalities to follow after Flagler in descending from the north; nor was Flagler the only one to make a significant investment in the new Eden. By 1898, colorful Chicago hotelier and gambler Colonel E. R. Bradley had relocated to Palm Beach to build his notorious Beach Club and, shortly afterward, a spacious home he called Pleasant View nearby. In 1903, the original town postmaster and longtime successful merchant E. M. Brelsford built the Banyans, an imposing Greek Revival home, not far from where the Royal Poinciana and Whitehall overlooked Lake Worth. And in 1914, noted Chicago portrait photographer William L. Koehne built the first private home overlooking the Atlantic side of the island, south of the Breakers, opening a cavalcade of such houses. It was named Zila Villa, after Koehne's wife, and some still contend that the residence (demolished in 1974) was designed by Chicago contemporary Frank Lloyd Wright.

Nor did all those who had followed in the Flagler footsteps hold their collective breath, waiting to see if Mary Lily would resurrect Whitehall following the death of her illustrious first husband. By most accounts, the heiress to Mary Lily's position as social doyenne of Palm Beach was Eva Stotesbury, wife of J. P. Morgan partner Edward T. Stotesbury, of Philadelphia. While the upstart Stotesburys were never fully accepted by Philadelphia's Main Liners, Eva's efforts in up-and-coming Palm Beach during the war years would come to earn her the sobriquet "grande dame of the winter set."

Edward was in fact the second husband taken by Eva, a native Chicagoan, who was widowed at the age of forty-four when her first husband, Oliver Cromwell (a descendant), died of a stroke in 1909. Though as Mrs. Cromwell she had been sponsored in New York society by the wife of John Jacob Astor, her first husband had frittered away much of his fortune in the stock market, and his death left Eva in serious need of one who might pick up financially where Mr. Cromwell had left off. Shortly thereafter, on a sea voyage to Paris, where her daughter was to make her debut, Eva met sixty-year-old Edward Stotesbury, himself recently widowed.

The smitten couple wed in January 1912, with "Ned" presenting Eva with a $500,000 diamond necklace and a loop of pearls said to descend to the floor between her feet. Following an elaborate ceremony, the couple traveled in Stotesbury's railcar to Palm Beach for a honeymoon, a choice that all but guaranteed the course of the enclave's future.

When he met Eva, Stotesbury was already a client of British art and antique dealer Joseph Duveen and had acquired one of the

News photo of Eva Stotesbury in 1919; she is described as "Mrs. Edward Townsend Stotesbury, wife of the great Philadelphia capitalist." Philadelphia banker Edward T. Stotesbury and his second wife, Eva, were prominent members of the Palm Beach society that blossomed in the 1920s.

leading private collections of European art, described as rivaling that of Henry Clay Frick.

With Eva as enthusiastic partner, the pair built Whitemarsh Hall on a three-hundred-acre plot outside Philadelphia, a 147-room house of a hundred thousand square feet with formal gardens that evoked comparisons to Versailles. The place is said to have been grand enough to elicit an unusually exuberant comment from guest Henry Ford (no. 11 on the Klepper-Gunther list of wealthiest Americans): "It's a great experience to see how the rich live."

Yet if all that was not enough for the Stotesburys to crack through the barriers preventing them from entrance into the highest ranks of Philadelphia society, they would find the going somewhat easier in Palm Beach, where the lineage stopped well this side of 1776. And Eva Stotesbury was by this time sufficiently self-assured to navigate almost any social gatekeeper's efforts. Shortly after her arrival in Palm Beach, one haughty matron took offense at Eva's outfit, a simple gingham dress enlivened by a strand of pearls.

"Pearls, in the daytime?" sniped the matron, only to be met with Eva's smiling riposte.

"Yes, my dear, I used to feel that way too. But that was before I had the pearls."

Hers was an ease that comforted others understandably uncertain about how one might crack the glass ceiling separating the would-bes from the very highest social layers. Another anecdote describes Mrs. Stotesbury finding herself somehow caught among a group of muttonchoppers trying to top one another with stories about their adroit business maneuverings. She listened to two or three such tales before cutting in: "My only astute business move," she said, "was to marry Mr. Stotesbury."

That may have been so, but the new Mrs. Stotesbury was also the possessor of good taste and a keen insight as to what attracted the interest of others seeking the finest. While the Stotesburys had been part of the scene in Palm Beach from their honeymooning days in 1912, the event that solidified their presence was the building of yet another of their fabulous residences, an undertaking that was itself the result of a seemingly impossible string of circumstances.

* * *

In 1917, Paris Singer, the twenty-second of twenty-four children born to sewing-machine titan Isaac Singer (in Paris, in 1867), paid a visit to Palm Beach, and like so many of the nouveau riche before him he found the island the perfect refuge from an often intrusive press and inquisitive public. Singer, whose father's company had sold about six million machines worldwide, was the offspring of Isaac Singer's third wife, Isabella, one of six children she bore the mogul. Following Isaac Singer's demise in 1877, Isabella Singer was declared the legal heir to the $13 million Singer fortune, and her children eventually divided the bulk of the money.

Paris Singer, whose trust fund was said to provide an income of about $15,000 a week at the time, studied for a while at Cambridge, but found it stifling and soon left the carrels to elope with his mother's maid. That was a short-lived union, however, and following an annulment, he went on to marry an Australian woman, Lillie Graham, with whom he had five children. In 1909, the adventurous Singer began a tempestuous affair with the internationally renowned and free-spirited dancer Isadora Duncan, with whom he fathered a child in 1910. It was the second child Duncan had borne out of wedlock; she had given birth to a daughter by actor Edward Craig in 1906.

Few novelists could conjure a more cataclysmic turn of fortune that what happened thereafter. In 1913, while Singer and Duncan were at lunch in Paris, the automobile carrying Duncan's governess and her two young children plunged into the Seine, where all were drowned. Terrible and guilt inducing as it was, the tragedy did not mark the end between the two, for Singer continued to quietly support her until a final quarrel in 1917 (she is said to have refused his proposed gift of Madison Square Garden—to be her very own performing palace—as a makeup gesture).

His affair with Duncan finally at an end (he would nonetheless send money to her until her death), the fifty-year-old Singer divorced his long-suffering Australian wife in 1918 and soon afterward renounced his British citizenship. He traveled to the United

States and eventually to Palm Beach where he found an unexpected new sense of purpose in life: he was to become the most legendary developer in Palm Beach since Henry Flagler himself.

Taken by the apparent possibilities of the new Eden, Singer purchased a home at 123 Peruvian Avenue and began to buy up property nearby. By the end of March 1918, Singer had, according to the *Palm Beach Post*, spent $250,000 on eight separate parcels on the island. "He has an architect and a lawyer and is incorporating a holding company to manage, develop, and build on the land," the paper said, adding that in the previous week Singer had painted his Peruvian Avenue cottage in Chinese colors and had also installed a stuffed alligator on the roof.

Paris Singer, twenty-second child of sewing machine manufacturer Isaac Singer, whose Everglades Club would transform the Palm Beach social scene.

On May 3, the *Post* offered more detail on Singer's development plans, noting that the aforementioned "architect" engaged by Singer was in fact California transplant Addison Mizner, who, though lacking formal schooling and a Florida license, would, with his work in Palm Beach, Boca Raton, and elsewhere, indelibly transform South Florida practice in his field forevermore.

Mizner was, in the words of just about everyone who met him, "a character." He had been a gold miner in the Yukon and a draftsman employed by an actual architect in California, and had, before his arrival in Florida, designed a number of country houses for wealthy patrons on Long Island. In 1907, he executed the design for White Pine Camp in the Adirondacks, a retreat that Calvin Coolidge later came to employ as his summer White House. A flamboyant bon vivant whose uncertain sexuality intrigues commentators to this day, the six-foot-two-inch, three-hundred-pound Mizner kept as pets a series of monkeys and macaws that often traveled about on his shoulder.

Though his work in Florida is generally categorized as Mediterranean Revival, Mizner had a more evocative way of describing it. It was often his goal, he said, to "make a building look traditional and as though it had fought its way from a small, unimportant structure to a great, rambling house." In Mizner's way of thinking, he was as much telling a story as building a house: "I sometimes start a house with a Romanesque corner, pretend that it has fallen into disrepair and been added to in the Gothic spirit, when suddenly the great wealth of the New World has poured in and the owner had added a very rich Renaissance addition."

Mizner and Singer became a legendary team (the precise nature of their personal relationship remains a provocative question), working together to transform the signature Mediterranean "look" of Palm Beach and much of South Florida in a way that endures to this day. The first of their undertakings was a set of fourteen villas that Singer announced would have nothing to do with the profit motive. Instead, the buildings once completed would be placed at the disposal of the U.S. government and the Allied nations for use as a convalescent center for military officers wounded in France, to accommodate "only such men in need of the invigorating influences of this climate." A clubhouse would anchor the project, Singer said, explaining that the planned Everglades Rod and Gun Club would allow men who were "discharged from hospitals [but] not yet ready to face life" to find "happiness and entertainment."

The soldiers' recovery would be stimulated by "deep-sea fishing, wild pig hunting, alligator hunting, and wild duck shooting." Stories meant to make all this seem plausible explained to readers that in fact Singer had in the early days of World War I converted his family's imposing British mansion, Oldway, into an American Red Cross military hospital.

By January 1919, the war was over and stories in the *Post* announced that what was now being called the Everglades Club for Convalescent Soldiers had neared completion, and Singer was said to have expended $1 million on the seventy-acre project. There were a dozen rooms for residential members in the vast clubhouse, which also featured a dining room that would accommodate up to two hundred guests, and seven of the villas were finished as well, each with seven residential suites. "The club offers a fleet of motor boats, tennis courts and a nearby log cabin, where hunting parties can hunt turkey, quail and deer. A golf course will be constructed later," the *Palm Beach Post* told readers.

Though no wounded officers, French or otherwise, ever hobbled on crutches or wheeled themselves through the portals of the Everglades Club, Singer was spending his own money on the project and had curried no apparent untoward favor by advertising the undertaking as charitable in nature. Furthermore, he had in fact already freely given over two palatial estates in Europe for the benefit of soldiers (he had also donated the use of Redcliffe Towers in Paignton for use by wounded Boer War veterans in 1900), so no one stood up to complain when he announced that the Everglades Club, for lack of subscription by the Allied wounded, would be converted to a private club.

The response to the conversion was electric among Palm Beach regulars. The *Post* reported in June that during the first season in 1919, the club enjoyed "three applications for every room" and that fifteen more sleeping rooms would be added to the facilities. Three hundred lockers for golfers were installed, along with a number of clay tennis courts, a garage for forty cars, and servants' quarters as well. Just prior to the 1920 season, the slate of club officers was announced, including Singer as president and E. T. Stotesbury as vice president. Listed among the new members for the season were Henry F. du Pont, Condé Nast, Herbert Pulitzer, and nobleman A. Leveson-Gower of London.

The meteoric emergence of the Everglades Club with its daily tea dances, its elaborate weekly member dinners, and the season showstopping gala costume ball was all it took for Eva Stotesbury to realize that she had found the perfect new canvas on which to work her architectural magic. In short order, she convinced her husband, E. T., that they should design and build a home to rival Whitehall itself, one that would be far more in keeping with the tropical spirit that surrounded them, a place where they might rise to heights of prominence impossible for them in Philadelphia.

The fact that a couple reportedly so personable and successful would have difficulty being welcomed into social circles within their home city at that time is not so surprising. The writer John McPhee quotes poet John Bossidy delivering a toast at a 1910 Holy Cross alumni dinner in Boston:

And this is good old Boston,
The home of the bean and the cod,
Where the Lowells talk only to Cabots
And the Cabots talk only to God.

While the doggerel targets snobbery among the illustrious denizens of the Massachusetts capital, the sentiment could be applied equally to certain segments of New York, Philadelphia, Washington, Newport, Charleston, and other places where "position"—or seniority in prominence—ruled supreme well into the twentieth century.

* * *

Americans were initially happy to swear off the despicable vestiges of European nobility in their new world—such distinctions were, after all, what led to the Revolution, the U.S. Constitution, and the Bill of Rights. Nonetheless, not long after the surrender of the British Earl Cornwallis, the "haves" in the new nation began a process of codification meant to distinguish them definitively from the "have-nots." In Europe and Great Britain, such publications as the *Almanach de Gotha,* first issued in 1763, and *Burke's Peerage, Baronetage and Knightage* (1826) purported to keep careful track of the family trees of royalty and the landed gentry.

In the States, the drive to delineate those of status, as distinct from the rabble, eventually found its way from word of mouth to printed form in the *Social Register,* first published in 1887. Money alone did not qualify one for inclusion in the pages of the *Social Register,* or in the various *Blue Books* and the like that followed along. Full acceptance required the cultural capital and cachet that only "old money"—inherited money—brings.

Thus, Edward T. Stotesbury may have been raking it in hand over fist in Philadelphia during the opening years of the twentieth century, but too many burghers lived there who had witnessed the signing of the Declaration of Independence—or somehow believed that they had—for an upstart like him to be brought into the fold. Key to the identity of a societal elite is exclusivity, and the great proliferation of wealth brought about in the United States during the Gilded Age posed a dilemma for the New World's old guard. Purported exemplars of a new society based on notions of merit and equality of opportunity, they were faced with an onslaught of new millionaires jostling for position at the trough of privilege. How else to distinguish between themselves and the newcomers except by invoking seniority?

For America's more recent wealthy, then, Palm Beach appeared at the perfect time and in the pluperfect place. It had been founded by a man who began his career as a shopkeeper's assistant, one who ran away from home jingling eight pennies in his pocket. Yet, despite such humble beginnings, in planting the flag on the island, Henry Flagler had displayed a vision to rival or even to surpass that of the early Spanish explorers. And he had gone on to variously decorate Palm Beach in a taste sufficient to attract a brand-new wave of aristocrats to a place where they could enjoy their freshly minted coinage free from the supercilious stares of hopelessly stuffy predecessors.

A sense of adventure thus bloomed in the minds of the Stotesburys when they realized they, too, had the opportunity and the means to re-create possibility itself. And what more appropriate phrase to describe the time of their ascendance than the Roaring Twenties?

- 8 -

GLORIA IN EXCELSIS

In 1960, Cleveland Amory published a paean to a lost era entitled *Who Killed Society?* Therein he quoted a Mrs. Edward C. Barry as lamenting, "Mercy! Society isn't a knit thing any more. It's everybody and his brother." Mrs. Barry had served as the editor of the *Social Register*, the directory of U.S. citizens presumed to be "elite," for sixty years. Mrs. Augustus Hemenway of Boston—at the time 103 and New England's reigning dowager (she was the founder of an institution called the Society of Those Still Living in the House They Were Born In)—added: "Society is a Nineteenth Century word in a Twentieth Century world . . . It's gone with the wind—kaput—kaflooey." And Chicago's Mrs. G. Alexander McKinlock, for many years a resident of Vita Serena, a cottage in Palm Beach, chimed in: "In the old days, everything was private. There were private houses and private parties and private balls and private yachts and private railroad cars and private everything. Now everything is public—even one's private life."

The sentiments might as well have been lifted from comments made in the twenties in Palm Beach by those aghast at what atrocities were being committed on "society" there. At the onset of the decade, notice had already been posted of dire changes at the highest levels of American society. The first of the well-known society columnists in the United States was a man named Maury Henry Biddle Paul who wrote under such pen names as "Dolly Madison," "Polly Stuyvesant," and "Billy Benedick." In 1921, Paul, who was recognized at the time as the final arbiter of who did and did not count in America, published a list dividing the upper crust into those he termed "Old Guard" and those who represented an up-and-coming "Café Society." Among the former were the names of Mrs. John R. Drexel, Mrs. J. Pierpont Morgan, Pierre Lorillard, Mrs. John King Van Rensselaer, Philip Rhinelander, and Mrs. Cornelius Vanderbilt. Those upstarts among the latter included Florida land and handsaw magnate widow Mrs. William Disston, Marion Tiffany, and Mrs. Edward T. Stotesbury.

Yet if the emergence of such new blood was disconcerting to the so-called old guard, it must have been an exhilarating boost to those such as Eva Stotesbury. News of the impending opening of the Everglades Club sent euphoria drifting through Palm Beach like the tides of night-blooming jasmine, enough for Eva to place an immediate call to Horace Trumbauer, who had designed the Stotesburys' palatial Whitemarsh Hall in Chestnut Hill. She wanted to join the bandwagon of splendor about to roll through Palm Beach and asked Trumbauer to formulate a design for El Mirasol, a private home that would make an equally spectacular splash in her winter retreat. Though Trumbauer undoubtedly gave the endeavor his all, Addison Mizner, in his unpublished memoirs, tells of happening on Mrs. Stotesbury at the tail end of the 1919 season, finding the matron with tape in hand measuring off the terraces outside the Everglades Club. When he approached to ask what she might be doing, Eva confessed all.

"Oh, Mr. Mizner, you have made me so discontented with the plans I have had done for El Mirasol." She glanced about at the splendor that surrounded them. "I don't think I will ever be content with them after seeing this."

It was a few short weeks later that Mizner received a summons from the Stotesburys. They had sacked Trumbauer, they told him, and wished for Mizner to undertake a proper design for El Mirasol.

The Stotesburys' forty-acre site at 348 North Ocean Boulevard lay at the very north end of that street and extended all the way across the island from oceanfront to lakeshore. Though it was bisected by County Road, the north-south artery that ran the length of the island, Mizner took pains to design landscaping that would conceal the road from view. Unless there were a momentous collision or car fire, anyone visiting might have wondered how on earth the architect had managed to make a major highway vanish. The grounds themselves had self-sustaining features such as a vegetable garden and a chicken coop (Mizner bowed to delicate sensibilities by noting it as a chicken *house*) along with lavish tropical gardens, orange groves, an aviary, and a zoo.

The house itself would become, in the words of Mizner's biographer Donald Curl, "the standard for judging later great Palm Beach mansions," even though Mizner found Eva more of a meddler as a client than he preferred. As Mizner wrote in his unpublished memoirs, he preferred a customer who signed a contract at the end of the season and then left for the North. By the time the next season rolled around, the client would return to find a house waiting to be occupied. He managed to do the same with El Mirasol, though it was not easy.

Even at long distance, he had been forced to make seven changes to milady's bathroom, he complained, despite the fact that "there are only three pieces that must go in." Hardly had those changes been settled on, furthermore, when the missus determined that the sitting room and the bathroom would have to switch places. It was the sort of thing that made him wish he had taken up another profession, Mizner observed, for a doctor could simply chloroform his patient "and do as he likes."

Still, the work got done, and on the twenty-ninth of January 1920, the Stotesburys returned to Palm Beach to find El Mirasol furnished and in readiness. What the Stotesburys discovered was a typical Mizner extravaganza, an opulent Moorish/Mediterranean design that he had ad-libbed along the way, with thirty-seven rooms occupying an area of thirty-five thousand square feet, half a dozen patios, an illuminated swimming pool, and an underground garage that could hold forty cars.

One entered from the north on a level below the main floors of the house and ascended a grand staircase to a living room where 175 might sit comfortably, enjoying a view—through unbroken banks of French doors—of the Atlantic to the east and the Versailles-worthy sculptured grounds to the west. Chandeliers that Mizner obtained from a Spanish castle dangled from a paneled ceiling, where the wood had been given an aged, distressed look by blasts from a small-bore shotgun and repeated stabbings from an ice pick. Where poured concrete might be visible on stairways or patios, a similar sense of age had been achieved by workmen shod in hobnail boots tromping back and forth before the surface had quite set. Though air-conditioning was yet to come in Palm Beach, a brochure prepared sometime later pointed out Mizner's ingenious placement of "grilled windows" in the ceilings of the rooms to "guarantee absolutely complete ventilation."

El Mirasol proved to be everything the Stotesburys had hoped for, propelling Eva to the station of hostess nonpareil in Palm Beach, a distinction she might have spent a lifetime fruitlessly chasing in Philadelphia. Local papers noted that her annual birthday party at the mansion on February 26 rivaled the Washington Birthday Ball as the social highlight of the season. At a later party a former ambassador to Spain opined that the Stotesbury mansion "far surpassed anything in Spain," with the possible exception of the king and queen's royal castle. Perhaps the grandest event to take place during those early years was the wedding of Mrs. Stotesbury's daughter Louise Cromwell to General Douglas MacArthur on the grounds, where the guest list reflected a prominence sufficient to make Jay Gatsby proud.

The Stotesburys would remodel and add to El Mirasol in 1925 and again in 1930, with Stotesbury's $100 million fortune more than sufficient to cover the costs, even if he often complained that it seemed Mrs. Stotesbury's spending habits would break him. As she once told a visitor who expressed astonishment at finding that the bathroom fixtures were gold plated, "They're very economical. You don't have to polish them, you know." Estimates of the original cost of the home were around $1 million, and one source says that Stotesbury finally put his foot down on his wife's weekly allowance in Palm Beach: she was to hold herself to $12,000 a week and not a penny more.

Though the house would be demolished in 1959, some evidence of its grandeur is still to be experienced in the form of its rebuilt gateway placed today on North County Road. Perhaps an even more effective evocation of its magnificence is to be found in the W. C. Fields film *It's the Old Army Game* (1926), where the comedian nonchalantly drives his automobile onto the front lawn of the estate and proceeds to lay out a picnic for his uninvited, Joad-like family. The seemingly endless trashing and destruction that follow are meant to be funny but at times are almost too painful to watch. "The owner of that house will pay dearly for this," Fields vows at the film's end, pointing at a dent his fender acquired as it smashed through a garden wall exiting onto North Ocean Boulevard.

The design of the Everglades Club and El Mirasol made Addison Mizner the most sought-after architect in the area for a considerable period, and while stories circulate to this day

regarding his technical shortcomings—he had forgotten stairways to second floors, had misplaced bathrooms in the middle
of kitchens, had never drawn a plan or an elevation until his
structures were complete—biographer Donald Curl suggests that
Mizner was well aware of the value of creating a certain mystique among the moneyed set and was likely the author of many
of even the most outlandish tales about himself. One young
draftsman recalls the sum total of Mizner's advice as "Never
design a staircase you can't walk up with a hat on" and "Never
design a fireplace that smokes."

*Addison Mizner, whose imaginative Mediterranean
designs characterize Palm Beach style and influence
South Florida architecture to this day.*

Biographer Caroline Seebohm recaps the familiar story that Mizner had forgotten to include a staircase in Casa Nana, a home designed for the Rasmussen family in 1926. According to legend, Mizner is supposed to have corrected his mistake by hastily adding an exterior circular staircase to the structure. The story persisted into the 1970s until the publication of an interview with Lester Geisler, a Mizner associate, who recalled that the architect had actually centered his design for the home on that impressive circular staircase. There was concern among the workmen who built the staircase, Geisler said, but that had nothing to do with its being added on at the last minute. There was no central support for the staircase, but Mizner pointed out that none was needed: like the blocks in an arch, each step within the spiral supported every other step.

Curl describes the architect's day as a well-planned one of rising before six to complete his necessary personal work before "office hours" and the inevitable stream of clients, customers, and contractors to be dealt with. His afternoons were devoted to inspections of projects under construction, and evenings were given over to what was equally important to his actual design work: attending Palm Beach parties, the chief source of his client stream. He might be exhausted by evening, might even be dreading the need to smile and make small talk, but as he wrote in his memoirs, "When I would get to a party, I always enjoyed it."

By 1922, the nation's economy had begun to roar like a locomotive's furnace, and over the next three years, Mizner designed more than thirty structures in Palm Beach, including villas for titans of industry, several shops and office buildings, and a new studio and house for himself. Mizner in fact built a number of his own residences in Palm Beach, but he did not stay in any for long. His first he called El Solano, built in 1919 about a mile south of Worth Avenue; here he installed three-hundred-year-old paneling along with furniture, red velvet, and tapestries from Spain, all enhancing a lovely sea view he enjoyed from the "cottage's" second-floor loggia. Within a year, Harold S. Vanderbilt had convinced Mizner that the house had to be his, and soon the architect was living in temporary quarters again, busily designing additions for another scion. It was a pattern he would repeat many times during his heyday in Palm Beach.

As Curl notes, there is no way to be sure just how many structures in Palm Beach were designed by Mizner (some contend there are thirty-seven still standing), for his office inventory includes designs for a number of houses that no longer exist or that cannot be matched with certainty to him. Also, some structures remain today that are known to have been designed by Mizner but that he never documented in his records.

What can be determined with certainty is the great impact that Mizner made on the town. Prior to his arrival in 1919, the architecture of Palm Beach was a mishmash: Beaux-Arts mansions were flanked by shingled bungalows (even on the Flagler property), which in turn were nestled beside Swiss chalets, with neighboring homes that might be reproductions of Cape Cod cottages. Mizner's work between 1919 and 1925 established a style that would dominate Palm Beach architecture—and much of South Florida—ever after. Only Santa Fe, New Mexico, might rival Palm Beach in architectural consistency, says biographer Seebohm, lamenting the inevitable transmogrifications that have overtaken most American resorts. While some might debate the purity of his design themes, Mizner cared not a whit for such cavils. "Most modern architects have spent their lives carrying out a period to the last letter and producing a characterless copybook effect," he told an interviewer. "My ambition has been to take the reverse stand."

Florida was an exotic place and Mizner gave the moneyed transplants to that place equally exotic habitations to root them there. In 1921, when Stotesbury's partner Leonard Thomas bought a lot on Lake Worth adjacent to the Everglades Club, he naturally sought out Mizner to design his home. Mizner took a look at the waterside setting and suggested that something on the order of a Venetian palazzo would be appropriate there. Thomas, who had spent time as a diplomat in Europe, was quick to agree and went off to Italy to find Renaissance furnishings, an Italian staff, and a gondola, while Mizner did his stuff. What rose on the property (and still stands there, as Casa de Leoni) looks for all the world like a structure plucked from Venice and rising straight up from the waters, with its arched and decorated trefoil windows and stone balconies linked to a style that Mizner called Venetian Gothic.

Whether one were to describe the structures as Venetian Gothic, Mediterranean, Mediterranean Revival, Moorish Mediterranean, or Ali Baba Comes to Florida, Mizner's buildings "worked," and not only did they contain their necessary complement of staircases and functioning bathrooms, but they also seemed to *belong*, with a casual glance at many suggesting centuries of existence in their environs. This patina of antiquity was central to Mizner's popularity, for aged ceilings, hobnailed concrete staircases, and worm-eaten furniture suggested precisely what so many of the newly wealthy so ardently sought: the stamp of approval from time itself. In any case, by 1925, as Curl aptly puts it, "Whether designed by Mizner or other architects, stucco walls, red-tile roofs, and Mediterranean architectural ornamentation had become the rule for Palm Beach."

And while a great many contemporary architects complain about the bland neo-Mediterranean style that dominates South Florida building and seems to plop down so many lot-line-to-lot-line mini mansions today, Sarasota architect Thorning Little points out that such shortcomings are hardly Addison Mizner's fault:

"Sensitivity to proportion and tuning" is key, says Little. "Some people get it—they have an ear for music. They have an eye for color. Or they have a sense for proportion. Mizner had it. He had a sense of those environments that few individuals have."

* * *

Certainly Mizner was aware of the influence he had come to wield in this new Eden. If he had not been, it is doubtful he would have had the courage or the hubris to embark on the new project that he intended as the summa of his career. Having stamped his vision on one of the most exotic and sought-after destinations in the nation, reengineering the American Xanadu in a few short years, he decided to design such an enclave of his very own from the ground up, incorporating every element that would make for the perfect living place. This new city would become the apogee of paradisiacal living and stand as a beacon for all those desperate to secure a foothold in Florida, and it would be known as Boca Raton.

Boca Raton had in fact incorporated as a city shortly before Mizner's arrival in 1925, but once he and the syndicate of investors he put together had purchased two miles of beachfront at Boca Raton Inlet and sixteen hundred acres on the estuary just inland, the city for all intents and purposes became his, the place where he would create, as he put it: "The foremost resort city on the North American continent." A Ritz-Carlton Hotel would anchor the project, along with three golf courses (one designed by Donald Ross), a polo field, a casino, and much more.

Soon, the Mizner Development Corporation was selling lots in offices located not only in Miami and West Palm Beach but also in New York, Philadelphia, Pittsburgh, Boston, and Chicago.

In short order, Mizner had sold more than $4 million worth of lots, and by May 1925, grateful city fathers appointed him as the city planner, with full authority to design and plat the city's entire area of incorporation. As one company brochure proclaimed: "Under the hand of Addison Mizner every public building shall take its form."

By June, Mizner had sold $6 million in lots and was employing three thousand men clearing land for his various projects. He drew up plans for his own residence in the city, a home that would take the shape of a "medieval" castle on an island in Lake Boca Raton (the estuary just back of the beachfront) that would require crossing a working drawbridge to reach.

Mizner was not the only one attempting to make a killing by selling lots in the new Eden of South Florida, and many of his competitors were far less scrupulous than he. Options on lots in new communities often changed hands as many as a dozen times in a day, driving prices to unrealistic levels, with the real estate industry in Florida plagued by so-called binder boys, who were making fortunes by repeating outrageous promises and collecting sizable commissions every time a slip of paper passed from hand to hand. Rumors of fraud and the failure of developers to live up to promises regarding their proposed new enclaves began to circulate, and reporters from northern papers were soon roving the state looking for any sign of scandal.

A number of prominent northerners whom Mizner had recruited to his new company's board of directors grew uncomfortable about having their names linked to the grandiose promises made in advertisements, and finally, fearing he would ultimately be found liable if the undertaking collapsed, T. Coleman du Pont, owner of New York's Waldorf Astoria Hotel, resigned from Mizner's board in November 1925, along with several others. The resignations, widely reported throughout the

Northeast, effectively constituted the beginning of the end for Mizner's dreams.

Though Mizner struggled to keep his enterprise afloat after his board's collapse, by the beginning of 1926, most of the purchasers of those $6 million worth of lots were defaulting on the payments required subsequent to their deposits, and without investors or cash flow, the Mizner Development Corporation was doomed. By May, the company was in receivership, and though Mizner was kept on as chief architect in hopes that his name might allow for something of a revival, a devastating hurricane in September 1926 swept across South Florida, virtually destroying Miami and the fledgling communities of Miami Beach and Coral Gables. It was the death knell, and with the Great Depression soon to follow, development in South Florida was virtually ended until after World War II.

Mizner returned to his offices in Palm Beach following the Boca Raton debacle, but his fortunes there were never to be revived to their former glory. Though Palm Beach would prove to be relatively safe from the effects of the Great Depression, other designers had come to town during Mizner's absence, just as eager to please their wealthy clients and some even more technically skilled, Maurice Fatio and Marion Sims Wyeth among them.

As always, public tastes wax and wane, and with Mizner out of the picture for an extended time, those propounding stylistic alternatives to the Mizner look and others offering the same thing only different became the new darlings. Though Mizner never went completely without work, his ability to sustain the grandiose lifestyle to which he had been accustomed was greatly compromised. Old friends were said to slip his staff members cash to pay the utility bills and the servants' salaries, but Mizner never lost his zest for life.

In the fall of 1932, he published a volume of his memoirs, *The Many Mizners*, featuring a colorful account of his early life and a number of amusing anecdotes describing his encounters with the rich and famous. A second volume was promised for 1933, and the 128 pages of manuscript that survive are studded with typically delicious Mizner jabs, including an episode in which he went to great lengths to convince a visiting Italian artist that Mrs. Stotesbury's name was to be pronounced "strawberry." But the second volume of *The Many Mizners* would remain forever unpublished. The architect died on February 5, 1933, at the age of sixty-one, from heart failure.

Shortly before Mizner's death, his brother, Wilson, a Hollywood screenwriter and notorious wisecracker, cabled, "Stop dying. Am trying to write a comedy."

Mizner's answer ought to have been emblazoned on his tombstone: "Am going to get well. The comedy goes on."

- 9 -

THE QUEEN IS DEAD—
LONG LIVE THE QUEEN

Marjorie Merriweather Post's first visit to Palm Beach and the Flagler resorts came in 1909, when she was twenty-two and still in the company of her first husband, Edward Close. At that time, visitors still reached the island by railroad bridge (trains would eventually be replaced by streetcars) or boat, and there were no cars on the island. Though the train stopped at both the Royal Poinciana and the Breakers, one thereafter got about "on shank's mare" as wits of the day might refer to walking, or by bicycle or in wheeled wicker carts pedaled by (invariably) black valets, leading to their designation as "Afro-mobiles." Marjorie and Edward were as taken by the beauty and the solitude as many others were and returned to the island every season for the next several years, until her father's death and World War I intruded on her virtually idyllic existence.

While Marjorie felt a natural obligation to step into her father's shoes at the Postum Company, Edward would have much preferred that they resume a previously unfettered life at the Boulders in Connecticut. An early compromise engineered by Marjorie was to shift a goodly portion of the business affairs of the company from Battle Creek to New York, where she and Edward could spend the week and then return to the Boulders and their daughters on weekends. The arrangement might have worked if the Fates had not intervened, but in late May 1917, shortly after the United States entered the war, an electrical fire broke out in the couple's splendid Connecticut home, burning it nearly to the ground.

For Marjorie, it was a turning point. Following the disaster, any notion that she would continue her life as a chitchatting suburbanite was over once and for all. They would move to Manhattan where she assumed her rightful place as a mover and shaker. By that time Edward was an army soldier, and a few months later he was on his way to a posting in France, where he would remain until after the armistice in 1918. When he returned home, he was bearing a medal from the French government for his heroics, but the embrace he received from his wife contained little trace of the passion he might have hoped for. In his absence, Marjorie Close had in effect transformed herself back to Marjorie Merriweather Post, the head of one of the most powerful business entities in the nation, and was also well aware of the shortcomings of a marital union she had engineered a dozen years before largely out of rebellion. Within months, she asked Edward for a divorce.

Without a great deal of protest, Edward relented. Neither was to spend a great deal of time alone. By the end of 1919, Close was back in Greenwich and happily remarried to a woman named Elizabeth Taliaferro, who would soon bear him two sons, one of whom would become the father of the actress Glenn Close. Marjorie, then thirty, had met well-known stockbroker E. F. "Ned" Hutton at a cocktail party on Long Island in 1917. Though she found the forty-two-year-old Hutton just as attractive and charming as most other women did, no sparks flew at that first meeting, for Hutton was otherwise entangled, having been married to Blanche Horton, by all accounts happily, for seventeen years.

Marjorie next encountered Hutton as she stepped aboard a houseboat in Palm Beach in the spring of 1919. During that party, held against the backdrop of a Palm Beach that had transformed itself from a sleepy vacation hideaway into a glittering showplace for a nation preparing itself to explode into excess on every front, she learned that Blanche Horton had died in the mass postwar Spanish influenza outbreak. Handsome, wealthy, impeccably dressed, and as brilliant and debonair as any man might be, E. F. Hutton was now a bachelor, one of the most eligible of his kind.

Under such circumstances, one might apprehend the sense of possibility that arose within both parties on that night, as two of the most attractive, powerful, available people alive met in a setting that could scarcely have been more

Marjorie Merriweather Post Close Hutton with the dashing E. F. "Ned" Hutton shortly after their "fairy-tale" wedding of 1920.

evocatively supposed or palpably charged. A bit over a year later, on July 7, 1920, E. F. Hutton and Marjorie Merriweather Post were, after a brief engagement, married in a private ceremony at her home at 2 East Ninety-Second Street in Manhattan, one block north of the spot where Andrew Carnegie had built his mansion scarcely two decades before.

Despite the magnitude of the two estates and the two personages being joined, there was little fanfare regarding the wedding, news of which came in a subhead of the *New York Times* society pages the following week. The piece put the size of Marjorie's portfolio at $20 million, noting that she had obtained a divorce from Edward Close the year before. Hutton was described by the paper as "a banker of this city" and a member of the New York Yacht Club, the Union League, and "other clubs." There might have been an asterisk placed after that last item, for despite Hutton's burgeoning wealth and popularity, he, like the Stotesburys in Philadelphia, had not been embraced by his city's old money. Directors of such venerable institutions as the Down Town Association and the Union Club were simply not ready to admit a parvenu such as he.

Marjorie, at thirty-three, had by that time found the perfect balance in her life as a hard-charging businessperson by day, counterpointed by the company of a dazzling array of accomplished friends and associates in the evenings. She delighted in being entertained and took just as much pleasure in entertaining. And to her, the latter required the proper venue above all.

Though she had no intention of returning to distant, stodgy Connecticut, she and Ned needed a home outside the city where weekends could be spent at leisure, away from crowds and traffic, and where her two daughters, Adelaide and Eleanor, might enjoy something of a "normal" existence. This home, to be known as Hillwood (there would later be a second Hillwood near Washington,

D.C.), was constructed in 1921 on a wooded 176-acre site in the Long Island community of Brookville, about thirty miles east of Manhattan. The estate was a rambling affair designed by New York's Charles M. Hart in the English Tudor style.*

Hart designed Hillwood with a rich and woodsy main house connected to a series of wings that gave the assemblage the appearance of a closely grouped collection of cottages more than a dominating estate. Massive wood-beamed ceilings, leaded windows, all manner of creaking staircases and nooks and crannies made the whole thing an Anglophile's delight. Outdoors were manicured gardens, including a topiary, stables, a tennis court, and, in deference to a new hobby Marjorie had picked up, a putting green.

Though Hillwood well served its principal purpose as a weekend and summer retreat for the couple, its idyllic setting provided only a vague simulacrum of the next of Marjorie's flights of fancy. Even as work on Hillwood was being completed, Marjorie was hard at work to convince Ned of the fabulous prospects at the Adirondack great camp of Lothrop, an assemblage of rustic cottages surrounding a main lodge on 207 acres of ridgeline wilderness property in far upstate New York, above Saranac Lake, about thirty miles south of the Canadian border. Marjorie had acquired the property in 1920, enamored of its isolation and rustic beauty, which recalled to her fond memories of similar retreats she had enjoyed during her Connecticut days.

Isolation might in fact be something of an understatement, for the "camp" itself, named after a prominent department store family from Washington, D.C., was situated atop an eighty-foot cliff some 310 miles from New York City, was served by no road, and could be accessed only by boat. Visitors would take the train to

---

* It stands today, housing the administrative offices and other facilities of Long Island University/ Post.

the hamlet of Lake Clear Junction, then be transported by car two miles to Upper St. Regis Lake. There they would board the yacht *Merriweather* for a jaunt across the lake to a private boathouse where a funicular would whisk them one hundred feet up to the sixty-eight-building compound. (The staff could drive around to the back of the property, but they would have to park there and hike up a steep switchback trail to reach the site.)

Such difficulties only enhanced the exotic character of the place for Marjorie, however, and soon she had a team of architects and builders hard at work renovating and enlarging the property, which she renamed Hutridge in honor of her new husband. After $500,000 worth of work, Hutridge had taken on the shape of a Hollywood fantasy. Most impressive was the splendid main lodge with two stone fireplaces in a great room studded with antlered chandeliers; a hanging birch-bark canoe; loon, porcupine, and fox trophies; an array of Native American rugs and exotic animal skins; and horseshoe- and spur-festooned lamps, all in all a set of western paraphernalia that would outdo any auction house's assemblage. Surrounding the lodge were eighteen meticulously retrofitted log cabins, with running water, electricity, baths, fireplaces, and sitting rooms, and each attended by a maid and butler (during the summer season and with a full complement of guests, there was a staff of eighty-five in all). To summon a staff member or arrange for a swim, a haircut, a massage, or an interlude with a dance instructor, guests had only to press a button on a panel that offered four dozen or so choices.

For amusement, guests might swim, fish, hike, hunt, or canoe, but in the evenings they were expected to be prompt for dinner in the main lodge and, furthermore, to be attired in dinner jackets and gowns. Such a juxtaposition of the raw and the cooked might seem somewhat bizarre, but the experience at Hutridge contained the selfsame appeal of a vintage Hemingway safari or a contemporary luxury cruise down a stately middle-European river, where one alights from a sleek glass-and-steel ship to dally about medieval ruins for an afternoon only to return to canapes and squab at dinner. For Marjorie, Hutridge constituted unalloyed pleasure, and though she would later change its name to Topridge, discarding the reference to her second husband, it would remain a favored center for the practice of her fabled feats of hospitality, maintained until the end of her days.*

Nor were Marjorie's instincts toward palatial grandeur restricted to Hillwood and Topridge. By 1926, wearied by the steady encroachment of traffic and hustle bustle on her home at the corner of Fifth Avenue and East Ninety-Second Street, Marjorie decided to accept the overtures of developer George Fuller, who wanted to demolish the five-story mansion and build a twelve-story luxury apartment complex in its place. Her agreement had only one condition attached: that Fuller would agree to essentially re-create her existing home on the top three floors of his new building.

If America was correctly described in the words of Edward, Prince of Wales, as "the country where nothing was impossible," Fuller would see no reason why Mrs. Post's wishes could not be accommodated. Indeed, when the building that was now entered at 1107 Fifth Avenue was completed, Mr. and Mrs. Hutton would occupy what was called the largest apartment in New York, a fifty-four-room, seventeen-bath triplex penthouse.

Though the main building's address had changed, the Huttons would in fact continue to use their own private entrance around

---

* Hutridge/Topridge was conveyed to the state of New York following Mrs. Post's death, and the camp limped along for a decade as a resort open to a public willing to pay $40 a night for a room, but receipts never rose to the level that would support the fifteen employees and some $325,000 a year required to maintain the facilities. In 1985, after reserving about half of the acreage to become a part of the Adirondack Forest Preserve, the state sold the principal structures and grounds of Topridge at auction to a Camden, New Jersey, businessman, Roger Jakubowski, who paid all of $911,000 for the privilege. Jakubowski was to go bankrupt in the early nineties, when Topridge was acquired by Texas businessman, collector, and conservative philanthropist Harlan Crow.

the corner at 2 East Ninety-Second Street, where ground-floor amenities included a drive-through entryway; a doorman's station; and a foyer with a fireplace, a fountain, and a concierge's apartment. The elevator there carried visitors to a twelfth-floor entrance to the residence proper, where one alighted into a foyer of forty-four by forty-four feet, a space that would prove sufficient for members of the Metropolitan Opera to perform at the housewarming.

The dining room could seat 125 guests, whose coats and cloaks were parsed into separate rooms for men and women. Many of the rooms offered glorious views of Central Park, and on the top floor, wraparound terraces provided 360-degree views of the entire city. Among a list of amenities that would surpass almost any expectations were a dozen fireplaces, a brace of laundry rooms, and quarters for a staff of twenty-one. There was a separate closet for ball gowns, a silver room, a wine closet, cold-storage rooms for furs and for flowers, and one guest bathroom where a guest might press a button to choose among a selection of French perfumes.

"I've never seen anything quite as luxurious as that apartment," said one veteran real estate executive in the 1960s, when tax concerns and the cost of a service staff had reduced the size of a "luxury" unit to eight or nine rooms. Marjorie held a fifteen-year lease on the property, for which she paid $75,000 a year. Following her 1941 departure, the triplex sat vacant for nearly ten years, there appearing to be no one who had the wherewithal to meet the rent. Eventually, the mortgage on the entire building was foreclosed and the triplex was converted into a half-dozen apartments.

* * *

For all these prodigious undertakings, the Huttons nonetheless found a special appeal available to them in Palm Beach, where none of the distinctions as to one's time in grade at the top prevailed and an arriviste's claim to status was just about as valid as any other multimillionaire's. Furthermore, those who had come to this new paradise in the tropics could lay claim to a certain rightful cachet, for they were founding fathers in their own right, pioneers hacking out a place on a new tropical frontier, albeit one of an exotic sort.

Marjorie would come to realize that in addition to the empyreans of pleasure and delight that she had created elsewhere, in Palm Beach she had found the perfect place to plant her flag of splendor. Her first move in that direction came in 1921, when she and Ned Hutton rented one of the apartments at the Everglades Club. However, two individuals who found appeal in living on an inaccessible wilderness mountaintop might understandably find life in a golf course townhouse a bit confining. As Marjorie would later recall, "[The place] was so horribly noisy on both sides of it that we just couldn't cope." Thus, "in desperation" as she put it, she and Ned went searching for a more secluded site on which they could build something more suitable.

One day, as the pair strolled down Golfview Road, the lane that approached the club just a block south of Worth Avenue, they bumped into Marion Sims Wyeth, a Princeton graduate and École des Beaux-Arts–trained architect who had recently moved to Palm Beach to open a firm with business partner Frederic King. The encounter would prove fortuinate for all parties. Following the completion of his training in Paris, Wyeth had returned to New York, where he worked for a time in the offices of Carrère and Hastings, the firm that had designed Flagler's Whitehall. Wyeth was thus well aware of the phenomenon of Palm Beach, including the work of Addison Mizner, and while he suspected there was room for more than one architect in the burgeoning town, he had not yet established himself there at the time he ran into the Huttons.

By the end of that day, Marjorie and Ned had handed over $100 for a golf-view lot to Paris Singer at the Ocean and Lake Realty Company and commissioned Wyeth to build a home on it. The result was Hogarcito, or "little hearth," a luxurious, if somewhat restrained, Spanish-style villa, still standing on its prominent site between the first tee and third green of the Everglades Club course, featuring a three-story tower with terraces, a salon dining area seating thirty or more, and many of the elements that Mizner popularized, including a spacious central courtyard; curved, grilled windows and balconies; and a red, barrel-tile roof.

Though Marjorie was pleased with the work of Wyeth, she soon found the place a bit too limiting for her purposes. Inspired by the notoriety and accomplishments of her newfound hostess friend Eva Stotesbury at El Mirasol, she recalled Wyeth to expand Hogarcito, originally permitted at a cost of $28,000, to its present ten-thousand-square-foot, eight-bedroom dimensions. Yet that was still not enough to provide the sort of canvas on which Marjorie intended to bring her stupendous social visions to life. Given that Hogarcito, described as "too small for their needs and not near enough to the ocean," had expanded to the limits of its footprint, Marjorie was soon prowling the island, searching for "the place" where the apex of her architectural ambitions might be realized.

Hogarcito, as it turned out, provided an auspicious jumping-off point for Wyeth's career in Palm Beach because Ned Hutton, who had opened an office of his brokerage firm in space at the Breakers Hotel, would go on to purchase a number of other lots on Golfview Road where he commissioned the architect to design several houses on speculation, later sold to Hutton's friends and clients.

Meantime, in December 1923, Marjorie gave birth to a daughter, Nedenia Marjorie (who was always called Deenie and who would, in time, become the well-known actress Dina Merrill), an event that only proved a further incentive to continue her search about the island for a site suitable for her residential pièce de résistance.

With the assistance of realtor Lytle Hull, Marjorie, whose wildest fancies were always grounded in certain practicalities, narrowed her search, intent on identifying a building site where the limestone shelving that constituted the most substantial under-pinning of the ancient landform most closely neared the island's surface. Marjorie would fasten her grand mansion to bedrock, or as close to such as a raised and calcified expanse of sea bottom could provide. There were some slightly elevated, jungled tracts near the south end of the ancient reef that might fill the bill, Hull told the heiress, but one would need vision to imagine a glorious structure placed on what now looked like forlorn scrubland a couple of miles from the center of town.

Lack of vision had never been an issue with Marjorie, how-ever, and soon enough the pair, guided by geological surveys as well as a realtor's zeal, were crawling on hands and knees through tangles of Brazilian holly and palmetto, sweating, sifting handfuls of sand and fossilized coral, until in 1924 Marjorie was finally cer-tain she had found the right place: a nearly eighteen-acre tract of solid, unspoiled land spanning the southern tip of the island from the Atlantic to Lake Worth, the characteristic that would lead to the estate's designation as Mar-a-Lago.

Whatever Ned Hutton might have thought of the prospects there, he was not inclined to quarrel with Marjorie about them. It was her money to spend, and he was no stranger to the good life himself. In essence, he had gone all in on the new relation-ship, becoming as much Mrs. Post's husband as she had become Mr. Hutton's wife. In 1923, at Marjorie's encouragement, he had stepped down from the management of his own brokerage house—maintaining his own branch office headquarters at the Breakers in Palm Beach—and had taken over the chairmanship of the Postum Cereal Company, a move that she believed would position the company for diversification and growth. One of the first steps toward repositioning the company as a food conglomerate was the relocation of the firm's offices to the newly renovated Postum Building near Grand Central Terminal in Manhattan. Furthermore, Marjorie soon appeared to be prescient in encouraging Ned's involvement. At the end of 1922, company receipts were $11.5 million, with profits at $1.4 million; by 1927, with the company having subsumed such competitors as Jell-O, Swans Down, and Minute Tapioca, Postum was doing some $37 million of business, with profits at $13.6 million.

* * *

With her chosen Palm Beach homesite in hand, Marjorie went back to Marion Sims Wyeth, who had designed Hogarcito, asking him to come up with a design that might vaguely suggest the spirit of Camp Hutridge transported to Florida, with a main building and a series of guest and family rooms arranged around a central courtyard. Wyeth was agreeable and worked with Marjorie through the remainder of 1924 and into the following year on the development of such a plan.

However rustic or modest their endeavor might sound, that impression was soon belied by a series of headlines in the *Palm Beach Post* of September 1925. It was announced that the Huttons had let a contract for the largest mansion ever to be built in Palm Beach, a structure that would far surpass Flagler's Whitehall and the Stotesburys' El Mirasol in scope and grandeur. The original Marion Sims Wyeth design had been augmented by input from a new source, writers said, revealing that Viennese architect, illustrator, and stage-set designer Joseph Urban, who had created sets for the Metropolitan Opera and the Ziegfeld Follies as well as for a series of silent films produced by William Randolph Hearst's Cosmopolitan Pictures, was now in charge of the Hutton mansion's design.

Marjorie in fact had found the look of the structure that Wyeth proposed a bit too conservative. Wyeth, who described his own work as "quiet, subdued and rational" had proposed facades that mirrored European models, which the practicing Christian Scientist Marjorie found "ecclesiastical" at best and "dreary" at worst. She wasn't exactly sure what she wanted, Marjorie admitted, but she did know that it would have to be different.

She found her solution almost by accident, during a spring 1925 fishing expedition to the Florida Keys in the company of her husband and noted impresario Flo Ziegfeld, who listened to her laments regarding Mar-a-Lago for only a few minutes before suggesting that she call in Joseph Urban. Before his arrival in the States, the classically trained Urban had designed buildings for Egyptian royalty, Hungary's Count Esterházy, and Emperor Franz Josef himself.

Urban's work in the theater had been lauded for his ability to heighten the effect of acting and singing far beyond their innate qualities by using set and costume design as well as inventive prosceniums to "suggest" more than literally "represent" the underlying substance of the dramas being presented, an approach that was being called the new stagecraft. Urban was a genius, Ziegfeld assured her, one who had heightened the role of theater architecture to a level equal to stage plays themselves.

Precisely such a difference was what Marjorie was seeking, and in short order she had summoned Urban to meet with her in

Palm Beach to look over her site, listen to her ideas, and review where matters stood. While some difference of opinion persists as to just how much of Wyeth is to be found in the completed Mar-a-Lago, it is clear that matters took a major turn following Marjorie's encounter with Joseph Urban. According to architectural historian Donald Curl, Urban examined Wyeth's plans for the new estate and, finding them too sedate, set about blending those Mediterranean traditions with his own more elaborate Viennese decorative notions that had found their way into the theatrical settings he produced for the Follies and the Met.

In May 1925, Wyeth was summoned to meet with his clients Ned and Marjorie aboard the Huttons' new yacht, the *Hussar*, which was anchored in the Lake Worth channel just off the planned site for the project. As the 202-foot, 585-ton yacht drew far too much water for any nearby dock, Wyeth had to climb into a launch to be ferried to the meeting. Once aboard, he found that the Huttons had already been joined by the imposing 250-pound Urban, and over lunch Marjorie explained how things were going to proceed. Though she very much hoped that Wyeth would remain on the project as associate architect, she said, she and Ned had decided to employ Urban to complete the decoration of the estate.

Under the circumstances there was little Wyeth could do but step back, though the fact that he was recalled by Mrs. Post to design a freestanding ballroom on the property suggests that relations between them were never completely sundered. It remains uncertain how much association Wyeth undertook with the exuberant Austrian going forward, but it is quite clear that, decoratively speaking, very little of a restrained Beaux-Arts influence remains in the finished product.

The result was a lavish architectural spectacle where the proportions may have stayed true to the original design (Curl describes the arrangement of Hogarcito as an obvious "ancestor" of Mar-a-Lago) but where the decorative touches went far beyond anything Wyeth might have suggested. Long after its completion, Wyeth sought to distance himself from responsibility for the finished product, telling a reporter: "It isn't my taste. It's the taste of Joe Urban. I don't want anyone to think I was the architect in charge."

But even those comments leave room for interpretation. As Curl points out, the basic layout of the estate, unchanged to this day, is similar to that of Hogarcito, where several self-contained

Viennese-born architect Joseph Urban, who designed stage sets for the Ziegfeld Follies, film sets for William Randolph Hearst, and the magnificent Mar-a-Lago for Marjorie Post and Ned Hutton.

structures with discrete functions are linked by a series of cloisters and loggias. To enter Mar-a-Lago, one passes through a set of massive iron and stone gates off Ocean Drive and drives a hundred yards or so past manicured grounds to alight beneath a porte cochere that offers access to the main house on the left and a separate guest house on the right.

Up a short flight of steps, a high-ceilinged foyer gives access to an even more impressive main pavilion where banks of windows and French doors offer views of the gardens overlooking the Atlantic on the east and the resplendent grounds (including a pool and a nine-hole pitch-and-putt golf course) that descend to Lake Worth on the west. Out the latter sets of doors one finds what Urban called a Baby's House and Master's Quarters—veritable apartments unto themselves gained off cloisters proceeding to the south—while the dining room, kitchen, and service and staff rooms are situated in a wing to the north. (Wyeth's later contribution, in 1959, took the form of a separate pavilion between the kitchen wing and the lake, where Mrs. Post was fond of hosting square dancing parties.)

Urban would likely have been less concerned with just how this assemblage of buildings was laid out (Wyeth's plan resembled "a tiny Spanish village" according to a *Palm Beach Post* article of the day) than with the facades of those structures, their decoration, and their "feel." Most important to that look and feel for Urban would be the installation of a centrally situated seventy-five-foot bell tower (some call it Moorish inspired, while others insist it evokes more of Vienna than of Spain) as the signature touch, looming over the large circular patio that tied all the structures and their collective 115 rooms together.

Urban proposed to style the dining room after one he had observed in the Palazzo Chigi in Rome, where, as he told Marjorie, Mussolini had installed his offices following the Great

War. Also, he intended to employ Viennese sculptor Franz Barwig and Barwig's son to execute the shaping and carving of the estate's stonework on-site, and he would bring Hungarian artist Louis Jambor all the way to Florida as well to paint frescoes on the extensive patio walls. As far as materials were concerned, doors and beams would be milled from native Florida cypress, complemented by three shiploads of Dorian stone from Genoa and antique floor blocks and roof tiles brought up from Cuba. There is no record of what murmurs of appreciation might have come from Marjorie as Urban laid out his vision, but they can be imagined. If different was what she was longing for, then Joseph Urban was the one to deliver it. That much would have been abundantly clear.

- 10 -

LITTLE COTTAGE
BY THE SEA

Work on Mar-a-Lago commenced at the height of frenzied speculation in Florida real estate and continued through its collapse in
1926, when the dreams of Paris Singer, Addison Mizner, and many
more evaporated once reality appeared on the doorstep, bearing
requests for payment due. The most affluent of the residents of
Palm Beach, Ned and Marjorie Hutton among them, were secure
against such setbacks, but working people and even whole munici-
palities, their dreams of burgeoning tax receipts now dashed, were
as profoundly affected as were rampant land speculators.

In her unpublished memoirs, Marjorie recalls the advice that
came their way in the dark days of 1926: Stop work immediately on Mar-a-Lago, where every week, it seemed, came news
of some unavoidable cost overrun from Joseph Urban. Stop, cut
your losses, and run. But that was a notion that ran counter to
everything she had learned from C. W. Post, who was in truth
echoing Henry Flagler himself. Money was made to be used, and
using it ended up helping everyone in the end. "We refused to stop
construction after nearly everyone advised us to stop," Marjorie
said. "Had we stopped and discharged workmen, this would have
added more unemployed. Hence we went ahead."

As completion neared, the cost of Mar-a-Lago, like that of so
many ambitious building projects, had escalated significantly, in
this case from an original estimate of $1 million to as much as $8

million or more, the figure nudged up by additions such as a tunnel bored beneath South Ocean Boulevard to allow unfettered access to the Atlantic beaches, incorporation of a thirty-six-thousand-item antique Spanish tile collection that Wyeth made available to the heiress, and the commissioning of a twenty-nine-foot, four-thousand-pound marble dining table inlaid with semiprecious stones that Urban assured his client would earn favorable comparisons to similar items found in the Pitti Palace and the Uffizi.

If these escalations were not fatal to the Hutton balance sheet, they nonetheless elicited notice, even at her stratospheric level of wealth. "Apparently, building estimates are not worth the paper they are written on," Marjorie would complain. "They have sunk our finances beyond anything we had imagined, so I have been having trouble with Ned about it." She went on to lament the most abhorrent of the prospects that could be faced by the superwealthy, an assault on the nest egg itself. As a result of the overruns, she said, "We have got to sell some of our pet Postum stock and you can imagine how unwillingly we part with it."

But part with it they did, for Marjorie Post was not the type to give up on a dream that was within her reach. In January 1927, Mar-a-Lago was completed, though not before one major hurdle was cleared. In March 1926, Hutton had ordered work on the project stopped when Anna Dodge, widow of the automaker, announced that she was giving up building plans of her own in the neighborhood and selling Causeway Park, a vacant tract that sat adjacent to Mar-a-Lago on the south, to developers who were planning a multiuse residential, commercial, and recreational project on the site. The very prospect of such a thing was scarcely welcome news to a pair of individuals whose idea of the perfect retreat was the virtually inaccessible Camp Hutridge.

The day was saved only when Hutton was able to put together a syndicate composed of friends and fellow property owners to buy out the developers and build a bath and tennis club on the Causeway Park site, a club intended originally for the use of a few dozen shareholders and guests, to keep away the "prying Fourth Estate Eyes," and to provide members "freedom from the annoyances that beset people on public beaches." Today, the luxurious Bath and Tennis Club—designed by Joseph Urban and serving perhaps 750 members—sits cheek by jowl with Mar-a-Lago, the property line scarcely discernible at beachside, the imposing club's design virtually indistinguishable from the mansion next door.

If visitors to the Hutton residence in Manhattan were treated to a previously unknown level of luxury, what they discovered at Mar-a-Lago trended into the outright flabbergasting. More than one guest was said to be stopped in midstep upon entering the main living room of the 115-room, 62,500-square-foot house, stunned by the opulence that unfolded there. Great cypress doors decorated with golden cherubs provided entrance, and beyond was a room of sixty feet long or so and half as wide, its ceiling forty-two feet high and decorated with the so-called thousand-wing effect that had been copied from the Gallerie dell'Accademia in Venice (the angels featured in the original had been replaced with sunbursts in deference to Marjorie's distaste for the ecclesiastical). Adorning the walls were tapestries that had come from another Venetian palace, and dangling from the ceiling were a pair of crystal chandeliers rivaling spiderwebs in delicate otherworldly intricacy. Carvings by the Barwigs, both elder and younger, adorned lintels, archways, and mantelpieces everywhere.

High up on the room's south wall were situated a pair of small balconies where Marjorie was fond of secreting herself as guests arrived at her home for one function or another. She reveled in each look of astonishment she witnessed, a pleasure that by all accounts was other oriented at its core. For Marjorie, performing as the consummate hostess carried its own reward. She was not interested in tallying up glances of envy from those bowled over as they entered her new home; she was taking guileless delight in witnessing a guest's awe at being transported on the instant from reality into paradise.

In time, she would come to present great musicians and vocal artists who might provide transcendent pleasure for her guests at Mar-a-Lago, along with illusionists, dancers, and even iterations of the Ringling Bros. and Barnum & Bailey Circus set up on her prodigious lawn. While Marjorie herself may not have been able to sing or dance or mime with talent sufficient enough to mesmerize, she could provide the most intoxicating setting her guests had ever experienced, and in that she took great pride.

The sheer size of Mar-a-Lago was not what so entranced visitors. After all, compared with the 135,000 square feet occupied by the Biltmore Estate built for the Vanderbilts in Asheville; Otto Kahn's 109,000-square-foot Oheka Castle in Huntington, New York; or the Stotesburys' own 100,000-square-foot Whitemarsh Hall outside Philadelphia, Mar-a-Lago was a virtual cottage, with a dozen or more mansions outdoing it in size at the time. Even in Palm Beach, the Huttons had barely outstripped Flagler's Whitehall and the Stotesburys' El Mirasol in square footage. The real impact of Mar-a-Lago was attributable to that elusive difference Marjorie had sought, coupled, of course, with her innate desire to please.

Of course, not everyone was enamored of this difference. From the moment of Mar-a-Lago's unveiling, some critics were unmerciful. A favorite line bandied about by Wyeth was supposed to have been uttered by the infamous Harry Thaw, who had shot well-known architect Stanford White, partner in the acclaimed Beaux-Arts firm McKim, Mead and White, as the latter was watching a show at Madison Square Garden in 1906. "My God, I shot the wrong architect," Thaw is supposed to have said after a look at Mar-a-Lago.

What seemed to trouble critics most was their inability to assign the finished product to any commonly agreed-upon category. Each of the guest bedrooms on the second floor of the south wing was done in a different style: one Dutch, another Spanish, yet another American Colonial. The exterior touches, including the barrel-tile roofs, Spanish lanterns, and marble sheathing, are predominantly Mediterranean, but then the distinctly un-Moorish tower is flanked by chimneys straight out of the Netherlands, and a bewildering array of iconographic stonework was added by the Barwigs, including rams, gargoyles, sunbursts, and other figures from Egyptian, Greek, Far Eastern, and Tudor mythology.

A piece published in the *Palm Beach Daily News* just before Christmas of 1926 declared Mar-a-Lago unclassifiable, pointing to features that were alternately Gothic, Dutch, Spanish, French, Persian, Tudor, and Indian. One writer suggested that perhaps the best designation would be "Urbanesque," and that may make the most sense, for almost no one was to complain that the overall effect was anything but entrancing.

In fact a replica of Mussolini's office had made it to Palm Beach, repurposed once again as a dining room and every bit as lavish as the Chigi Palace original, with its gold chandeliers, golden candelabras, and jewel-encrusted multiton table. Of the last, of which Marjorie became greatly fond, latter-day superintendent Jimmy Griffin would say:

> It would take four men to put one section in
> this table because the sections weighed 350–400
> pounds apiece. It was gorgeous, and it weighed
> as much as 6.5 tons. It was a major job to set it
> up. We'd have to know a day ahead if she was
> going to use it for dinner and how many guests,

to know how many sections to put up, and then
again to take it back down [to two ends and a
middle section].

In the Master's Quarters, Ned and Marjorie had their separate and commodious bedrooms, each with its own bath, though
Marjorie had hers configured as a spa cum office, with a desk and
phone placed every bit as prominently as the tub and dressing
table. There she spent most mornings alternating the writing of
memos and making of phone calls with attention to her toilette
and daily massage.

Inside Deenie's House, as the child's room was called, was
a fireplace built to resemble a beehive with walls adorned by
bas-relief plaster rose vines and foliage where a pair of yel-
low canaries peeked from their resting place. The carpet in the
room was woven to Urban's specifications, featuring a series of

*A 1967 view of Mar-a-Lago's Chigi Palace–inspired grand
dining room featuring the ornate dining table now at
Hillwood Museum in Washington, D.C.*

characters he had created for a volume of fairy tales: embroidered there were goblins, elves, and fairy princesses. One would scamper across all this to a four-poster bed whose intricately carved posts each culminated with a wooden squirrel at play.

In addition to the guest bedrooms, Master's Quarters, and Deenie's House, which included bedrooms for both her and a nurse (and with a twenty-four-hour armed guard stationed just outside following the kidnapping of the Lindbergh baby in 1932), there were twenty-seven rooms for servants and several cottages for groundskeepers and maintenance workers. In all, the estate could comfortably house about seventy. A staff of sixty, including some day help, was employed to maintain ordinary operations, though when elaborate entertaining was planned that number might rise to eighty.

When Ned Hutton was asked by friends for his opinion of it all, his reply was unvarying and diplomatic, daughter Dina Merrill recalls: "Marjorie said she was going to build a little cottage by the sea. Look what we got."

* * *

The year 1927 began auspiciously for the Huttons: on Wednesday, January 19, they gave away Marjorie's oldest daughter, Adelaide, then eighteen, to twenty-eight-year-old Yale graduate Tim Durant in a ceremony at St. Thomas Church in New York, where young Deenie served as flower girl. Edward Close was not listed among those in attendance. Marjorie commissioned a cottage to be built for the pair on the grounds of Hillwood, purchased a seat on the New York Stock Exchange for her new son-in-law, and then she and Ned were off to Palm Beach for what they hoped would be a season to beat all seasons.

On January 30, 1927, the *New York Times* reported that the Bath and Tennis Club had opened for the season "with all its facilities, including swimming pool, five tennis courts, sun rooms for men and women, restaurant service and clubrooms," the formal opening set for February. One month later, the paper reported on the first public affair hosted at Mar-a-Lago, the largest of a number of dinner parties that preceded the annual costume ball at the Everglades Club on the evening of March 1. The hosts were identified as "Mr. and Mrs. Edward F. Hutton," who seated their guests on the spacious patio, which was described in breathless terms: "Its vista from ocean to lake a veritable fairyland at night, with a 'moon' [a bit of stagecraft courtesy of Joseph Urban] shining down from the tower of the house and wrought-iron lanterns swinging from limbs of banyan trees which rise from clumps of tropical shrubbery." Tables were decorated with bouquets of orange blossoms, gladioli, freesias, sprays of kumquats, and roses; and an orchestra and a Neapolitan quartet stationed in the nearby loggia provided entertainment.

The Stotesburys and the Urbans and the Singers were there, as were Addison Mizner and the likes of Mrs. William Randolph Hearst.

The ladies were said to be attired splendidly: Mrs. Hutton wore "an afternoon gown of the Louis XV period, with green striped bodice and bouffant skirt opening in front over a peach-color crepe de chine skirt trimmed with ecru lace," said the paper, which added: "Her large hat of green silk was trimmed with ostrich plumes of blue and pink." A few years later, Eva Stotesbury, her husband gone, her fortune dwindling, her health in question, would take Marjorie aside to say, "You'll have to carry on now, dear." But it was apparent to just about everyone in attendance at those events who had become the social doyenne-in-waiting in Palm Beach.

Things would go well for the Huttons throughout the rest of that year and the next: in December 1927, Marjorie presented Eleanor, her second daughter with Edward Close, at a coming-out party in the grand ballroom of the Ritz-Carlton Hotel in New York, with decorations and lighting design by none other than Joseph Urban. And in May 1928, longtime Anglophile Marjorie had one of her fondest dreams realized when Eleanor was presented at the Court of St. James's before King George V and Queen Mary. In the back of Marjorie's mind was that this event might signal the possibility of a match between her daughter and an eligible member of the European nobility, even though Eleanor wanted no part of an arranged marriage.

A favorite family tale, in fact, tells of Marjorie contriving to have Eleanor seated next to an eligible Bulgarian prince at a dinner given in the Plaza's Persian Room by a hostess friend. Eleanor went along, but when she came to the table, she found that the prince was not only cross-eyed but insufferably cross-tempered as well. After what seemed an eternity of princely declamation, Eleanor excused herself from the table. Shortly after her return, their waiter arrived to dispense the soup course, but hardly had Eleanor been served when there was an unfortunate accident. The clumsy waiter poured the entire contents of his tureen down the shirt and tailcoat of the elegantly attired prince. There was some attempt at mopping up the mess, but the outraged prince would finally have to leave. Later, Eleanor cheerfully admitted her part in the scheme. Though she did not disclose the amount of the bribe she paid the waiter, she pointed out that the cost was more than worth it: "I never had to go out with the prince again."

Marjorie, however, only had her appetite for royalty whetted by Eleanor's presentation at the royal court. Though she had despaired lest her status as a divorcée might forever keep her out of favor, connections she had forged to other British nobles over the years finally paid off: in June 1929, she herself received an invitation to Buckingham Palace where she was introduced to the king and queen, delivering a curtsy that daughter Eleanor claimed they had all been forced to practice from the time they were children. "Mother had always wanted to be presented at the Court of St. James's. From the time I was a little girl she had talked about it." More than twenty years had passed since the heiress had heard those dismissive comments regarding her status as she walked down the aisle for her first marriage. It may well be that she left the Court of St. James's with some satisfaction finally in her mind.

The first part of 1929 was also propitious for the Postum Company, given that in June of that year another of Marjorie's longtime dreams would come to fruition. As early as 1925, while the Huttons were enjoying a summer sail up the New England coast aboard the *Hussar*, their cook served up a meal of goose. As the story goes, Marjorie found the goose especially tender and tasty and wondered how on earth the cook had managed to come up with a fresh goose to serve on a boat that had been at sea for several days. Cook told Marjorie that he was glad to hear of her report, for he had bought the goose frozen, in Gloucester, Massachusetts, and had been wondering if the taste would be satisfactory.

One version of the tale has it that Marjorie ordered the yacht turned back to Gloucester on the spot so she could find the person responsible for freezing the goose. What is known is that Marjorie did eventually learn who was responsible, a man named Clarence Birdseye who had set up a small food-processing plant in Gloucester. Birdseye was a former employee of the U.S. Biological Survey who had stumbled on the idea of "flash freezing" foods while observing fishing methods in Labrador. While Eskimos and others

Men of Brains
Know and appreciate
the brain-food strength of

Grape-Nuts
"There's a Reason"
Postum Cereal Co., Ltd., Battle Creek, Mich., U. S. A.

Prior to C. W. Post, few thought of food as an "industry." In 1985, General Foods (originally Postum Cereal Company) was sold for $5.6 billion, the largest non-oil acquisition to that time.

had long used freezing as a means of preserving foods, most consumers who sampled defrosted frozen items found that the process had rendered them mushy and flavorless, owing to the tendency of ice crystals to form during freezing, thereby shredding the cell walls of foodstuffs.

However, during his time in Labrador, Birdseye had noted that when fish were pulled out of the water during the winter and subjected to temperatures that might reach thirty or forty below zero, they froze solid virtually instantaneously and when defrosted tasted as if they had just been caught. It did not take long for Birdseye, a naturalist by inclination, forced from his studies at Amherst College by a lack of funds, to ascertain the reason: when foodstuffs are frozen quickly, the ice crystals do not have time to cluster and grow large. Thus, when defrosted, flash-frozen items retain their cellular integrity and taste perfectly palatable.

To Marjorie, Birdseye's work seemed miraculous. Access to frozen foods would be a godsend to a housewife, she reasoned, allowing for the preparation of farm-fresh meals year-round and without the need for a daily trip to the market. Hutton and others within the company were not so smitten, however, for in the eyes of the American public at the time, "frozen food" was a phrase virtually synonymous with "something you'd eat only as a last resort." Even Birdseye himself was aware of the negative connotations afloat and referred to his products as "frosted" foods. By 1924, he had developed something of an assembly line for freezing and packaging and had formed the General Seafood Corporation in Gloucester, where he was selling enough flash-frozen fish to revive what had been a flagging Massachusetts fishing industry.

Beyond the issues of bad press for frozen food were more practical considerations. How would the products be transported to grocers from processing facilities, given the general lack of refrigerated trucks and railroad cars? And furthermore, unless grocers were willing to invest in big, expensive freezers to store the foods, what would be the point? To top it off, at a time when most home refrigerators were simply glorified chests cooled by a block of ice, how many American households would be willing to go out and buy a freezer of their own? Hutton and others within the Postum company argued that there was no practical future in so-called frosted foods. This was one instance where Marjorie simply needed to come back to earth.

Marjorie, however, was not one to give up on an idea she thought revolutionary. She kept careful tabs on Birdseye and his operations in Gloucester and persisted with her lobbying efforts to convince Postum executives of the assuredly glorious future of frosted foods. Finally, in early 1929, with Birdseye's operations at long last turning a profit, Hutton relented and dispatched an agent from Goldman Sachs, Postum's investment banker, to discuss terms with Birdseye for the acquisition of his holdings and his technology. After some negotiation, Birdseye proposed a final figure—$22 million—a sum to which Postum agreed.

That was something of an uptick from the $2 million Marjorie might have had the company pay for Birdseye back in 1925, but nonetheless, she was gratified by the purchase. In fact, the acquisition of the Birdseye product line was momentous enough to prompt a reevaluation of the company's very profile. The breakfast line that had been the cornerstone of the company from the beginning still produced significant revenues, but it had long since been outstripped by many other products within Postum's diverse lines and no longer seemed to represent the full breadth or might of the organization. The acquisition of Birdseye was simply the capstone of a trend toward diversification. Thus, the board announced a momentous change: as of July 24, 1929, the Postum Cereal Company was no more. In its place was the corporation known as General Foods.

- 11 -

HARD TIMES

It may have seemed a grand and glorious moment, watching one great institution disappear only to rise up like the reincarnated phoenix in the next instant, but little did the Huttons know just how many other companies were about to vanish, never to return again. On Black Tuesday, October 29, 1929, a few months after General Foods had become a reality, Wall Street investment collapsed when 16 million shares were traded and the Dow Jones Industrial Average closed at 230.07, after having been as high as 381 the previous month. Thus began the twelve-year period known as the Great Depression, putting a definitive end to the exuberance, excess, and unbridled enthusiasm of the Roaring Twenties. By July 8, 1932, the Dow Jones would decline to 41.22, its lowest modern level, marking a loss of almost 90 percent of all the market's stocks in less than three years.

Though the earlier crash of the Florida land market had taken its toll on Palm Beach, sending Paris Singer scurrying from creditors and forever ending solvency for Addison Mizner, the effects of the Great Depression on much of the town were relatively modest. While the value of the Huttons' portfolio fell, along with that of everyone else's, many of the island's most prominent residents were not speculators but rather moguls, all but impervious to complete ruin.

One 1930 visitor to the Royal Poinciana Hotel, Wall Street analyst E. W. Kamelbert, was quoted as saying, "There has been a crash and a big one. But we're still carrying on." Kamelbert insisted that America would only be getting "bigger and better," as evidenced by the robust activity in Palm Beach. Though the town council tightened its budget somewhat, owing to a projected uptick in delinquent taxes, that body forecast expenditures of more than $200,000 for 1930 and the chamber of commerce said that the town "was enjoying one of its largest seasons."

Railroad bookings were up that year, more than $3 million in building permits were issued, and horseman Joseph Widener broke ground on his mansion, Il Palmetto, a $2.5 million, sixty-thousand-square-foot house on five-plus acres spanning the island from ocean to lake not far north of Mar-a-Lago. Things were somewhat precarious at the Everglades Club, as it was in receivership, its owner Paris Singer having pledged the property as security for a number of failed real estate ventures on what is called Singer Island today. By the midthirties, however, club members banded together to form the Everglades Protective Syndicate to purchase the property from creditors, and in the midforties, the establishment became a completely member-owned club. By the spring of 1933, Wall Street seemed to be creeping up from the previous year's nadir, and by December 1933, Palm Beach hotels were reporting an 80 percent occupancy rate.

If the rest of the nation was gripped by doubt and fear, things were proceeding pretty much as usual in Palm Beach. In January 1931, the society pages of the *Palm Beach Daily News* (often called the Shiny Sheet, for its use of a glossy stock) noted the efforts of one matron, Mrs. Charles Hall, to pick up the spirits of her friends and neighbors in the enclave. Her "novel amusement" featured guests dressed in elegant pajamas, sipping champagne brought to them by waiters while they stood at various stations on a fifty-foot canvas painted to resemble a giant backgammon board, waiting for the toss of a giant pair of dice to move them along.

The Huttons, though, were not content to confront the economic collapse by posing as board game pieces. In the aftermath of Wall Street's collapse, Marjorie placed all her jewelry in a safe-deposit box where it would stay for some time, pledging the resulting savings in insurance premiums to various charitable causes, including the establishment of the Marjorie Post Hutton Canteen in New York's Hell's Kitchen where women and children could get a decent meal well into the mid-1930s. Downtown, on Seventeenth Street, was also the Edward F. Hutton Food Station for Men. And by February 1930, Marjorie had become head of the special gifts campaign for the Salvation Army's Women's Emergency Aid Committee, just one of a number of civic undertakings she immersed herself in during the period.

If such actions by the Huttons were admirable, they could not altogether prevent a backlash from among the nation's many millions of the far less fortunate. Later in 1930, Marjorie's niece, Barbara Hutton (the daughter of Ned Hutton's brother, Franklyn, and the granddaughter of five-and-dime tycoon F. W. Woolworth), was introduced to society at a coming-out ball at the Ritz-Carlton in Manhattan just before Christmas. One story previewing the event allowed that the young heiress had lived "rather quietly" since receiving her $60 million inheritance four years previously, but the reporter nonetheless grumbled that in selling $10 million of Woolworth company stock (one of the largest private stock transactions ever) just before the crash, the heiress had saved $4 million.

No expense was spared for the ensuing party. One thousand guests attended Miss Hutton's Brilliant Ball, for which the entire ballroom suite had been decorated by Joseph Urban to resemble the moonlit courtyard garden of a country estate. Sprays of eucalyptus branches freighted in from California covered the walls, which were flanked by stands of ceiling-high birch trees surrounded by banks of roses and poinsettias. Guests enjoyed entertainment by the Russian Ensemble and Rudy Vallee, the Howard Lanin Orchestra, and dancer Mademoiselle Argentina.

By all appearances, her debut marked the end of quiet living for Barbara Hutton. In April 1931, New York and Palm Beach society was shocked by the apparently inexplicable suicide of James P. Donahue, husband of Jessie Woolworth, Barbara's aunt, characterized as the "wealthiest woman in New York City." The Donahues had built the forty-five-thousand-square-foot mansion Cielito Lindo, the largest house designed by Marion Syms Wyeth, in 1927 on sixteen acres of sea-to-lake property just north of Mar-a-Lago. The property was one of the "show places" (as they were then called) of Palm Beach; and the Donahues, married for nearly twenty years, were recognized as stalwarts and dedicated party givers in the community.

If Donahue's ingestion of a fatal quantity of mercury capsules suggests that life at the top is not always what it is cracked up to be, it seems that niece Barbara set out to prove it. Page-one headlines in March 1932 trumpeted Barbara's insistence that there was no husband-to-be in her future. She was "Daddy's girl," she told reporters as she stepped from a plane in Los Angeles, bound for a cruise with her father, Franklyn Hutton. Added Hutton, "Barbara has had a hard time living down all this fortune publicity. Let's give her a break: she's just a real American girl after all."

But that image was soon to change. By January of the following year, Barbara was stepping onto another ship in San Pedro, bound for an around-the-world cruise and denying rumors that she was contemplating an impending marriage to one of two suitors: Count Emanuele Borromeo d'Adda of Italy or Prince Alexis Mdivani of Georgia. The count waved good-bye to her from the pier shortly after confiding to reporters that he was on the verge of announcing his engagement to "a beautiful and wealthy American society girl." For her part, Barbara said, "I'm not going to marry anybody, and it's final."

On April 16, her father, Franklyn, was confronted by reporters in Palm Beach brandishing stories that his daughter had in fact married during a stopover of her ship in Bangkok. "So far as I know, she is still unmarried and had no intention of marrying anyone in Siam or anywhere else," he said. "When she does marry I think her father will be right by her side, at least I hope so."

The allegations that Barbara had married in Siam turned out to be untrue, but gossip columnists were quickly assuring readers that the heiress would soon be announcing her engagement and that her choice was not the count but the prince. By mid-May, Franklyn and Jessie Hutton were aboard a ship en route to Paris where they hoped to meet with Barbara and divine exactly what was going on.

At first, conflicting statements were issued, but soon enough the matter was officially settled: news outlets worldwide announced that Barbara Hutton would marry Prince Alexis Mdivani in Paris on June 20. The announcement stirred controversy among the Russian émigrés in Paris, who disputed the notion that Mdivani was part of the Georgian nobility. "Prince, my eye, he's a secretary," huffed one authentic royal, pointing out that *divani* in Georgian means "secretary," an apparent reference to Alexis's father who was an aide-de-camp to the late czar of Russia. "Prince in Georgian means to be a descendant of the royal family of the Bagratids, who never had any connection with the Mdivanis."

Alexis, whose previous marriage to Louise Astor Van Alen, descendant of John Jacob Astor, ended in divorce after a year, refused to take up the issue with reporters, saying, "I don't think it would be dignified."

A tempest in a relatively small teapot, this nonetheless confirmed the advice of Barbara's aunt Marjorie, who reportedly told her: "Barbara, forget this cheap Russian. All of the Mdivani brothers are bad news. You don't want to be taken and made a fool of, do you?" By this time, reporters were beginning to refer to the phenomenon of the "Marrying Mdivanis," with brother Serge having formed a short-lived union with actress Pola Negri and brother David having married actress Mae Murray.

Though she was both bright and undeniably beautiful, it might seem that Barbara Hutton had something of a masochistic streak or at least spectacularly poor judgment in choosing mates. Her marriage to Mdivani lasted less than two years, a period marked by astronomical expenditures by her new husband on homes, clothing, polo ponies, and almost anything else that would strike a prince's eye. Hutton, who would become increasingly dependent on alcohol and drugs to make her way through life, eventually married seven times, including a brief union with actor Cary Grant. Reporting on her marriage to Dominican diplomat and international playboy Porfirio Rubirosa, one writer was to quip: "The bride, for her fifth wedding, wore black and carried a scotch-and-soda." At the time of her death from heart failure in 1979, Barbara Hutton was said to be virtually penniless.

Even had Marjorie devoted an unending amount of time to tending her niece, it seems doubtful that she could have materially altered the trajectory of that troubled life. She also had troubles much closer to home occupying her attention. Her own stout-minded daughter Eleanor, who had scotched any number of her mother's attempts to pair her with nobles and blue bloods, came to Palm Beach early in 1930 to announce that she had finally found her man.

The Huttons might have been pardoned for feeling wary about such news, and inquiries soon confirmed their fears. Eleanor had in fact fallen in love with thirty-one-year-old actor and playwright Preston Sturges, whom she had met at a dinner party in December. Sturges's father had been a traveling salesman and his mother, Mary D'Este, a clothing designer and friend of Isadora Duncan (the scarf that strangled Duncan had been given to her by D'Este).

Sturges, who would go on to considerable acclaim as a Hollywood screenwriter and director of screwball comedies such as *The Great McGinty, Sullivan's Travels,* and *The Palm Beach Story,* had recently found substantial success. His play *The Guinea Pig* had made the jump from regional theater to Broadway in 1929, and later that year his second play, *Strictly Dishonorable,* began a sixteen-month run on Broadway that would earn him more than $300,000. That success led to calls from Hollywood as well, and indeed Sturges was riding high, by his own lights at least.

The Huttons, however, were dubious. Eleanor was only twenty, and Sturges was thirty-one, with one failed marriage in his past. His mother, with four marriages of her own, had lived an unconventional life, and Sturges, as his work would demonstrate, was hardly a devotee of societal elitism. Finally, Ned Hutton called Sturges in for a man-to-man discussion as to the latter's intentions. As Sturges recalled in his biography, Hutton wanted to know just what sort of financial means were at the playwright's disposal. Sturges replied that at present, he had two shows on Broadway, one of which was netting its writer $1,500 a week. Hutton waved a hand, saying, "That's pin money to her."

When pressed by Hutton as to whether he truly thought himself capable of supporting his daughter in the style she was accustomed to, Sturges uttered the caliber of line that would eventually garner him an Academy Award in a much different setting: "I would hope in better taste."

All this accomplished little for Marjorie but to fuel her daughter's ire. Despite the Huttons' plea that she wait at least a year before going forward, on April 14, 1930, the *New York Times* broke the news on its front page: "Eleanor Post Hutton, younger daughter of Mrs. Edward F. Hutton, . . . it was learned yesterday, and despite the objections of her mother was married to Preston Sturges, author of the play 'Strictly Dishonorable.'" Though Eleanor's intentions were well known to the Huttons and their set, seeing such news on page one of the newspaper of record would scarcely have been pleasing, especially given the notation in the story's coda, "The marriage of Adelaide Hutton [where Eleanor had been maid of honor] was one of the biggest social events of the 1926[–1927] season."

The next day the *Times* followed up with an interview with Sturges, who disclosed that the pair had been wed on Saturday by a justice of the peace in Bedford Hills and motored on to Woodstock, where they spent the night. In a couple of weeks the two of them would embark on a proper honeymoon, he said, to consist of a sail on his fifty-two-foot motorboat, *Recapture*, though Sturges said they had no real destination in mind. The two of them would "just sort of wander along." Regarding all this, said the paper: "The bride's mother and her stepfather, Edward F. Hutton, who was also opposed to the match, made no comment."

All of it made considerable fodder for gossip columnists who reported that Marjorie had disinherited her daughter in a fit of pique, that the Sturgeses had only $7 to their name the day they wed (even that much a loan from Sturges's mother), and that Eleanor's stepfather, Ned, was less upset than her mother, Marjorie, about it all. But the most substantive result of the union might have surfaced in late November 1930, when the 1931 edition of the *Social Register* was mailed out, revealing that the name of Eleanor H. Hutton had been erased from its pages. Another name mentioned as vanished was that of one William J. Willock, Jr., who had committed the transgression of marrying one of his family's maids. Evidently, to the *Register*'s keeper, wedding a successful Broadway playwright was equally damning.

In any case, Eleanor needn't have fretted unduly about her future. In December 1930, when she turned twenty-one, she came into possession of a bequest of $1.5 million left for her by her grandfather, C. W. Post. Nor should the Huttons have worried too much about the actions of their headstrong daughter. Just two years and one month after her elopement, Eleanor filed for an annulment of her marriage to Sturges on the grounds that his divorce from his first wife, the former Estelle Mudge, filed by Estelle in the Mexican city of Nogales, had never taken effect. In November, Eleanor's request for dissolution of the marriage was granted and in April 1933 she would be wed again, this time to Étienne Gautier, a Frenchman and noted polo player.

In later years, both Sturges and Eleanor would recall this interlude in colorful if curious fashion. In a letter written shortly before his death in the late 1950s and quoted by biographer Wright, Sturges told colleague Chris Chase: "In 1930, I was in Palm Beach—at the Everglades Club and various places—helling around and romancing a very rich young girl I would have been better off never to have married—her name was Hutton, I believe."

For her part, Eleanor would tell an interviewer some sixty years after the fact: "Not that I was in love with him, but he was fascinating. He would say, 'It's such fun taking your mind out of baby ribbons.'"

- 12 -

SEA CHANGE

Most who knew the Huttons during their Palm Beach heyday would have assumed that any essential conflict between the pair could be traced to their political differences. As the Depression worsened, the deeply charitably inclined Marjorie became more and more convinced that the New Deal policies of Franklin Delano Roosevelt promised the only way out of misery for the country. Hutton, on the other hand, despised Roosevelt and characterized his policies as socialism in disguise. He himself argued fiercely in support of classical "trickle-down" theories in which governmental encouragement of big business investment would eventually raise all foundering boats. In fact, following the completion of the *Hussar V*, the 316-foot, four-masted sailing ship he had built in 1932 (it was the largest private sailing yacht in the world), Hutton told friends that with enough such extravagant expenditures by the wealthy, "the nation might yacht its way out of the depression."

But given the size and scope of their holdings it is doubtful that differences on economic policy alone would have led to such a couple's dissolution. It seems just as compelling a notion that Ned Hutton, despite his own charm and accomplishments, ultimately felt threatened by a woman as assured and resolute as Marjorie Merriweather Post. As the physically attractive, adroit, and wealthy man he had been from early adulthood, he had never wanted for the attentions of women, and one could argue that any occasional dalliance he may have indulged in constituted no more than the bee's casual pass across the flower. If that were so, a woman as intelligent and worldly as Marjorie might have managed to overlook such lapses.

However, Marjorie had never been able to forgive her own father for his weaknesses. C. W. Post not only had deserted her mother for another, younger, woman but had, in the end, terminated his own life rather than carry on a battle against illness. It seems entirely possible, then, that what galled Marjorie most regarding Ned's various infidelities was that she saw them not as "crimes of passion" but rather as pathetic attempts at combat, displays of swordsmanship meant to demonstrate that he was without doubt the man of the Mar-a-Lago house.

In any case, Marjorie forced the issue, just as she had when she realized that the end had come between herself and Edward Close. And since adultery was the sole grounds for divorce in New York state, she persevered until she could prove the fact. The *Times* reported on August 16, 1935, that the couple had been separated for several months, with Marjorie at that time secluded at their Adirondacks camp. That story also took note of her active role in relief work in Hell's Kitchen, adding that her efforts had earned her the title of Lady Bountiful in the downtrodden neighborhood.

All of this was reported, ironically enough, just days after publication of the news that Prince Alexis Mdivani, recently divorced from Barbara Hutton, had died in a car crash while driving "at high speed" in an attempt to catch a train in Palomas, Spain. Traveling with him was Baroness Maud von Thyssen, a lovely—and also married—German aristocrat who reportedly lost an eye in the accident.

On September 7, New York supreme court justice George H. Furman signed the divorce decree that Marjorie had sought, ending her fifteen-year marriage to Ned Hutton, with *Times* reporters noting that though Hutton had "denied the charges of infidelity made by his wife," papers in the suit had been sealed by the court and none of the principals would discuss the evidence upon which the judge had based his decision.

The court awarded custody of eleven-year-old Deenie to her mother, with E. F.'s visitation rights restricted to the occasional holiday and one summer month each year. Though Marjorie's attorney noted that his client had sought no alimony and that no financial settlement pertaining to the matter had been made, it was later learned that Marjorie would retain ownership of Camp Hutridge, Hillwood in Brookville, the grand apartment in Manhattan, and Mar-a-Lago, as well as that of the *Hussar V*.

In December came the news that Ned Hutton had resigned his unpaid post as chairman of the board at General Foods, with stories noting that his outspoken criticism of Roosevelt had not always dovetailed with the opinions of other directors. One piece noted that Hutton would continue as a member of the board of directors (he was in control of 1 to 2 percent of the outstanding stock of the company, with Marjorie owning about 10 percent of the shares). Marjorie would the following year take his place as chair.

Also, in that month came somewhat more surprising news: MRS. M. P. HUTTON TO WED was the headline in the *Times* on December 14, over a story noting that on the following day, the former Mrs. Hutton, forty-eight, would become the bride of Washington attorney and FDR adviser Joseph E. Davies, fifty-nine. If this union, coming on the heels of her divorce, was a surprise to the public, it was not to those close to Marjorie, for members of her family would often say later that she would never leave one man until the next in line was already chosen. Even much later, when she was eighty and contemplating a fifth union, she snapped at her daughters, who had gathered to try to dissuade her of the notion: "You're not the one sitting here alone at night."

Marjorie had met Davies in Palm Beach the previous winter, when she was already certain that she would leave Hutton. Even though Davies was married at the time and had been for almost thirty years, the two apparently fell in love instantaneously. The story is told that Marjorie paved the way for Davies's divorce by having one of her attorneys contact Mrs. Davies to discover just what size of financial settlement might allow her husband to have his freedom. If it is to be believed, Mrs. Davies was not completely astounded by this overture; in essence she agreed to sell her still politically ambitious husband to the former Mrs. Hutton for the sum of $2 million. This charge is not endorsed by descendants of Mrs. Davies, who contend that she was never in need of money.

With the termination of her marriage to Hutton, Marjorie may have kept title to her Palm Beach mansion, but the onset of the Depression had already dimmed her enthusiasm for the over-the-top displays that marked her early years with Hutton at Mar-a-Lago. In February 1929, for instance, they had given a luncheon in honor of abdicated Russian grand duke Mikhailovich, father of the heir presumptive to the Russian throne, Prince Nikita. And later that same season she brought a version of John Ringling's circus to the grounds of the estate, with two performances benefiting the Animal Rescue League and other charities and one reserved for the delight of friends. In the one-ring extravaganza were included: "French and Belgian midgets, a living skeleton, monkey man, an armless wonder, a sword dancer, magician, Scotch piper, and a dainty little woman weighing 700 pounds."

In 1930, following the commissioning of famed golf course architect Donald Ross to scheme up a nine-hole pitch-and-putt range on the estate's grounds during the off-season, Marjorie came up with the notion of importing the entire theatrical production of *The Merry Wives of Windsor* from New York City to Mar-a-Lago. Act 1 of the play was staged on the patio, the second act on the terrace, and the final act in the spacious living room, with an orchestra assembled for entertainment at intermissions and during supper.

By the middle of the 1930s, however, the soup lines were still long and her glamourous marriage to Ned Hutton was over. With her new husband, Davies, about to receive a posting to Moscow as the ambassador to the USSR (he had been promised Germany, but the gathering political storm precluded that), Marjorie made the startling decision to close Mar-a-Lago and go to Moscow with Davies, a decision that would stand for five seasons. In many ways, it was the end of an era.

While belt-tightening would always be a relative term in Palm Beach, and even if some residents might have idled away the doldrums of the Depression posing as backgammon pieces, the completely unalloyed excesses of the twenties were gone for good, a casualty of, among other things, the Sixteenth Amendment, enacted in 1913, and the subsequent rise of the personal income tax, whose top rates reached 63 percent during the Depression and 94 percent on income over $2 million during World War II. Just as potent as rising taxes were rising wages, which were multiplied by a factor of ten in the years leading into the 1950s, meaning that the monthly outlay for a staff of sixty had increased from $4,500 to $45,000.

What might have seemed like "pin money" in the twenties had become significant overhead for multi-mansioned titans whose businesses were beset by higher labor costs as well. Such considerations led Marjorie to determine in the 1950s that the *Hussar V* (renamed the *Sea Cloud* following her divorce from Hutton), which required a crew of seventy to keep it afloat, had outlived its usefulness. Advertisements revealed that she was willing to sacrifice the craft for $1 million, though she had invested seven or eight times as much in it over the years. Even at that price she found no takers.

Finally, her old friend Rafael Trujillo, the infamous dictator of the Dominican Republic, who had always been enamored of the yacht, offered to trade Marjorie one of his planes, a forty-four-passenger Viscount, itself worth about $1 million, for the yacht. As only one pilot was needed to fly an airplane, with a copilot and a steward or two for good measure, Marjorie quickly saw the advantages, and a deal was struck. From then on, she traveled about the world much more quickly and signed many fewer paychecks along the way.*

* * *

Any fears that Mar-a-Lago might languish until it met the kiss of the wrecking ball proved unfounded, however, for Marjorie would maintain a particular fondness for many of her several landed estates up to the day of her demise. Rising tensions with the Russians required the Davieses' departure from Moscow in 1938, but their retreat was only as far as Brussels, where Davies was briefly installed as ambassador to Belgium and Luxembourg. Following the fall of Poland in 1939, Davies was remanded to the United States, where he was appointed special assistant to Secretary of State Cordell Hull and served FDR in various capacities through the war years.

During the 1940 season, the couple returned to Palm Beach for brief stays at Mar-a-Lago, where they entertained groups of a decidedly more political cast than in former days, including a convocation of southern governors and their wives. Marjorie also lent out the estate for a fund-raising concert by Metropolitan Opera star Doris Doe to benefit the local Episcopal Church. They would

* The *Sea Cloud*, which Marjorie had made available for the use of the navy during World War II, passed through various hands following Trujillo's assassination in 1961 and still sails today as a cruise ship.

return for visits the following season as well, throwing a party at Mar-a-Lago for friends just before the New Year and entertaining Senators Alben Barkley and Millard Tydings and their wives in April 1941, all events that were covered by the *New York Times* and other papers.

The season of 1942 again saw the Davieses in residence for brief periods, though in that year, they would share the attention of society columnists who were atwitter over various appearances made by the glamorous seventeen-year-old Gloria Vanderbilt, heiress to grandfather Cornelius's railroad fortune and newly married to Hollywood agent and reputed mafioso Pat DiCicco. "This 17 year old bride carries her youth gallantly and combines with it unusual poise and graciousness," one writer gushed. "None of the newspaper pictures does her justice." In an afterword was the brief notice: "Mrs. and Mrs. Joseph E. Davies have arrived from Washington and are at their ocean front villa, Mar-a-Lago."

The demands of Joseph Davies's wartime duties—rather than any perceived decline in the quality of company at Palm Beach—kept the couple away from Mar-a-Lago for another extended period. The two returned for the 1944 season, but by then the fear of depredations from German U-boats lurking just offshore had resulted in strictly enforced dim-outs of oceanfront properties. That year, the couple rented a much more modest home fronting Lake Worth, and in April Marjorie turned Mar-a-Lago over to the government for use as an occupational therapy center for returning soldiers. Many of the men were outpatients from the five-hundred-bed Ream Army General Hospital that had been temporarily established at the former Breakers Hotel, three miles up the street.

The Davieses would not return for some time following the war, prompting lament among the locals. "In its extremity, Palm

Beach directs anguished looks towards those three unoccupied estates: Mar-a-Lago, owned by Mrs. Joseph E. Davies; Cielito Lindo, Mrs. James P. Donahue's villa; and Playa Riente, owned by Mrs. Hugh Dillman," one columnist put it. The last was the largest designed by Mizner, its seventy rooms sprawling over a twenty-seven-acre ocean-to-lake parcel, while, at forty-five thousand square feet, Cielito Lindo, or "beautiful sweetheart," was the largest Palm Beach home designed by Marion Sims Wyeth (for heiress Jessie Woolworth Donahue and her husband). Again in 1947 Mar-a-Lago stood vacant, along with Cielito Lindo, by then sold off by the Donahues and stripped of its elaborate furnishings, with El Mirasol, the once grand Stotesbury estate, soon to go on the auction block.

But even if others had lost heart or at least their fortunes, Marjorie Post was in command on both counts. She and Davies reopened Mar-a-Lago in 1948 and by the following season were once again hosting grand functions, including a New Year's Day dance, a benefit for the Animal Rescue League, and a "genuine glamour party" for friends and guests that capped the year. Marjorie would redouble her activities at Mar-a-Lago in the 1950s and in 1957 founded the annual Red Cross Ball, a lavish fund-raiser that would continue at the estate for more than sixty years—and to this day. By 2016, Red Cross officials said, the five-hundred-invitation event, with a procession of ambassadors in white tie with their wives and escorted by marines in dress blues, would raise nearly $1 million and cost about $400,000 to stage.

Marjorie's relationship with Davies, however, had been deteriorating for some time, exacerbated, it is said, by Davies's descent into ill-tempered old age (Davies turned seventy-one in 1947, Marjorie sixty). They had enjoyed a decade of compatibility during which Marjorie found herself exposed to a type of worldly travel and high-level statesmanship she had never experienced in

Marjorie Merriweather Post and Mrs. Joseph P. Kennedy during the Red Cross "Snow Ball" at Mar-a-Lago in January 1965, taken by legendary celebrity photographer Bert Morgan.

the company of Ned Hutton, but the ten years she spent with Davies after the war are described as dour indeed, with Davies sometimes appearing at social functions by himself, having "forgotten" to mention these engagements to his wife.

Though Davies enjoyed considerable attention for his pro-Stalinist memoir published in 1941, *Mission to Moscow*, which sold seven hundred thousand copies and was made into a 1943 film starring Walter Huston, his political career was on the downside by the end of the war. Thus, he began to chafe as his star dimmed and Marjorie's continued to brighten. In 1955, with herself almost sixty-eight and the perpetually grouchy Davies nearing eighty, Marjorie made her way to Sun Valley, Idaho, where following the required six-week stay to establish standing for such proceedings, she was granted a divorce from her third husband. Questioned by reporters as to her reasons, Marjorie had a succinct response: "The Ambassador had a funny lack of basic straight thinking that was awfully hard to live with."

It would not be the end of Marjorie's interest in men, however, nor the end of her career as hostess extraordinaire. In 1947, she had decided to sell her seldom-used Hillwood estate on Long Island to the trustees of Brooklyn-based Long Island University. Though nearly eight years passed before the transfer went through, owing to the opposition of nearby residents worried about the devaluation of their own holdings, in 1954 the $200 million sale was completed, the transaction doubtless brightened for Marjorie by the decision of the trustees to name the new Brookville campus C. W. Post College.

Thus in 1955, with her marriage to Davies over, Marjorie undertook the building of a second Hillwood in the Washington, D.C., that she had come to know and love. The site was an estate overlooking Rock Creek Park formerly known as Arbremont, which Marjorie would gut and spend the next two years remaking into a glittering showplace for a staggering array of portraiture and art objects, many of which she had acquired during the days she and Davies spent in Moscow. It took two years for her to finish the work on Hillwood II, and by the time she did, at seventy, she was ready to commence a new round of vigorous hostessing. She lacked only the presence of a handsome man on her arm.

Her choice was Herbert May, a former Westinghouse executive originally from Pittsburgh, well connected with social circles in Washington and Palm Beach and, most important, well liked. At the time of their wedding in June 1958, May was sixty-five and Marjorie was seventy-one. In many ways, May was the perfect antidote to the curmudgeonly, politically ambitious Davies. He was a tall, bluff, good-natured, and good-looking man whom people naturally gathered around, and he was good for Marjorie as well, encouraging her to have that second drink and enjoy herself instead of worrying so much about others enjoying themselves.

But while May was not completely averse to joining Marjorie in her bedchambers (he had been previously married and was the father of three grown children), neither was he averse to the occasional stint with another man. While others had known that May was bisexual, none of them—not even daughter Eleanor—had found the gumption to convey their knowledge or their suspicions to Marjorie Merriweather Post.

For a time, no one seemed bothered by the fact that May might enjoy the odd midnight frolic with a group of boys at the oceanfront pool he had added at Mar-a-Lago. Marjorie had grown so hard of hearing she couldn't have made out the bleat of an elephant from Herb's bedroom, and the servants, though aware of what sometimes went on across the road, simply shrugged and looked the other way. According to biographer Wright, the situation reached a crisis only when Herb May learned that his new wife was being taken advantage of by certain employees at Mar-a-lago and decided to intervene.

Though it was not uncommon for a supplier or contractor to slip a majordomo or secretary a few dollars in appreciation of an order or the awarding of a maintenance contract, May discovered that the situation at Mar-a-Lago had gotten completely out of hand, with one major grocery chain refusing to do business with the household owing to the size of the kickbacks required. When word of May's intentions to rectify things at Mar-a-Lago reached certain members of the staff, a counteroffensive was undertaken. Soon, one of Marjorie's attorneys on the island arrived at his office one morning to find an anonymously delivered packet on his desk. Inside was a stack of photos taken of a naked Herbert May cavorting with a number of similarly unclad young boys at the oceanfront pool.

Marjorie was certainly no sybarite, despite all that she had been exposed to over the years and despite the fact that she apparently had a healthy sexual appetite of her own so long as it was good, old-fashioned sex. In fact, it is said that May complained to a confidant shortly after the marriage: "My God, she wants to do it every night."

However, guests who wanted more than a drink or two at one of her parties would have to be willing to quietly grease the palm of a willing waiter, and couples found to be dancing in what might be construed as a scandalous manner on the ballroom floor were quickly called out. The photos that her attorney shared with her made whatever "evidence" she had produced against Ned Hutton look like child's play.

She and her attorney are said to have marched directly into May's bedroom at Mar-a-Lago, where they produced the photos and demanded to know what May had to say for himself. To his credit, May leafed through the photos with aplomb, handing them back with a steady hand. They were obvious fakes, he told Marjorie, the work of devious scoundrels out to get him. According to Wright, May's denial was all that trusting Marjorie needed to hear.

Perhaps no more might have been said about the matter, if May had been willing to drop his plans to root out corruption among the pantry staff. As it was, however, shortly after May had issued his denial, news came to Marjorie and her legal team that an unnamed "author" had completed a tell-all book detailing the sordid secret lives of certain Washington insiders. One chapter would feature the shameful exploits of Herbert May and would be illustrated with the very photographs that Marjorie had seen. The readers would have to distinguish for themselves between what was real and what was fake.

It was simply more than staid-to-the-core Marjorie could endure. A check was written to forestall publication of the "manuscript," no copy of which has ever materialized, and soon the couple were separated. By 1964 they were divorced, though Marjorie continued to support May until his death in 1968. At the end of her fourth marriage, at age seventy-seven, Marjorie reassumed the name she had been born with, Marjorie Merriweather Post, and she would carry it for the rest of her days.

Other men entered her life—"escorts" they would ever remain—and she gave many more parties, at Topridge, at the new Hillwood, and at Mar-a-Lago, where, in addition to the ocean-side pool and cabanas and renovations to the Master's Quarters initiated by May, Marjorie built three basement bomb shelters, built a loggia for outdoor dining, and made various additions and improvements to the staff quarters. Marjorie had also by this time brought the miracle of air-conditioning to the estate, adding wall units first to the servants' quarters and then to her own bedroom. In the mid-1960s, what a staffer called "an enormous" mechanical unit was brought atop the mansion by helicopter, providing relief for the main living areas.

In 1961, Marjorie also completed the ballroom for which Wyeth was commissioned, with a stage and a thirty-by-fifty-foot dance floor where were staged the fabled square dances. "She liked the women to wear full-skirted dresses, and everyone gathered at 7 p.m. sharp for cocktails," one frequent guest told the *Miami Herald* in a 1973 interview. A buffet dinner commenced at 8, and at 9 p.m., "sharp," the dancing began.

Though some sophisticates in Palm Beach might have rolled their eyes at the thought of square dancing, an invitation to one of Marjorie's parties was rarely dismissed. Rose Kennedy, who became a regular at the affairs, once wrote to Marjorie: "I have not had so many attractive dancing partners since I was a debutante."

Nor was a coveted stay at Mar-a-Lago quite like any other. Once when Marjorie's estate planner Henry Dudley was invited for a visit with his family, his wife explained to their two sons that each would have to pack two bags, because everyone would need to be "properly dressed" for dinner. Furthermore, Mrs. Dudley told her sons, "just wait until you see what they do with your luggage on the way home." Explained son Spottswood Dudley sometime later, "The valets repacked your bag for you with everything cleaned and in tissue paper so nothing wrinkled. I would arrive home with my mother happily rubbing her hands and declaring 'no work this week.' On a visit to Mrs. Post you came back looking better than you arrived."

As a result of her donation of Long Island's Hillwood, Marjorie was eventually named honorary housemother of the Sigma Alpha Epsilon fraternity at C. W. Post College. Anyone else might have accepted the designation as a pleasantry, but that was not Marjorie's style. She visited the fraternity house, regularly corresponded with members who sent her Mother's Day cards and flowers, and each year invited the fraternity's president and a companion for a two-week stay at Mar-a-Lago.

One such guest, John Convery, remembers being included in the square dancing and elaborate dining, as well as a side trip one day to a nearby attraction, Lion Country Safari. In the gift shop, Marjorie saw some copper bracelets she wanted to buy, but she had no money with her. John took a hundred-dollar bill from his travel funds and handed it to her. That night at dinner, he found a little card at his place setting. "She gave me a little bonus," he said. "I think it was a hundred and fifty bucks in there. That was the best loan I ever made."

The dinners at which the Dudleys and the SAEs were present were seldom intimate affairs. According to Anthony Senecal, who came aboard Marjorie's staff in 1959, typically thirty-six gathered in the dining room, seated around the duplicate of the grand table at Chigi, "with one butler and thirty-five footmen also present, the butler for the missus and one of us for each of the other guests. I don't think the Queen of England went that far." Such affairs were like living in a scene out of history, says the West Virginian–born Senecal. "And I was a kid, maybe twenty-five. I didn't have the slightest idea what I was doing at first. But the thing was, everybody who worked for Mrs. Post absolutely loved her and wanted to live up to her expectations that everything be just so. They took me under their wing, so I could learn to do as well as they did, because in the end only one thing mattered: that she would be happy."

One of the things that Senecal came to learn was the unwritten rule that you simply did not speak to Mrs. Post unless you were spoken to first. "First of all there were seventy-five or a hundred of us running around most of the time and we were always getting ready for one thing or another. [Until her last few years at Mar-a-Lago, Marjorie strictly observed the 'season,' arriving at the beginning of January and departing after Washington's Birthday.] She didn't have a lot of time to chitchat. But that didn't mean she didn't care about you. I would watch her walk through the gardens in the morning, stopping to talk with everyone working out there. She knew the gardeners by their first names, the names of their wives, the names of their children, how everybody was doing in school. It was amazing."

One of the special occasions on the docket for Marjorie during that period was the marriage of her daughter Deenie, by then forty-one and well known as Dina Merrill, to the equally famous Cliff Robertson, also forty-one. Their ceremony took place on December 21, 1966, at the second Hillwood, which was described as "the baronial Rock Creek Park estate" by the *New York Times*. The marriage was the second for both, and Robertson was to become a favorite of his new mother-in-law. "Cliff lived in mortal terror of Marjorie," says Anthony Senecal. "But she was intimidating to a lot of people. She liked him a lot, though, well enough to tell him she wanted him to deliver her eulogy when the time came."

* * *

By this point in her life, Marjorie's thoughts had begun to focus increasingly on her legacy. The second Hillwood had always been intended as much as a museum as a home, the same way Henry Clay Frick had planned his Fifth Avenue mansion, now the museum known as the Frick. (Frick is said to have vowed his home would make archenemy Andrew Carnegie's digs "look like a miner's shack.") In fact, shortly after its completion, Marjorie announced her intention to leave Hillwood and its many treasures—one of which was the mammoth Chigi table reproduction she moved from Mar-a-Lago—to the Smithsonian.*

As for Mar-a-Lago, Marjorie was greatly concerned that following her death her Palm Beach property would not meet the same fate as had befallen El Mirasol, the Stotesburys' fabulous compound. Accordingly, in 1964 she invited Farris Bryant, Florida's governor at the time, for a tour of it, telling him that she wanted to bequeath Mar-a-Lago to the state for whatever

---

* Citing the burdensome costs of upkeep, that institution would decide against assumption of Hillwood and its many splendors, and today Hillwood is operated as an independent museum.

uses might be appropriate. Bryant was as impressed as anyone else by the grandeur of the compound, but he was also a practical man and asked what might be needed to keep Mar-a-Lago going for a year. At the time, there were about seventy-five staff members, half of them maids, valets, kitchen workers, drivers, secretaries, laundry workers, and watchmen; the other half were groundskeepers and maintenance men, including an electrician, a painter, and a carpenter.

Marjorie was quick to flip open the ledger book for 1962 and find the sum required for help, supplies, and utilities at the bottom of a page: $259,512.47. There is no record of Bryant's expression as he studied the figures, but neither is there doubt as to his answer. Mar-a-Lago was a bit too rich for the state of Florida's blood.

Alternatively, a news report of 1968 sheds a slightly different light on her dealings with the state. According to the piece, the Florida legislature had actually favored the idea that the grand mansion might become a kind of tropical Chautauqua, an international gathering place where great talents in the arts and politics might convene for the public good. The state was so appreciative of Mrs. Post's offer, it is said, that the legislature invited her to the capitol in Tallahassee where she was named an honorary citizen, the only time it had ever done so. The sticking point in the deal was said to be not so much the amount of the upkeep as the pressure brought to bear by a number of Marjorie's well-heeled and politically connected neighbors who were concerned about the amount of additional traffic and the general bother that any such use might bring to a neighborhood where zoning permitted only private residences.

Whatever the reasons for the state's demurral, Marjorie turned her sights on the next logical candidate, the federal government. Mar-a-Lago was very well suited to become a sumptuous retreat for high-ranking officials and visiting foreign dignitaries, she reasoned. After all, the far more modest La Querida ("the beloved"), a Mizner design purchased by Joseph Kennedy in 1933, had served as JFK's winter hideaway earlier in the 1960s, and even if the elder Kennedy had used the place to entertain his many mistresses—including Gloria Swanson—the president had brought back a certain amount of respect for the so-called Kennedy Compound and had undoubtedly provided Marjorie with precedent for her idea. In fact, Marjorie was certain that Mar-a-Lago would make the perfect winter White House.

- 13 -

A PLACE IN READINESS

By the time Marjorie Merriweather Post had gone in search of a proper future custodian for her beloved Mar-a-Lago, Palm Beach itself had long since become part of the national lexicon where wealth and privilege were described. From the days of the W. C. Fields silent movies, film had done its part to make Palm Beach synonymous with unbridled means, and by the time Preston Sturges released his 1942 film *The Palm Beach Story*, the mention of the town was all it took to alert moviegoers that this "screwball comedy" about a young fortune-hunting woman's unlikely travels there would be fueled at the expense of the uncommonly rich.

By 1952, Cleveland Amory had included Palm Beach among the baker's dozen of the nation's established spas he had sport with in *The Last Resorts*. There, along with the venerable playgrounds of the Berkshires, Southampton, Newport, Bar Harbor, Saratoga, White Sulphur Springs, and Jekyll Island, was Palm Springs, where Amory—after detailing how Mrs. Stotesbury had once chafed under her weekly allowance of $12,000 or so—characterized Palm Beach as a transcendent destination. "From the moment you cross over the drawbridges over Lake Worth from West Palm Beach . . . you enter what amounts to an island of privilege, in many ways the most remarkable one left in this country."

Though a goodly part of Amory's book poked gentle fun at how the elderly rich had been forced to downsize and adjust their notions of who belonged to "the club," and what scandalous behaviors would have to be countenanced at mid–twentieth century, there was no suggestion that social distinction had ended. And while such spas as Saratoga, White Sulphur Springs, and Hot Springs were in decline, Palm Beach, with most of its eight square miles built out and playing the role of the only true winter destination for the wealthy, was going strong. That bastion might have changed in some cosmetic ways, with the likes of legendary Eva Stotesbury long gone and the sixty-thousand-square-foot El Mirasol shuttered, but still, even if Cadillacs were soon to lose their fins, they remained Cadillacs. A *New York Times* story of 1960 called Palm Beach "one of the world's most exclusive playgrounds," noting that where once stood but two Flagler hotels and a handful of houses, there now sat thirty-five hotels, 192 apartment houses, and 1,905 residences.

While Henry Flagler had started the flow of the privileged south to Palm Beach, Paris Singer and Addison Mizner broadened that stream to a flood. The construction of the Everglades Club, along with the shops, hotels, and homes soon to come, turned Palm Beach from a distant spa centered on one grand hotel into a multifaceted resort destination. As one commentator put it, their mission was nothing less than the "transformation of American high society. Their elaborate plans set the stage for post-Puritan America; they taught rich Americans how to enjoy their wealth, how to relax, how to have fun in the sun."

Along with the genre-bending homes Mizner designed, each one leading to more commissions from patrons eager to outdo the last, the effect of his work on the public life of the enclave is equally profound. In 1923, he completed a three-story building opposite the Everglades Club on Worth Avenue, where he moved his offices and studio to the second floor with space for his draftsmen and a studio apartment for himself on the third. On the first

An 1823 map drawn by City of St. Augustine surveyor Charles Vignoles, the first to show Florida as an American territory, much of it then described as "Unexplored Lands."

A seldom-seen image of Marjorie Post Hutton at 35, two years after her marriage to Ned.

A rendering of Hutton in Byronesque repose, date and artist unknown, still in the Sea Cloud collection.

A meditative Henry Flagler on the docks at Knights Key, at the halfway point down the line of the Oversea Railway.

The only surviving photograph of Flagler's Ouija-bewitched second wife, Ida Alice Shourds, in her bridal gown.

A postcard rendering of the 1,150-room Royal Poinciana Hotel in Palm Beach, opened in 1894 and soon dubbed the "Newport of the South."

Whitehall—Flagler's stately home and museum in Palm Beach—as it appears in the catalog of Historic American Buildings.

Opened in 1898, Bradley's Beach Club offered fine dining, roulette, and chemin de fer within walking distance of Flagler's hotels.

On June 9, 1903, the wooden Breakers Hotel was destroyed by fire. It burned again in 1925, and was reconstructed in its present form in 1926.

A view of the north loggia of the Everglades Club, the Paris Singer/ Addison Mizner creation that would transform Palm Beach and the American social scene.

Addison Mizner, with his beloved companions. The spider monkey, Johnnie Brown, occupies one of only two marked gravesites on Palm Beach island.

Mar-a-Lago as it appeared while under construction in August of 1926.

*Mar-a-Lago as it looked in 1967 in the closing years
of the Marjorie Merriweather Post era.*

Marjorie Merriweather Post Hutton Davies,
during the World War II years.

Marjorie Merriweather Post Hutton Davies (right), on the set of Mission to Moscow,
in 1942, with Barbara Hutton (center), and actress Yvonne Hendricks (left).

Pictured in 1993 are Anthony Senecal (right), the only person to serve as majordomo to both owners of Mar-a-Lago, and Donald J. Trump (left).

Typical Via Mizner shops and courtyards as they appear today.

Looking north along the Lake Worth trail in Palm Beach.

floor, he fashioned a street-front arcade with shops that purveyed antiques and pottery and tile of his design. The following year, he created an adjoining shopping complex, the Via Mizner, consisting of a pair of buildings flanking a twisting lane that connected Worth Avenue to residential Peruvian Avenue behind it. The effect was to make pedestrians feel transported to a European village and the Via Mizner concept to this day anchors high-end boutique-studded Worth Avenue, ranked with the likes of Rodeo Drive as among the most desirable shopping streets in the country.

Mizner was the most important and prolific and certainly one of the most flamboyant of the architects to have an impact on Palm Beach, but those who followed in his wake during the 1920s and '30s also contributed significantly to the mystique of the community. Joseph Urban's flair for the dramatic made Mar-a-Lago an iconoclastic sensation, but his design of the Bath and Tennis Club (1926) also proved to be an enduring concept, working as well in the twenty-first century as it did in the twentieth.

Also in 1926, Urban designed the Paramount Theater and Sunrise Building complex, about a mile and a half north of Worth Avenue, which included a phantasmagorical-themed thousand-seat theater, shops, apartments, and offices around a spacious courtyard that served as the performing arts center of the community for decades, hosting shows by the likes of George Gershwin, Will Rogers, Ed Sullivan, Bob Hope, and Barbra Streisand. Though the theater ceased movie screenings and performances in 1980, the building still houses a church and offices and is listed on the National Register of Historic Places.

More widely influential for residential design in Palm Beach than Urban were those among the so-called second generation of architects there, including Marion Sims Wyeth, Maurice Fatio, John Volk, and Howard Major. Wyeth continued to design homes in Palm Beach for more than fifty years after the Huttons gave him the commission for Hogarcito, and while he was influenced by Mizner in such undertakings as the Donahues' Cielito Lindo, he also worked in other vernaculars, including the two-story Louisiana-themed Southwood for Dr. John Vietor (1934) and Gemini, a sleekly modern version of the Mizner style, for pharmaceutical heir Gerald B. Lambert (1947) in Manalapan, just to the south of Palm Beach.

Maurice Fatio was a Swiss-trained architect who opened an office in Palm Beach in the mid-1920s and who was said to be as personable as the popular Mizner. With Mizner frequently overwhelmed by requests, Fatio was often able to pick up work, including some commissions passed along by the overburdened Mizner himself. Much of Fatio's work follows in the Mizner vein, though he designed a Norman half-timber house for his mother-in-law, Mrs. Charles Curry Chase, in 1928 and a house in the Le Corbusier International style for Mrs. Barclay Douglas in 1936. The Reef, as the latter is known—purchased by Miami Dolphins owner Stephen Ross in 2010—is one of the few remaining modernist structures in Palm Beach and is generally considered the apex of Fatio's work. Had his career not been cut short by his death from cancer in 1943, Fatio would have undoubtedly gone on to further exploration of styles.

John Volk was an Austrian-born, classically trained architect who arrived in Palm Beach in 1926 after a year in Key West. He began working in the Spanish style, producing some designs that could have been taken for Mizner's; but eventually he moved away to other forms, including a Regency-influenced renovation of the Royal Poinciana Playhouse and Shopping Plaza in 1958 and the highly futuristic residence La Ronda, built for James J. Ackston in 1969 and demolished in 2003.

Perhaps the most influential architect to work in Palm Beach after Mizner was Howard Major. Trained at Pratt Institute, Major caused something of a stir soon after arriving in Palm Beach in 1925 by dismissing the use of Spanish styles in Florida as "fumbling with a foreign element." Major was said to be motivated more by his disdain for slapdash imitation of Mizner's approach than by outright antipathy toward his predecessor. But eager to carve out a niche for himself, he fastened on Georgian architecture as it was found in Bermuda and the British West Indies as the appropriate vernacular for Palm Beach. In 1925, he completed Major Alley, six attached houses built in the Georgian classic style on a narrow Peruvian Avenue lot, an undertaking that provided the basis for what would eventually supplant the Mizner style in the resort by the late 1930s.

In large part because no vast swaths of land to be developed remain on the island, there has been no cadre of notable architects to set up shop there in the wake of those mentioned. And when such imposing Mizner masterpieces as El Mirasol, Playa Riente, and Casa Bendita fell to the wrecking ball and their footprints were subdivided for smaller homes, Mar-a-Lago's survival seemed all the more notable.

Even that Flagler's grand mansion Whitehall survives is something of a minor miracle. Following the death of Mary Lily Kenan in Louisville in 1917, Whitehall was conveyed to her niece Louise Wise, who had become Mary Lily's favored companion following Flagler's death. Louise also inherited, the Flagler home in St. Augustine, Kirkside, which she found far more practical as a residence.

For seven years, Whitehall sat vacant, falling victim to the decay that is particularly virulent in the seaside tropics. In the mid-1920s, the Kenan family opened Whitehall as a club, then converted it to a hotel, constructing a ten-story, three-hundred-room addition on the west side of the mansion overlooking Lake Worth. This renovation, designed by Carrère and Hastings, removed Flagler's office and a housekeeper's apartment and made significant changes to the kitchen and pantry areas in preparing the building for commercial use. The grand original structure was converted for use as an entranceway and lobby, bar, card rooms, and offices, with the Flaglers' bedrooms converted to luxury suites. The Whitehall Hotel, characterized by the *Palm Beach Post* as an "apartment hotel . . . more formal than the Royal Poinciana," opened on December 31, 1926, just in time for the Florida bust. In 1929, $3 million in debt, the hotel was sold to a group of Boston investors for what might seem an impossible $2,600, and operations continued on. A 1939 guidebook called the Whitehall a $4 million structure and, with the Royal Poinciana having been demolished in 1935, described it as the town's second largest, after the Breakers.

Whitehall operated as a hotel well into the 1950s, until Jean Flagler Matthews, daughter of Harry Harkness Flagler and granddaughter of Henry Flagler, stepped into the picture. In a letter quoted by David Leon Chandler, Mrs. Matthews spoke of hearing little of her illustrious grandfather while she was growing up, despite having been bequeathed $1 million in Standard Oil stock when she was three. She knew there was an estrangement between the elder Flagler and her father, she said, but that was about it. When she came to Palm Beach in the 1940s—she purchased Via Serena, a Marion Sims Wyeth creation—and those aware of her lineage started to pepper her with questions that she could not answer, she began digging into family history and went to have a look at Whitehall.

"The more I learned, the more I gazed at Whitehall," she said, "and started the mind thinking about what should be done." Ultimately, in 1959, word reached Mrs. Matthews that soon the matchless 110-foot-by-40-foot marble entrance hall of the mansion would be converted to dressing rooms for a spa.

"That did it," she said. The next day she told her lawyer that she wished to acquire Whitehall and turn it into a memorial: "To grandfather." Though her lawyer was dubious, Mrs. Matthews— her various trusts reportedly grown to some $42 million—was resolute. "It all happened in the nick of time, as hammer and chisel were about to be lowered," she said. As a result of her tireless efforts to summon community support for such a move, not to mention an initial outlay of $2.5 million, Whitehall opened as the Henry Morrison Flagler Museum on February 6, 1960, a development that surely gave Marjorie Merriweather Post confidence that a similar outcome lay ahead for Mar-a-Lago.

- 14 -

HOUSE WITHOUT A HOME

The disinterest of the state of Florida might not have been the first prompt that Mar-a-Lago would have its status indelibly elevated by a U.S. president. Reports have it that during the Kennedy administration, Palm Beach County officials had floated to Mrs. Post the idea of turning the mansion into a winter White House for JFK and his successors. While subsequent events ensured that JFK would not have a part in determining its future, in early April 1968, Marjorie turned again to Washington, this time inviting Lady Bird Johnson down for a look at Mar-a-Lago.

Though the official reason given for the visit was "for rest," the president's wife was accompanied by U.S. chief of protocol Angier Biddle Duke and National Park Service director George B. Hartzog, Jr. Given that an important diplomatic officer and the director of the agency sure to be purposed with caring for Mar-a-Lago were along for the ride, Marjorie's proposal was clearly being taken seriously. Reports said that Mrs. Post had pitched it as potentially "a more luxurious Camp David" where presidents could get away for working vacations and which the State Department might use to extend the stays of visiting heads of state following official tours in Washington. White House sources had allowed that the matter was a "long-range possibility" but were playing it all close to the vest, given that questions of cost and zoning were still problematic. Mar-a-Lago, valued at $2 million at the time, employed among the maintenance staff twenty-two year-round gardeners tasked with, among other things, moving ten thousand potted plants indoors to greenhouses when Mrs. Post was not in residence.

The first lady's visit put the rumor mill into high gear: cheek by jowl with society columnists' notes that Jackie Kennedy was expected in Palm Beach the following week were whispers that Mrs. Post had struck a deal with the government, one that would preserve the property intact after her death and forestall the plans of developers who, according to ominous stories that had begun to circulate, were poised to level Mar-a-Lago once Marjorie was no longer around to protect it. There was talk of building as many as fifty homes on the site. Marjorie was mum on the subject, however, telling reporters only that she planned on continuing to live at Mar-a-Lago and referring all other questions "to Washington."

Columnists all the while also continued to speculate that the heiress was not done marrying. The appearance of handsome Colonel C. Michael Paul at her final square dance of the 1968 season was noted with lifted brows, "but not to be counted out of the picture are Mrs. Post's other dear friends like [Russian nobleman] Serge Obolensky, Victor Bowman and former Secretary of the Navy Fred Korth, who [20 years her junior] escorts her to parties. She's 80 and still beautiful."

The following season of 1969 saw a resumption of the routine of square dances and benefit luncheons for the Animal Rescue League and others by Marjorie, and a wrap-up of the calendar identified her as still "the empress of Palm Beach." Even at eighty-one and "of failing hearing," she remained the enclave's undisputed social leader, eclipsing such Johnny-come-latelies as the Kennedys.

"She was getting pretty frail those last two or three years," says Anthony Senecal, by that time one of Mrs. Post's most trusted assistants. She had for years used the Moorish tower overlooking the grounds as her personal retreat: there was a bedroom on one level, a sitting room on another, and an observation deck at the top that offered a 360-degree view of the island and its surroundings. "But there were more than one hundred steps to climb to get up there," Senecal says. "It was hardly ever used at the end."

Still, extravagant activities, such as the annual Red Cross Ball that drew a crowd of movers and shakers and politicos from across the country and around the world—including ambassadors

Mrs. Post with daughter Dina Merrill and granddaughter Nedenia at Mar-a-Lago, shortly before the actress's 1966 divorce from Stanley Rumbrough, Jr., and her remarriage to Cliff Robertson.

from India, Italy, Luxembourg, Nicaragua, Panama, France, Spain, and elsewhere—continued unabated through the seasons, though a lengthy *New York Times* piece of 1970 spoke of dire changes in the works for the enclave. The very fact that the Florida grocery chain Publix was bringing a supermarket to the island was discussed in the same terms as if Marjorie Merriweather Post had been spotted frugging in a discotheque, barefoot and wearing cutoffs. "The supermarket is a symbol of the waves of change breaking over the shores here," the story warned. "To wealthy residents, the change means the select few are being surrounded by the anonymous many."

The town had burgeoned from 1,200 year-round residents shortly after the first season of Paris Singer's Everglades Club to 9,000 in 1970, a figure that would swell to 36,000 at the height of the season. Counting plebeian West Palm Beach, scarcely a drive and an approach shot across Lake Worth, at times 150,000 people were clamoring for beach access, parking spots, and restaurant tables where once there had been a few dozen genteel types with boaters and parasols being pedaled about by valets.

Moreover, the newly renovated and enlarged Breakers Hotel announced that beginning in 1971, it would keep its doors open throughout the entire year, quite a blow against the concept of a season, which itself had expanded over the years from the six-week period beginning with the New Year and ending on Washington's Birthday. Now it was understood to last until the end of April. Pollution had put an end to swimming in Lake Worth, and West Palm Beach was pushing for a sewage outfall line into the ocean, one that would have to cross the island's pristine grounds. Clamor from increased vehicular traffic had combined with the roar of airliner approaches to Palm Beach International Airport in sufficient degree for the town government to draft its first-ever noise ordinance.

As for those privileged residents inhabiting the "glamourous coconut-shaded properties" of Palm Beach, "the select few are being surrounded," the 1970 *Times* piece lamented. "Gone are many great estates including those of Hearst, Kingsley and Untermeyer. Tourists still hear the famous names, but numbers are beginning to speak louder than names in determining the fate of this area."

The fate of Mar-a-Lago would finally come before Congress in 1972, some four years after Lady Bird Johnson's hoedown with Marjorie and friends in its ballroom. LBJ's interior secretary Stewart Udall had begun the process for the designation of Mar-a-Lago as a national historic site. By 1972, under the Nixon administration, things had progressed somewhat. It was now clear that the gift would be accompanied by an endowment that would provide the funds for upkeep, and Democratic congressman Wayne Aspinall of Colorado introduced a bill authorizing the National Park Service to take over development and administration of the property following its eventual transfer from the Post estate.

While Aspinall's bill was being discussed, representatives of the Palm Beach Town Council appeared before a House National Parks subcommittee to say that they were opposed to giving the Park Service sole authority for determining what uses might be made of the property. The town council wanted to reserve "something resembling a veto power" concerning such decisions, said Councilman Robert Grace, adding that perhaps a part of the mansion could be set aside for town meetings and an office for the mayor.

Whatever he may have thought of Grace's notions, National Park Service director George Hartzog saw even bigger problems with the proposal. He doubted that the attached endowment would be sufficient to cover actual operating costs, he said, and his initial prediction was that if Mar-a-Lago were to open as a museum, as many as sixty-five thousand to seventy-five thousand visits to the facility might be made annually, a number that Councilman Grace said would appall local residents. Not only would turning Mar-a-Lago into a national park create impossible traffic problems, town leaders said, but it would also mean the loss of $25,000 a year in taxes on the property, which was on the tax rolls at the time at $1.5 million. As for the idea of visiting dignitaries making use of the property as a retreat or a home away from home, Grace wondered why taxpayers should have to pay for such a thing.

Marjorie's Washington attorney, Henry Dudley, attempted to assure town officials that the gift of Mar-a-Lago to the government came with restrictions that limited its use to that of a retreat for the U.S. president or foreign heads of state and that any attempt to turn it into a museum would mean the reversion of the property to the estate. But residents were hardly convinced. Once the camel's nose was under the tent, chaos was sure to follow, argued town fathers, if to little avail. On October 12, 1972, the bill designating Mar-a-Lago as a national historic site cleared Congress, and on October 23, President Nixon signed the bill authorizing the secretary of the interior to accept title to it upon Marjorie's death. Five advisory commissioners would be appointed to establish operating policies, two of whom would be selected from nominees proposed by the Palm Beach Town Council. The $3 million endowment attached to the bequest was projected to provide somewhere between $140,000 and $150,000 annually.

* * *

During a chat with reporters following the announcement, Mar-a-Lago's head butler—Mr. Livingston—confided that while things had slowed down a bit, Mrs. Post, eighty-five, with seven grand-children and eight great-grandchildren, still enjoyed strolling down to the pavilion and watching movies, usually Disney films featuring animals. Anything smacking of violence or cruelty was a major turnoff for the heiress, however. The staff had tried to talk her into watching an episode of *Flipper*, but when the week's program began with an evildoer's attempt to kidnap the genial creature, Mrs. Post ordered it switched off.

As hale and active as she had been, time would eventually catch up with Marjorie. In February 1973, she was taken by ambulance to Good Samaritan hospital in Palm Beach suffering from pneumonia, and though she rallied, she remained seriously weakened. "The most vivid memory I have of my days there," says Tony Senecal, "is of watching her being taken down the long hallway to the front door, on her way back to Washington. Jimmy Griffin was pushing her wheelchair and all the staff was lined up to say good-bye. He zigzagged her chair down the hall-way first to one person and then the other and she would take each person's hand and whisper, 'Thank you,' in a voice so soft you could barely hear it. I think we all knew it was the last time we would see her."

Marjorie would not return to Mar-a-Lago. On September 12, 1973, she died of heart failure at her Hillwood home in Washington, and at her funeral, her eulogy was in fact delivered by Cliff Robertson. Her will divided most of her property, val-ued at $117 million, among daughters Eleanor, Adelaide, and Deenie, with bequests earmarked for operations at Hillwood and Mar-a-Lago (Camp Topridge was given to the state of New York) and gifts of $5,000 to $50,000 going to various long-term employees, including lifetime annuities to a few. In the press, she was widely hailed for her graciousness and her generosity. "She was probably the most considerate person I've ever known," said Charles Carey, for many years the chief of protocol for the annual Red Cross Ball. "I've never known anyone who was so thoughtful for all the welfare of her guests." As for her Palm Beach friends, Mrs. Harold Whitmore likely best summed it up, saying, "There is only one Mrs. Post. There will never be another."

"She could be tightfisted," recalls Anthony Senecal. "She'd raise hell if a driver ever got a ticket, even a parking ticket. She just wouldn't tolerate carelessness. But she was also very generous. A bunch of us were sitting around the courtyard of the servants' quarters one day just before Christmas back in the 1960s when somebody walked up holding an envelope. 'Isn't that great?' the guy says. 'Mrs. Post giving us fifty bucks for Christmas.' I didn't say anything because I hadn't been given my envelope yet, but a couple of other guys chimed in saying, 'Yeah, I got my fifty, too.' Well, I was thinking, great, I can use fifty bucks, but Mrs. Post's driver Jimmy was there, too, and he had a really funny look on his face. 'You guys got fifty bucks apiece?' Jimmy asks, and a bunch of people are nodding. 'The superintendent's been handing the envelopes out.' So Jimmy just nods and walks off. A little while later Jimmy comes by my room and hands me my envelope. I open it up and there's twelve hundred dollars inside. 'What the hell?' I said to Jimmy. 'I saw the size of the check Mrs. Post wrote out to the super for you guys,' Jimmy said. 'I had a little talk with him. He agreed with me that he made a mistake in his math.'"

It is a story that underscores Marjorie's generosity, for a $1,200 Christmas bonus was a stunning windfall for Tony Senecal and his fellow footmen in the 1960s. But it also illustrates the truth of the problems that the unfortunate Herb May was trying to root out on behalf of a far too trusting Marjorie. Another story passed along by Senecal is tied to the death of Mrs. Post's private secretary, whom he and several of his colleagues referred to as "the wicked witch of the North."*

"As Mrs. Post got older, this person took over most of the day-to-day operations," Senecal says. "It was pretty hard for anyone to get past her to talk to Mrs. Post about anything. But shortly after Mrs. Post died, the witch died, too. When they went into her apartment to go through her things, they found a lockbox under her bed. There was $250,000 in cash inside."

* * *

If Marjorie Merriweather Post was one of a kind, most would agree that the same might be said of Mar-a-Lago. But the heiress's funeral was scarcely concluded before the future of the property was back in question. One National Park Service official announced that if the agency was to be barred from opening it as a public park or museum, it would likely be transferred to some other government agency such as the Secret Service. "After all, we run public parks," said Park Service director of information Gerald Waindel, who pointed out that even if Mar-a-Lago were to be used principally as a southern White House, such a designation would not necessarily prevent the Park Service from giving public tours there. After all, Waindel pointed out, "We have tours at the White House." It would all be hashed out in the coming months by the advisory commission, he said, reminding reporters that two members of that commission would be representatives from Palm Beach.

Shortly after the Fourth of July, then president Richard Nixon interrupted a holiday vacation on Miami's Key Biscayne to make

* Senecal and several other men occupied a suite of eleven rooms above what is now the spa. The "witch" lived in a private apartment above today's store, just to their north.

an unscheduled helicopter flight to Palm Beach for a closer look at Mar-a-Lago. Along for the ride was his longtime confidant Bebe Rebozo. The visit, taking place as Nixon faced charges in the Watergate cover-up and the threat of impeachment, lasted less than half an hour, and though it generated speculation as to whether he was intending to leave behind the two villas he owned on Key Biscayne, Park Service and Secret Service spokespersons downplayed the notion.

By that time, State Department officials had already opined in a memo to the Park Service that the property's location would present significant problems in maintaining security for a president; for one thing, the fact of its location in the middle of the flight path of Palm Beach International Airport presented an apparently insurmountable safety concern. The Park Service had also already determined that making any public use of Mar-a-Lago would require an additional appropriation from Congress. "The costs would be prohibitive," said Park Service spokesperson Gerald Cadieux. "You can't just turn 10,000 people loose to walk through there. The place wouldn't be the same when they left."

Nixon's subsequent implosion put an end to his involvement with Mar-a-Lago, though the question of what use the government might make of it was still very much up in the air. In March 1975, a report surfaced that the State Department had floated the notion of housing the shah of Iran at Mar-a-Lago during an official visit by the potentate scheduled later in the year. Park Service officials indicated that the possibility of such a thing happening was slim. Associate Director Richard Curry said, "There would be some real problems to that. We don't have the money or the staff to open it up." Since assuming the property, the Park Service had been maintaining it in what was termed a "closed door manner." Regional Director Charles Watson said that two months would be needed "to fix the place up for somebody to visit," with all furniture and movable fixtures having been removed and stored. It was his intention, Curry said at the time, to ask Congress to divest the Park Service of the property and return it to the Post estate. Complicating that scenario, however, was the fact that the estate was without the funds to operate it.

Indeed, the $180,000 that the Post Foundation (a charitable endowment) donated to maintenance costs each year was from the beginning inadequate, and by 1974 the government was forced to contribute more. By 1978, the annual line item subsidizing the Foundation's contribution had escalated to $48,000. With no apparent interest on the part of any U.S. president in taking up residence there and most of the town's power brokers opposed to any use of the property that would attract tourists, some legislators began to complain that the government essentially had an expensive white elephant on its hands. As far back as 1975, the Palm Beach Civic Association had already written to then president Gerald Ford, urging that the property be returned to the "original donors," arguing that even as potential residences lavish "little White Houses" were no longer popular with the public.

But Phillip Burton, a congressman from California and chairman of the subcommittee on National Parks, toured Mar-a-Lago in early 1979 and came away convinced that the government would be foolish to return what he considered to be a national treasure into private hands. "You should spend two hours in just one room to do it justice," Burton glowed. He said that to do otherwise would be like "racing through a Rembrandt."

The Palm Beach County legislative delegation, however, heavily lobbied by influential local residents, had succeeded in efforts to quash the government's maintenance subsidy for 1978 and Representatives Paul Rogers and Dan Mica were pushing legislation to return Mar-a-Lago to the Post Foundation. Just to keep it in what he called "mothball condition" would actually cost

Les Standiford

$390,000 per year, Rogers claimed. In response to Congressman Burton's fears that returning it to private hands would be tantamount to its destruction, Palm Beach councilman Grace argued that in its mothballed state it was already effectively dead to the public. "I think it could live under private ownership," he added.

Burton, however, was resolute, and given his position as chairman of the National Park Service committee, he saw to it that the bill in support of returning Mar-a-Lago never reached the House floor for debate. Burton's successor, Sidney Yates from Illinois, took up the baton and in fact announced support for a $100,000 supplement to Mar-a-Lago's operating budget for 1980. "It would be a big lift to us," said the property's maintenance superintendent Jim Griffin, a longtime employee of Marjorie Post. Griffin said that the house itself was still in good shape, but the grounds had deteriorated significantly. They had given up long ago on the golf course, he said, and much of the shrubbery was withered. To maintain the home and grounds in residential condition, he said, would in truth require between $800,000 and $1 million a year. Despite the opposition of Mica and others, the House of Representatives in August voted in favor of the $100,000 boost, and it seemed as if Mar-a-Lago's place as a federal keepsake was for the time being secure.

But then in December 1980 came a surprising reversal. In a bit of canny maneuvering, Representative Mica attached an eleventh-hour amendment that would return Mar-a-Lago as part of a pet-project bill sponsored by Burton, and the latter had little choice but to accept Mica's rider. The omnibus bill (ironically, Burton's measure authorized the return of federal lands near Lake Tahoe to private interests) was passed unanimously, and with a concurrent measure already having passed the Senate, seven years of uncertainty regarding Mar-a-Lago were ended. The palatial mansion would be returned to the Post Foundation, which for all intents and purposes meant Marjorie's daughters Eleanor, Adelaide, and Dina Merrill.

Shortly before Christmas, President Jimmy Carter, former peanut farmer and no aficionado of mansions, signed the reversion bill into law. The transition of the property from public to private hands was to take four months, providing for the completion of paperwork and the like, meaning that the Foundation could, if it wished, have Mar-a-Lago on the real estate market by late April 1981.

A prospective buyer showed up well before then, however. In early February, Sheikh Mohamed al-Fassi, a member of the royal family of Saudi Arabia, came to Palm Beach on a house-hunting and investment mission. The young sheikh had already purchased half a dozen South Florida properties as investments, it was reported by the *Miami Herald*, but none seemed worthy as a potential domicile for himself until he saw Mar-a-Lago. He had heard rumors that the Foundation would be asking $30 million for it, but that was not an issue, said the sheikh. "It would make a good buy."

However, by the time the property was actually placed on the market, young Sheikh Mohamed was no longer anywhere to be found. When Sotheby International Realty Corporation's Charles H. Seilheimer was asked just how much he expected Mar-a-Lago to fetch, he was vague. "We won't discourage any offer," he said.

"How about five million dollars?" someone asked.

"I can discourage five million dollars very quickly," Seilheimer replied. After all, the mansion had cost somewhere between $2 million and $8 million to build and furnish. "This is a very valuable property," Seilheimer insisted. "It will set a new record for price."

At the time, the most ever paid for a private residence was said to have been $14.5 million, handed over in the early 1980s by singer Kenny Rogers to producer Dino De Laurentiis for his estate in Bel Air. The Foundation had authorized four Palm Beach realty offices to list the property and soon reports emerged that the expected sale price was in the neighborhood of $20 million. Adding an annual maintenance bill of $1 million and taxes of $350,000 meant that the pool of prospective buyers would naturally be limited, but the Foundation was already mulling the possibility of allowing the grounds to be subdivided. Though the mansion Mar-a-Lago itself was inviolate, there might in fact be room for a number of smaller properties or a series of "$1.5 million bungalows" as a Foundation spokesperson quipped.

Even dangling the possibility of permission to subdivide Mar-a-Lago did not bring a rush of prospective buyers. By early 1983, the Post Foundation could only say that "several genuine prospects" had appeared, all with the ability to pony up $15 million to $20 million. Former Palm Beach Zoning Commission chairman Benjamin Oehlert reaffirmed the notion that a buyer could build six to eight sizable homes around the perimeter of the grounds without the need to seek a variance. Oehlert said he had heard from the Foundation that three serious contenders were vying for the property, but he declined to name them.

* * *

All the while, Palm Beach was undergoing something of an identity crisis as modern-day development continued its various assaults on the enclave's exclusivity. STATION WAGON CROWD USHERS IN NEW SEASON, cried one headline shortly after Marjorie's death, the article going on to lament: "The season, they say, is no more. Gone the way of Mrs. Post's Mar-a-Lago, black-tie champagne openings of first-run films at the [Joseph Urban–designed] Paramount Theater, taking tea at Henry M. Flagler's Whitehall."

The threatened opening of the Publix supermarket had actually taken place, though in deference to Palm Beach sensibilities the occasion was an invitation-only event, featuring a 9 a.m. champagne get-together. Since 1924, there had been those Mizner shops on Worth Avenue, directly across the street from Paris Singer's Everglades Club, but by the 1980s the premises were occupied by the likes of Saks, Cartier, and Gucci, with promotional literature describing the boulevard as "the most distinctive, most exciting shopping street in the world." Now, town preservation leaders banded together as the Preservation Foundation of Palm Beach and, fearing the same forces that had bulldozed El Mirasol and were threatening Mar-a-Lago, were urging that all two hundred buildings on Worth Avenue be designated as a single historic district, protecting the entirety of what was often called "the richest little street in the world" from the wrecker's ball.

Still, the likes of the Biddles and the Kennedys, including Rose and Caroline, and the Du Ponts—having fled Miami's Coconut Grove after an armed theft of Willis du Pont's coin collection in 1967—were in residence in the winters, and the Breakers Hotel continued its distinction as one of only nine five-star resorts extant in the United States. Said Cleveland Amory at the time, "To its credit, Palm Beach has lasted longer than many of the other places of its era, such as Newport. And while some resorts seem to be 'in' and then go 'out' again, Palm Beach always seems to stay at least somewhat 'in' . . . It still has the aura of being the sandpile of the rich. And it has done it in a more secure way than Palm Springs did it as a western sandpile for the rich. Palm Beach is based on society rich rather than celebrity rich and that's more enduring."

As for the Breakers, visitors might have a glance at the imposing twin-towered structure on the ocean, approached by a sculptured drive worthy of Versailles, and presume that its preeminence among public buildings in Palm Beach had never been in question. But such is not the case, for the hotel as it appears today is actually its third incarnation on the site. Built originally as the Palm Beach Inn and opened in 1896, it was enlarged and remodeled in 1901, when it was also renamed. On June 9, 1903, a fire broke out while some welding was going on in what was then a wooden hotel, and the volunteer firefighting force from West Palm Beach had to be called to combat the blaze. As is recounted by *Palm Beach Post* columnist Eliot Kleinberg, the volunteers were stopped by the tender of the railroad bridge that crossed to the island. The tender was demanding that each man turn over the nickel toll for a crossing. Under such circumstances did the original Breakers burn to the ground, though most agreed that it would have likely done so even without the delay.

Given the hotel's popularity, Flagler did not hesitate to rebuild. Its second incarnation stood until March 18, 1925, when fire once again broke out, thought to be caused by a curling iron. This time, the blaze spread to other structures on the island and a ladder truck was ultimately dispatched from Jacksonville, several hours away, to help fight it. One person died in the mishap, and a six-hundred-pound hotel guest had to be plucked from a balcony and brought down by aerial bucket.

Within a week, the board of the Florida East Coast Hotel Company (spun off from the railroading empire following Flagler's death to manage the hotel properties and headed by William Kenan, Mary Lily Kenan's brother), announced that it would again rebuild the hotel, this time as a five-hundred-room, $3 million fireproof structure, a decision that was in part influenced by the announced plans of both Paris Singer and Addison Mizner to build $10 million luxury hotels in the area. Neither of those proposed projects came to fruition, and the Breakers opened for the third time, on December 29, 1926. The construction, featuring a team of some seventy-five Italian craftsmen brought over to reproduce the look and feel of Rome's Villa Medici, proceeded at a breakneck pace, at a final cost of $6.5 million. When in 1935 the Royal Poinciana was demolished, the Breakers, with its vast, ornate public rooms and commanding aspect, became the preeminent hostelry on the island.

Its reign was interrupted during World War II when the hotel—along with a number of other notable establishments, including the Biltmore in Coral Gables—was converted for use as a military hospital. In 1944, Ream General Hospital, as it became known, was returned to the FEC Hotel Company by the army, and the Breakers once again commenced operations, albeit on a seasonal basis, usually opening during the third week of December and closing after Easter. It was not until 1971, in fact, that the hotel began to operate year-round.

The hotel would make the news from time to time over the years. In 1944, William Kenan was called to Washington to testify before the War Investigating Committee, countering claims made by Florida senator Claude Pepper that "special interests" had pressured the army to return the property to the hotel company. And in 1965, the Anti-Defamation League of B'nai B'rith filed charges that the hotel was guilty of "a pattern or practice of religious discrimination." The league said it had tested the Breakers' compliance with the new Civil Rights Act of 1964 by sending out a series of letters requesting reservations, some signed with "Jewish-sounding" names and others with non-Jewish names. The latter were given reservations, while the former were denied, the league claimed. Schuler Dodge, manager of the hotel, called the charges ridiculous, saying, "Certainly, we have Jewish people here." Ultimately, the FEC Hotel Company wrote to the Justice Department pledging that the Breakers would obey the law and the matter was dropped. By the mid-1980s, the Anti-Defamation League was holding its annual convention at the hotel.

Still, trying to run a hotel the size of the Breakers on a seasonal basis was difficult, and the Flagler System, the entity that subsumed the FEC Hotel Company and managed other property interests for the Flagler heirs, was by the mid-1960s some $14 million in debt. Upon the death of his uncle William Kenan in 1965, nephew Frank Kenan reorganized the Flagler System, selling off interests in Jacksonville newspapers and other assets to retire the company's debt and focusing on restoring the Breakers—boarded up most of the year—to its former grandeur.

It was no simple matter to make the conversion to year-round operations. For one thing, central air conditioning would have to be added to a building nearly half a century old, a task complicated by the need to maintain both the exterior and the interior appearance. And to ensure a steady income stream, the hotel would have to attract a whole new market in addition to the leisure crowd it had traditionally relied upon. To bring in the so-called "group market" required adding some 150 rooms to the 300 existing, building an expansive oceanfront ballroom and meeting complex, and creating a sprawling beach club that could also be marketed for the use of island residents. "Now, it's open twelve months of the year, has five stars, and runs around the clock," Frank Kenan told an interviewer in 1990.

* * *

As far as boarded-up Mar-a-Lago was concerned, the Palm Beach Preservation Foundation obtained permission from the Post Foundation to open portions of the property in 1982 and 1983 to stage fund-raisers for its operations, but for the most part, visits consisted of realtors trooping potential buyers through shuttered rooms with furniture cloaked in dust covers and across once verdant lawns now parched and dusty. Realtors' hopes for a deal on Mar-a-Lago were raised in March 1983, when news came of the sale of the Perry House at 240 Banyan Lane for $4 million. That sale, for a property that lacked so much as an ocean view, set a new record for Palm Beach.

Still, no buyer for Mar-a-Lago came forward, unless one counted the attempt of a Robert J. Ewing, a guest at the Breakers Hotel, who told the beautiful young woman seated at a dinner table next to his one September evening that he was a prince about to be crowned as king of Switzerland and in fact had purchased the mansion, where the shutters would be coming off the very next day. Furthermore, as he told Ms. Patricia Welsh, herself on vacation from Pennsylvania, he thought he would have a job for her once the place was opened up. Though Ewing never made it clear exactly what sort of work he had in mind for her, Welsh was intrigued enough to drive by Mar-a-Lago the following day. Noting that the shutters had not yet come down, she made a few inquiries about "Prince" Robert Ewing, which led to the discovery that Ewing was a con man who had left a string of unpaid bills at a series of noted hostelries across the country, where no one seems to have recalled Switzerland's lack of a monarchy.

Finally, in January 1984, the Post Foundation announced that a preliminary contract had been drawn up with a purchaser, with a rumored sale price of $15 million. The property was described as comprising "58 bedrooms, 33 bathrooms, 27 servants' rooms, 12 fire places, three bomb shelters [added by the ever-prepared Mrs. Post in the 1960s], two greenhouses, a wine cellar, a theater, a nine-car garage, a nine-hole golf course, a citrus grove, a cavernous living room and a two-ton marble dining room table that could seat 50 . . . filled with Ming vases, Persian rugs, silverware for 200 and busts of Homer and Hadrian." Despite all that, one broker sniffed, "It seems like an awful lot to pay for a residence."

Estimates of annual maintenance costs for Mar-a-Lago had risen to $2 million, in addition to property taxes of around $400,000. Foundation attorney Doyle Rogers disputed the notion that it had been difficult to find a buyer, however. "It's not unsellable at all," he said. "We've had a lot of people interested in it for different things. We could have entered a number of contracts."

Those may have sounded like brave words, but the following month the prospective buyers were in fact identified as two shopping-center developers from Boca Raton who planned to make Mar-a-Lago their home. Reminded that Palm Beach zoning rules would allow the construction of up to eight other residences on the property, partner William Frederick said, "We're not planning any development. We will leave the residence in the state it is in."

For months there followed much ado about the plans of Frederick and his associate Thomas Moye, who had struck a deal to buy Mar-a-Lago for $13.5 million and had reportedly placed a deposit of $500,000 on the purchase price. While many speculated that the two planned to subdivide the property, and Fredrick and Moye seemed to bask in the attention paid them by the press (Frederick claimed to have been attacked by the ghost of Marjorie Post, warning him off the purchase), it all fell apart in May 1984 when a spokeswoman for the Sotheby office that had brokered the sale announced that the buyers had forfeited their deposit and backed out of the deal. Though no official reason was given by the prospective buyers, doubts had been raised in the press as to the propriety of their past business practices, and a hint of a chronic issue regarding the property also came from the broker. "They were going to turn it into a development," the Sotheby spokeswoman said. "The neighbors don't want the traffic problem."

As if that disappointment were not enough of a blow, more bad news came in August 1984, when the county tax assessment figures were announced. Though the valuation of Flagler's mansion, Whitehall, then operating as a private museum, had increased to nearly $11 million, leading the list of residential properties was Mar-a-Lago, now valued at $15.2 million (it had been pegged at a mere $1.7 million as recently as 1972).

Yet even this was not enough to deter Houston developer Cerf Stanford Ross who announced, just a few days after the tax assessor's figures came out, that he had agreed to purchase Mar-a-Lago, contingent on the approval by the town's Landmarks Preservation Commission of his plans to build eight or nine homes on the grounds. It might take as long as six months for details to be finalized, Ross said, but meantime, "I own it. It's mine."

As the Ross deal percolated, Palm Beach itself prepared for yet another season of paradise, with visitors still fascinated by the singular pleasures of the place. One writer for the *Wall Street Journal* hinted at why those such as developer Ross might yearn to possess a property such as Mar-a-Lago. Though the journalist was rhapsodizing about the pleasures of the Breakers Hotel, the essential, other-era appeal was the same.

"Even when it is sold out, which is usually the case in winter, the 568-room hotel has loads of uncluttered public space—inner courts with splashing fountains, colonnaded loggias . . . The Breakers is a throwback, an anachronism. How often do you find a hotel with poky elevators operated by hand, a tie and jacket requirement for men after 7 p.m., eating to string music in a huge vaulted dining room, or croquet on the front lawn? There is even a croquet pro . . . who looks more like a linebacker and favors shorts over the traditional long whites." As Fitzgerald so accurately portrayed him, Jay Gatsby, smitten by the concept of grandeur, was willing to do anything to possess its symbols. Frederick, Moye, and Ross lusted for the same.

Ross's intoxication with the project would run him afoul of town leaders, however, for in mid-January 1985, he placed a series of ads in the *Palm Beach Daily News* offering the main house and a number of surrounding lots he intended to carve from the grounds up for sale well in advance of a mid-March date for final review of his plans by the town council and the Landmarks Preservation Commission. Insiders suggested Ross planned to sell the main house for $11 million and would ask an additional $1.5 million for the furnishings. A four-foot wall would surround the mansion to separate it from the eight adjoining sites to be developed, with those sixty-thousand-square-foot lots to sell for $1.5 million each, on average.

Said town mayor Yvelyne Marix: "I think it's somewhat premature to advertise something to the public prior to the matter being resolved. There are a great many things to be resolved."

In the end, the fact that Ross had jumped the gun soured neither the town council nor the Preservation Commission on the prospect of seeing the eleven-year-shuttered Mar-a-Lago become a subdivision. On March 12, the council gave its approval, and on the next day the Preservation Commission followed suit.

Those who had observed the many twists and turns of the estate's disposition might be forgiven for suspecting the story had not closed, however. One of the conditions for Ross's development plans was that by September 15, 1985, he provide a letter of credit proving he had the wherewithal to implement them. In late June, rumors came that Ross was about to flip his grand investment to another private buyer, for cash. Additionally, this mystery buyer was said to have no interest in subdividing but intended to keep the property whole, welcome news to town fathers who were quick to extend Ross's deadline by another month.

Finally, however, just days before Ross's "final" deadline of October 15, came unexpected news. Another well-known developer, this one from New York with an imposing sixty-eight-story tower on Fifth Avenue as part of his résumé, had come forward wishing to purchase Mar-a-Lago from the trustees. While Ross dithered, waiting for a never-to-arrive down payment from his mystery buyer and waffling about going forward with his own plans, a report surfaced that Donald "Tower" Trump himself had approached the Post Foundation with an offer, saying that he planned to use the entire property as his private residence. With Ross unable to comply with terms, the Foundation had accepted the offer from the new suitor, sources assured the *Miami Herald*, with the closing to take place later in the year.

"That's mind-boggling that someone is going to come in and live there," Palm Beach Town Council president Paul Ilyinsky said. "But this is what we wanted. This will solve a lot of problems. I'm looking forward to meeting him." Indeed, it must have seemed a miracle, the appearance of an angel who would not create one single wave to add to those gently lapping at the shores of the most privileged bastion on earth.

- 15 -

ANGEL FROM AMERICA

On Friday, December 27, 1985, Donald Trump officially became the new owner of Mar-a-Lago, with the purchase price undisclosed in the press but rumored to be somewhere between $10 million and $15 million. Eventually, it would be discovered that the figure recorded by the county clerk was $5 million, with Trump reportedly paying another $2 million for 358 feet of previously attached beachfront that the Post Foundation had sold separately and another $3 million for the mansion's furnishings. At $10 million, all told, it would have seemed something of a bargain, considerably less than what the Foundation and Ross had settled on (Ross later said that his agreed-upon price had been reduced to $12.3 million with furnishings but without the beachfront parcel). Then again, there had been eleven long years of waiting and the bird-in-hand principle had surely come into play. Had the Foundation been certain that Ross would have been able to swing the deal, it is hard to believe the directors wouldn't have waited a few more days.

Stories have circulated that Trump had previously made somewhat more substantial offers. Anthony Senecal, who stayed on as steward for Mar-a-Lago from the time of Mrs. Post's death, resumed his employment as a butler for its new owner and says that Trump told him he had made an offer of $25 million for the house and furnishings to Adelaide, Eleanor, and Deenie (Dina Merrill) well before Ross had come along but that they had said it wasn't enough, even though—says Senecal—"none of them ever really liked it. The only one of the girls who did was Marwee [the daughter of Marjorie's daughter Adelaide] and she was out of the will." In the scenario related by Senecal, parts of which Trump himself recounted to the *Washington Post* in 2015, the spurned bidder took off his gloves and went looking for a way to construct a deal that could not be refused.

In this 2015 version of events, Trump said that he had actually offered $28 million to the trust. When he was turned down, he said, he used a third party to purchase the ocean frontage and then let it be known to the Post sisters and the trust that with the beach frontage under his control, he planned to build a god-awful monstrosity there, one that would not only turn the stomach of anyone who saw it but block Mar-a-Lago's sea view forever. "That was my first wall," he told the *Washington Post*. "That drove everybody nuts. They couldn't sell the big house because I owned the beach." In this version of events, and with Ross unable to produce his mystery buyer or the capital to back up his development plans, the Post Foundation came scurrying back to Trump to see if he might still be interested in making an offer.

"Sure," Trump is supposed to have said. "I'm happy to make you an offer. Five million for the house, three for the furniture. Take it or leave it." Whether the trust had wistful thoughts of Sheikh Mohamed al-Fassi and his $30 million offer is not recorded.

Setting aside exactly what dealings led up to it, Donald Trump—said to be worth $600 million at the time and suddenly the wealthiest resident of South Florida—had his offer accepted and did in fact become lord of the manor at Mar-a-Lago, at age thirty-nine. He and wife Ivana set about quickly to restore the place, including buildings, furniture, and fabrics, to its original splendor. "They've tried to be very careful about restoring the home so that it remains the same," said one Foundation director. "Naturally, we're tickled pink."

For his part, Trump characterized Mrs. Post as "highly intelligent and extremely graceful. I think every bit of that aura should be preserved." In an interview with a writer for *Palm Beach Life* magazine in July 1986, Trump said of his purchase: "I thought I was buying a museum. I never thought it was going to be a particularly comfortable place, but I thought it was so incredible as a statement that it would be wonderful to own. The fact is, it has turned out not only to be a museum, but also a very comfortable home."

Tony Senecal, who took over as Trump's chief butler shortly after the property's purchase, confirms that Trump wasn't just making nice. "I think he was more comfortable at Mar-a-Lago than he was in his New York apartment," Senecal says. "He was down here almost every weekend, and sometimes he'd come in on Thursday and go out at the last minute Sunday. He and his wife Ivana had a lot of close friends living here even in those early days and they made the most of it, entertaining at the house and going out a lot."

Nor did Senecal ever find Mar-a-Lago stuffy or museum-like himself. "When the Trumps were out, I'd be sitting there in the living room by myself, sometimes for hours at a time, but I never felt like I was alone. That's the effect the place has on you. It makes you feel comfortable. It just has a character of its own."

For a time, all went swimmingly between Trump and his new neighbors, until the tax assessment came for Mar-a-Lago in 1986. Mar-a-Lago was appraised at $11.5 million, Trump learned, $4.5 million more than he had paid for it and the beachfront parcel the previous year, with the tax bill soaring to $206,540, up more than $80,000. Trump appealed, and at a hearing before the special master in charge, Foundation lawyer and now Trump advocate Doyle Rogers argued that the noise of airplanes in the Palm Beach International Airport flight path had grown to the point where the value of the property was diminished. "I seriously doubt Mr. Trump would have offered what he did for this property had he known the effect of that airport noise," said Rogers.

"He called me up and he was so mad about the airport noise," Rogers continued. "He wanted to go right to senators and everybody else. 'How can they possibly permit all of the airplanes coming out of that airport to come right over my house?' And I mean he was furious."

In the end, Special Master Bob Groover was unmoved by the appeal. He said he wished he could set a compromise figure, but he was constrained by law to either find for the appellant's request to set the value at $7 million or let the new assessment stand. He chose the latter.

Trump was no more pleased with the outcome than any other aggrieved property owner would have been, but one Palm Beach property appraiser who had served as an arbiter in such cases points out that hard-luck complaints such as Trump's rarely had an effect on evaluations. Only obtaining independent valuations by professionals or pointing to comparable sales might work. And in the case of Mar-a-Lago, nothing else was comparable. By vague way of comparison, the Breakers Hotel was valued for the year at $46.5 million, with a tax bill of $835,000; the Everglades Club was appraised at $30.5 million, with taxes of $547,780. But both of these were assessed as commercial properties, not as private homes.

Early in January 1987, Trump exercised his sole remaining option, filing suit against the property appraiser in circuit court, where he reiterated his claims about airport noise and argued that the property, which had gone unsold for eleven years, was worth no more than what he paid for it—or $7 million, not $11.5 million. In response, Palm Beach County property appraiser Rebecca Walker told the court that Trump had paid a "grossly disproportionate" share of his tax bill for 1986 and asked that the court levy an additional 10 percent penalty. As it turns out, Trump had gone ahead and figured his own tax bill for the year, based on the valuation of $7 million, then sent in a check for $121,743, which included a 4 percent discount he availed himself of for early payment.

Meanwhile, Trump carried his complaints about the airport to the public, forming a lobbying committee of well-to-do noise-averse neighbors on the island and telling reporters: "Palm Beach is the worst regional airport I've ever seen. Palm Beachers should riot over what's happening there. It's a disgrace . . . the airport should never have been built in that location. It's not a matter of flight patterns or the time of flights, it's just in the wrong place." He advocated selling the airport and moving it about ten miles south instead of embarking on the current $188 million renovation. The response of Bruce Pelly, county director of airports, on the odds of relocating the airport: "Zero."

In late March 1988, when the tax case went to trial, appraiser Walker introduced a quote from Trump's recently published book, *Trump: The Art of the Deal*: "I first looked at Mar-a-Lago while vacationing in Palm Beach in 1982. Almost immediately I put in a bid of $15 million, and it was promptly rejected." The statement (which of course is at variance with the $25 million and $28 million offers suggested elsewhere) undercut Trump's insistence that the property was worth only $7 million, Walker argued, supporting her contention that Trump "stole" the estate at that price.

Though Foundation board member and attorney Doyle Rogers said that no $15 million offer had ever been received from Trump, Rogers did testify that Trump had in fact made one previous bid on the real property for $9 million in 1983, contingent on various rezoning issues. The fact that he eventually acquired the property for $7 million does suggest that, whatever the merits of the story told to the *Washington Post*, he had played some version of hard-ball with the Foundation once the Ross bid had collapsed, saving himself $2 million, at the very least. At the trial, an appraiser hired by Trump testified that he valued the house at $8.1 million.

The matter was resolved on April 8, when in a widely reported verdict, county circuit judge Richard Burk found for Trump, saying that there was no other private residence in the area to which Mar-a-Lago could be compared. And given that the house had been on the market for such a long time without a bona fide offer having been made, the ultimate purchase price was what determined the value. The judge also scolded Walker for some slipshod math. Had she conducted her own calcula-tions more carefully, Burk said, her own appraisal would have totaled $7 million.

The judge's decision had no effect on the assessments that were levied on the estate for 1987 and 1988, however, each of which tallied $11.8 million. Perhaps of equal interest was word that surfaced in October that Trump had taken out a mortgage of $12 million on the property with the Boston Safe Deposit and Trust Company, suggesting that the officers of that company found Trump's literary flourishes more compelling than his court-room testimony.

Soon came word that the Boston loan was in fact a second mort-gage taken out on the property by Trump. While it was assumed that he had paid cash for Mar-a-Lago back in 1985, the truth was that he had financed the deal by means of an unrecorded mortgage he obtained from Chase Manhattan Bank in the amount of $8.5 million. He used $8 million to cover the cost of Mar-a-Lago and its furnishings, then plopped down the remaining $500,000 as a deposit on the beachfront property that had been acquired from the Foundation by Jack C. Massey. Massey reportedly took a personal note from Trump for the $1.5 million balance. Trump used the second mortgage from Boston to pay off the loans to Chase and to Massey in 1988, providing himself with $2 million in fresh capital. Observers said that Trump's cash outlay for the purchase of Mar-a-Lago and all its treasures probably totaled about $2,800, or the cost of the paperwork involved. Much of this is at odds with the acquisition story Trump told the *Washington Post* in 2015, but it nonetheless bears out his abilities as a dealmaker. Whatever happened and in exactly what order may never be determined, but it is undeniable that Donald Trump became the owner of Mar-a-Lago and that he did so at a very good price.

While news of a second mortgage on a property was one thing, the prospect of a second marriage for the mogul had come to occupy far more of the news surrounding Trump. By the time details of the nature of the deal he had engineered for Mar-a-Lago emerged in 1988, gossip was rife that Trump's thirteen-year marriage to Ivana was on the rocks and that she would end up with the Palm Beach property, even though a prenuptial agreement she had signed limited her to custody of their three children (Donald, Jr., twelve; Ivanka, eight; and Eric, six), a forty-five-room home in Greenwich, Connecticut, and a payment of $25 million. Ivana was angered by Trump's reputed philandering—reports indicated that he was intending to run off with a former Miss Georgia, Marla Maples—and as a hardworking manager for several of their business ventures, she felt she was entitled to far more.

Even more diverting news came in June 1990 when it was reported that, in the midst of a nationwide downturn in the real estate market, Trump's fabled business empire was said to be on the verge of collapse. He was in arrears on interest payments of $2.3 billion owed to various New York banks, it was said, and was so strapped for cash that Palm Beach sources were predicting he would either dump Mar-a-Lago for a song or simply walk away and leave it in the bank's hands. *Forbes* magazine slashed its estimate of Trump's wealth from $1.5 billion to a third of that, well below what he had been worth when he arrived in Palm Beach five years previously.

Closer inspection of Trump's business activities suggested that a significant portion of his success was fueled by the practice of acquiring properties at distressed prices, then leveraging those properties as security for loans far in excess of what he had paid, which he had done twice with Mar-a-Lago. At the point at which the real estate downturn curbed his ability to sell off assets or secure further loans on his properties, many of which required significant debt service and operational costs, he had been forced into a reckoning.

Whether that reckoning would include the sale of Mar-a-Lago to help stanch the bleeding was anyone's guess. While the interest and term of Trump's second mortgage on the property were not divulged, anyone might roughly calculate what that place was costing him as opposed to the outlay of a homeowner living quite large by most standards in South Florida, where a monthly payment on a $500,000 place in a desirable neighborhood might run $5,000, including taxes. The annoying and ever-escalating costs of insurance in a hurricane-prone area would tally another $1,000, and other incidentals like the pool man and the lawn service another $1,000.

Mar-a-Lago, on the other hand, and depending on the exact loan terms, would have required $65–$70,000 monthly payments on principal and interest alone. Taxes, if paid at the posted rate, would have been another $15,000 per month. If the widely reported maintenance costs had not escalated greatly, they would have added another $200,000 a month to the total, making Donald Trump's monthly outlay somewhere around $300,000 to maintain his place of residence in Palm Beach, exclusive of insurance.

While all this might seem somewhat speculative, certain facts are known: after a meeting with his principal creditors in June 1990, Trump agreed to find a way to manage on a very frugal monthly budget; he was not to spend a penny more than $450,000, his creditors demanded, or they would foreclose on everything in sight. At the time, however, it was also widely reported that interest payments on his private Boeing 727 and his yacht alone were said to total $2 million per month. Clearly, something would have to go.

In September came word that Boston Safe Deposit and Trust Company, a subsidiary of American Express, had done some math of its own and modified the terms of the $12 million mortgage Trump had taken out on Mar-a-Lago, clarifying that the bank could at any time require additional outlays for insurance, taxes, or upkeep without Trump's approval. Running up a huge unpaid tax debt, for instance, would no longer be an option, as that would attach to the property if the owner walked, affecting prospects for a clean sale and diminishing the likelihood that the mortgage would ever be fully satisfied. Nor would the bank any longer run the risk of being stuck with property leveled by a hurricane or another disaster (a minor fire had broken out earlier that year in the servants' quarters, causing $50,000 in damage). Trump might have been willing to live on the edge, but Boston Safe Deposit—which had also lent him $15.7 million on his yacht *Trump Princess* and extended to him a $10 million personal line of credit—was not.

Given that Trump owed $3 billion, including $725 million on his woefully underperforming Trump Taj Mahal casino in Atlantic City alone, he had little choice. In contrast, his Palm Beach obligations, including the $12 million note on Mar-a-Lago and another $27 million outstanding on the condo tower Trump Plaza of the Palm Beaches just across Lake Worth in West Palm, might have seemed relatively insignificant. Trump had purchased the latter property at public auction in July 1986 for $40 million, intending to upgrade the 224 units with what was left over from a $60 million loan he secured from Marine Midland Bank, but sales had stalled.

As analysts pointed out, shedding any significant debt under such circumstances was the prudent thing to do, and some thought that Mar-a-Lago might fetch as much as $30–$40 million from the right buyer. The property was "the best private residence in America," Trump had been assured, outdoing such fabled estates as Cornelius Vanderbilt's summer home the Breakers in Newport and William Randolph Hearst's California masterpiece at San Simeon. But as if simple covetousness were not enough motivation to hang on to such a property, Ivana had obtained a restraining order preventing him from selling any of their homes, including Mar-a-Lago, to satisfy creditors.

Some proof that the otherwise hard-nosed businessman had damned reason and determined to find a way to hang on to Mar-a-Lago at all costs came in early 1991, when he filed a proposal with the Palm Beach building department to build eight homes on lots subdivided from the main property, a revival of the same plan that Houston builder Cerf Ross had floated six years before. At the time, as a result of rising taxes and maintenance costs, there was only one other equally large property remaining on the island, but even that—the eighteen acres of Casa Apava to the south—had been carved into seven lots already up for sale. As for Mar-a-Lago, a resolute Trump told reporters, it wasn't going anywhere. "It's mine," he said. "It will always be mine."

Predictably, Trump's plan to subdivide it ran up against immediate opposition from town fathers and preservationists, who up until this time viewed the developer in relatively neutral terms. His was not old money in the eyes of some burghers, but he had saved Mar-a-Lago from the wrecking ball and, with the exception of his prolonged feud with the property appraiser, he had not to that point entered into significant combat with his neighbors or local government.

The proposal to subdivide the property, however, galvanized considerable opposition from the same quarters that had opposed such plans of previous prospective buyers. This time, the town council went so far as to hire a consultant, whose August 1991 report recognized the need for some way of mitigating the expense of maintaining Mar-a-Lago but recommended a much-diminished subdivision, perhaps with half as many mini estates added. It was a Solomonic suggestion that satisfied no one, with Trump insisting, "If anyone else but Donald Trump owned it, they would approve it," and the preservationist Dr. Donald Curl opining, "Any subdivision would be a mistake."

Ultimately, the town landmarks commission rejected the plan, and when Trump appealed the decision to the town council, that body upheld it, asking only that the landmarks commission work with Trump to find a feasible plan. Trump next tried an end run around both the council and the commission by attempting to find approval on a technicality from the town's zoning commission, but that, too, was rejected as "contrary to the public interest." That Trump's plans were subjected to delay after delay by the various town agencies led one wag to liken the process to "death by duck peck."

In July 1992, Trump filed a $50 million lawsuit against the town for denying his requests to subdivide, claiming that the various decisions against him were motivated by conflicts of interest and had been tainted by private meetings, special-interest lobbying, and biased board members. As this litigation hung fire, word came in November that Trump had fallen far behind on mortgage payments to Boston Safe Deposit and Trust. As part of its investigation into Trump's fitness to hold a gaming license for his Trump Taj Mahal casino, the New Jersey Casino Control Commission discovered that he was in arrears to the tune of $495,000 in interest payments on that Boston Safe Deposit and Trust loan. The commission ordered Trump to begin immediate $33,000 monthly payments to bring the loan current by December 1993 and, in addition, to make $65,000 monthly payments to cover current obligations. This was no sign of financial weakness, Trump assured reporters, or the bank would have not agreed to rework the terms of the mortgage. "Only very strong people can get extensions on mortgages," he said. As to the pending suit against the town of Palm Beach, he was not backing off. "I have a constitutional right to subdivide," he said. "I'm in no mood to settle."

Shortly after news broke concerning the BSDT's successful demand for payments on the Mar-a-Lago mortgage, an element that some thought had potential for breaking the impasse entered the situation. Complaining that he could buy the nicest house in Miami for the $3 million annually that Mar-a-Lago was costing him to maintain, Trump commissioned well-known Palm Beach attorney Paul Rampell to do a bit of backroom inquiry to see if there was anything that the entrenched interests on the island would find palatable regarding the future of Mar-a-Lago.

With this encouragement, Rampell kicked around a possibility that surprisingly enough found some favor in the community: if Mar-a-Lago were to be turned into a private club along the lines of the neighboring Bath and Tennis Club, with most of its physical plant remaining intact, well-heeled residents and town fathers just might be able to stomach the idea. Trump was enthusiastic about it, and attorney Rampell had found a number of flexible townsmen who, as he put it, "seem to think the idea has a great deal of logic about it." As Trump pointed out, "The beautiful thing about it being a club is it'll be preserved and it'll give somebody the right to see it. Now, only I can see it."

By the following March, Trump filed plans for such an endeavor with the town council, promising among other things to open up a long-dormant service entrance to the property off Southern Boulevard to ease concerns about added traffic on South Ocean Boulevard. After Trump appeared before the town council promising to build a wall and a hedge on the northern boundary of the grounds and to hold to a stipulated limit on daily entrance and egress at the club, the town council voted tentative approval of the plan by a 4-to-1 margin, the first gesture of conciliation between the two sides in some years. In turn, attorney Rampell said he would begin immediate efforts to settle Trump's $50 million suit against the town.

By June 1993, a formal agreement had been drawn up and the council confirmed its approval of the plan. Overnight guest suites were to be limited to ten in number, with those among the allowable limit of five hundred members restricted to three stays per year, no more than seven days at a time. Trump's suit against the town was no more. At long last, it seemed, Mar-a-Lago's future was assured.

- 16 -

NEVER SAY EVER

Hardly was the ink dry on the agreement between Donald Trump and the town, however, when two of Trump's neighbors, Robert Grace (former town councilman) and John Callahan, filed suit in the Circuit Court of Palm Beach County, seeking to invalidate the town's approval. "The area is zoned exclusively for highly desirable, single-family residential estates," the suit said, "and is nationally known for its private and exclusive character." The operation of the club with guest suites, it contended, "will significantly change the character of the neighborhood, rendering it more transient, and will decrease the value of the plaintiffs' property."

As if that were not enough, less than a week later, Boston Safe Deposit and Trust was back in the mix, said to be dragging its feet in signing off on Trump's plans to convert the residence into a club, where the addition of a thirty-five-hundred-square-foot spa had been announced. It would take nearly a year for the dispute to be settled, with the bank concerned that the conversion of Mar-a-Lago to a club threatened the value of the mortgage and Trump contending the opposite. In the end, all legal cross-claims in the matter would be dropped, with Trump agreeing to pay off the $12 million loan before opening the doors to the club. The agreement removed barriers to the issuance of necessary building permits, and work could go forward on various projects: the spa, the northern privacy wall, and others.

Soon, an early-bird membership fee of $50,000 was announced, set to increase to $100,000 after the doors opened. Annual dues were set at $3,000, and members would enjoy a spa, a bar installed in the library, croquet greens, tennis courts, and a refurbished saltwater pool at oceanside. An ebullient Trump threw the estate open for a gala benefiting Miami's Jackson Memorial Hospital in late October, when Julio Iglesias performed, singing "Happy Birthday" to Trump's new wife Marla Maples at midnight, suggesting that perhaps the glory days had in truth returned to Mar-a-Lago.

Late in the year, it was announced that those who had bought memberships included the likes of Andrew Lloyd Webber, Henry Kissinger, Frank Gifford, Lee Iacocca, Denzel Washington, Steven Spielberg, Arnold Schwarzenegger, Norman Mailer, and Elizabeth Taylor. As the New Year approached, Membership Director Katherine Merlin announced the somewhat astonishing news that Prince Charles and Lady Diana had as well bought memberships—separately, of course, given the sad fact of their divorce. Ms. Merlin had not seen the royals' applications herself, but she had been told about them by her boss. "That, Mr. Trump handled," she said.

Some doubts were raised when spokespersons at Buckingham Palace called the reports that Charles and Di were Palm Beach–bound "rubbish," and eventually, new club impresario Trump was forced to clarify. In fact, he had simply written to both the prince and Lady Diana to extend "honorary memberships" to Mar-a-Lago, as he had to certain others previously announced, including Steven Spielberg and Andrew Lloyd Webber. "That is extremely, extremely common for a club of this nature," Trump said. None of those luminaries—or the ten or twelve others that Trump said were on his personal list—would be asked to pay the membership fee or annual dues; rather, they would be his guests. "These are people I like tremendously or have a great deal of respect for," he added.

In March 1995, Trump agreed to terms with the National Trust for Historic Preservation, formalizing Mar-a-Lago as one of some fifteen hundred National Historic Landmarks. It meant that the structures on the property would be safe from demolition or from significant change, that the ocean and lake views would be maintained, and that the estate would be opened at least once each year for public viewing.

Years later, in 2017, a story suggested that the working out of this agreement in fact lengthened the timeline for the opening of the club. According to the *Palm Beach Post*, the agreement from the town was contingent on Trump's willingness to grant what is called a preservation easement on the property, ensuring that neither he nor any future owner could change various of its "critical features." Such restrictions diminish the value of properties, and thus IRS regulations allow for the claiming of tax credits based on verifiable estimates. Trump was willing to grant the easement, but had he put his intentions in writing, the IRS might well have characterized the arrangement as a quid pro quo undertaking, thus voiding the tax advantages. Without his agreement in writing, the town was reluctant to grant final approval. Trump wanted the signed approval from the town before he donated the easement.

"Suppose I put preservation easements in place and then they decide to not sign the agreement," he told a *Palm Beach Daily News* reporter in a story published on August 1, 1993. "Nobody has ever accused me of being stupid." At stake was the possibility of a $5.7 million deduction. In the end, Trump got his agreement from the town, with the understanding that no certificate of occupancy would be issued for the club until the easement was in place, though none of it was in writing. All of that maneuvering took two years.

Finally, on Saturday, April 22, 1995, Trump and wife Marla Maples hosted the official black-tie opening at the Mar-a-Lago Club. Some two hundred were said to be in attendance, including a number of new members who had paid as much as $100,000 to join. Celebrities were in somewhat short supply, with only Frank and Kathie Lee Gifford on hand, but no one seemed to mind. Said Saul Jacobson, a retired DuPont chemist, it was an easy decision for him to join. "When you're 82 years old, how much longer are you going to live? I had a doctor friend who said, 'You economize all your life, fly coach, while your kids go first-class.' *I* want to go first-class."

In December 1995, just before the club opened for its first full season, one member who had paid a $25,000 deposit on a membership the previous year caused something of a stir when he sued in county circuit court asking for his money back. He had been promised an exciting venue reflecting the "new Palm Beach," said thirty-one-year-old West Palm Beach stockbroker Joseph Visconti. Instead, Mar-a-Lago had provided Tony Bennett for entertainment and its tables were occupied by white-haired folks playing backgammon. "I mean, it's ridiculous." Visconti said. "It's too old."

Trump brushed off Visconti's claims when questioned by reporters, saying that Madonna had recently been to the club and that Bon Jovi was expected at the opening that night. "It's our policy. We don't give money back," he said. "I can't be extorted. We're very happy not to have him as a member."

In fact, the December 1995 opening proved a great success, with an overflow crowd watching the ballroom entertainment from tables that had to be hastily set up on the lawn, and guests including actors Lee Majors and Joe Pesci as well as members of the Palm Beach Town Council. Asked about his history of conflict with the last, Trump was unfazed. "I enjoy working with the council. I see it always as a new challenge. And I always win because this is a good thing," he said, indicating the splendid setting surrounding him.

In many ways, it might have seemed a Gatsby-like moment for Trump, whose German immigrant grandfather had been a saloon keeper and whose father had been a real estate speculator and developer in Queens and Brooklyn. His money may have been newer than new in the opinion of some, but his new home was the showpiece of them all, and the well-to-do were crowding shoulder to shoulder at his side.

* * *

If Trump seemed to be extending an olive branch to city and county officials on that evening, it was an illusory one, for his jousting with community leaders over noise-abatement issues at the airport would continue, as would his fights with the tax assessor over valuation of the Mar-a-Lago property. The latter issue was not resolved until 2003, when Trump took a major step toward compromise. In August of that year, citing eight years of success in the operation of Mar-a-Lago as a club, Trump agreed to sign away any rights to subdivide the property, in perpetuity to the National Trust for Historic Preservation. As a result, the Palm Beach property appraiser's office agreed to change the basis on which the club was valued from "residential estate" to "private club." It meant a sizable reduction in taxes, from $551,195 in 2002 to $302,163 for 2003, when the value of the property was placed at just over $18 million. At the time, the club, which Trump continued to make available for charity and fund-raising events, had 443 members on its rolls, even with initiation fees said to have risen to $150,000.

By that time, Trump had also set aside a $75 million suit against Palm Beach International Airport in which he alleged that jet noise and fuel emissions had devalued and damaged the property. He agreed to drop the suit in 1996 in exchange for the county's agreement to award him a lease—at $438,000 per year—on a 215-acre site south of the airport where he built Trump International Golf Club, a luxurious sporting counterpoint to Mar-a-Lago that opened in 2000. Between 2000 and 2005, Trump renovated the oceanside pool area, adding a pair of two-story cabana buildings and a casual restaurant, refurbishing the saltwater pool, and also adding a seventeen-thousand-square-foot grand ballroom on the south side of the grounds, the largest such facility on the island.

Occasional flare-ups occurred, such as the 1998 incident in which club guests Sean "P. Diddy" Combs and Jennifer Lopez were spotted by a local gossip columnist performing what was termed "the horizontal rhumba" on a beach chair in full view of nearby patrons of the staid Bath and Tennis Club. And in 2006, a much-publicized tiff began between Trump (who had married his third wife, Melania, in 2005) and the town council, when officials took offense at his installation of an eighty-foot-high flagpole displaying a fifteen-by-twenty-five-foot American flag on Mar-a-Lago's front lawn without first seeking a permit.

The town argued that Trump had violated any number of agreements and code requirements, while he claimed that the attempt to make him take down the pole and flag deprived him of his rights to free speech, not to mention its being outright unpatriotic. He announced plans to sue the town—first for $10 million, then for $25 million—but in April, facing fines of $1,250 daily, he agreed to reduce the height of the flagpole by ten feet, apply for the appropriate permits and variances, move the pole closer to the residence, and donate $125,000 to veterans' charities. As a result, the suit was dropped and the fines were rescinded.

* * *

With such exceptions, the twenty-one years that passed between the founding of the Mar-a-Lago Club and Donald Trump's assumption of the U.S. presidency passed relatively smoothly. One well-established resident who joined the club on the first day applications were accepted was quick to explain why. "I'm a Jew," said a well-respected insurance broker and longtime Palm Beach resident bluntly. "And it was not so easy for me to gain membership to certain of the other private clubs here."

In 1992, Florida outlawed discrimination based on race, color, religion, gender, pregnancy, national origin, age, handicap, or marital status at private clubs with more than four hundred members and where meals are served regularly. However, proving that violations of the law have taken place is difficult, and conversely, individuals are naturally loath to seek close association with those who don't want their company. One would find little argument in Palm Beach that the Everglades Club and the Bath and Tennis Club were throughout the twentieth century predominantly composed of white, Anglo-Saxon, Protestant members, with the Palm Beach Country Club predominantly Jewish. From the outset, however, Trump made it clear that he did not care about such distinctions. "I wanted something totally different," Trump has said. "We have a great relationship with the other clubs, but no, we certainly didn't set out to be in any way like them."

Many of the Palm Beach old guard sniff at such comments. "It's ridiculous to even lump Mar-a-Lago in the same group with those. It's an entertainment club with a razzle-dazzle showman at the helm, and it boils down to the dollar. If you have enough money, you can get in," one said. Sniped another, using the ultimate put-down for wannabes: "Mar-a-Lago is more of a Boca [Raton] idea than a Palm Beach idea. Mar-a-Lago is a new-money idea at an old-money location." Shortly after Mar-a-Lago opened, when its initiation fees had climbed to $100,000, it was said that the equivalent fee at the Everglades Club was about $35,000, while membership at the Bath and Tennis Club was about $30,000. Initiation fees at the Palm Beach Country Club, established in 1954, had risen to $100,000 in the 1990s.

Trump dismisses put-downs, saying, "Even people who hate me are joining the club." And perhaps some are, drawn in part by the desire to rub shoulders with what is surely a somewhat younger, more worldly set. At the time of Mar-a-Lago's opening to the public, the average age of an Everglades Club member was seventy-five.

The undeniable splendor of Mar-a-Lago is also a lure. Though some of the original furnishings such as that grand marble dining table are gone, almost everything durable enough to withstand a bit of traffic and the inevitable spilled drink or ill-placed sweating glass remains. Given that following the presidential election of 2016, annual dues are said to have risen to $14,000 and initiation fees increased to $200,000—sources say that the latter figure has always been a negotiable one—only a privileged few will enjoy a regular dip in the saltwater pool or a spot of croquet on the manicured lawns. But as a National Historic Landmark, the premises will ever remain intact and the occasional guest of a member or an "ordinary" gala attendee can have a glimpse of bygone grandeur that simply must be seen to be believed. Had Donald Trump not become involved with Mar-a-Lago or had he indeed been duck-pecked to a symbolic death by councils and committees, it is an open question what might have become of Marjorie Merriweather Post's grand accomplishment.

A stately portrait of the mature Mrs. Post hangs on a wall in the former library, and across from it a notable one of Trump himself: youngish, attired in a tennis sweater. The latter is the work of Ralph Wolfe Cowan, a Virginian transplanted to West Palm Beach, and according to a knowledgeable staff member, the source of a tough-to-trump tale. In this version (there are others), Cowan produced the painting without prior consultation with its subject and had it delivered to Mar-a-Lago, suggesting that Trump have a look. Trump did have a look, as the story goes, and he liked Cowan's rendition very much, but there was something about it that needed to be discussed. Trump got Cowan on the phone and told him how much he liked the painting.

"That's great," Cowan replied. "It's all yours."

"But you left out one of my hands," Trump said. "There's just a white space where my left hand ought to be."

There was a pause on the other end of the line. "Well, if you want me to add the hand," Cowan said, "that'll cost you fifteen thousand dollars." While it is difficult to ascertain the truth of all this, visitors can be certain of this much: in the portrait as it hangs the subject of *The Visionary* clearly has two hands.

When asked if he might corroborate any of the details of the portrait's provenance, longtime butler Senecal shrugs. "I was there when Cowan brought the painting over. I can tell you that much. He says to me, 'Show it to Donald.' Which I did and Trump says, 'Where the f--- is my hand?' It hung on the wall for a couple of years and finally the hand got added." Senecal laughs. "What I can tell you for sure is that Cowan's part of Mar-a-Lago history long before that. He was one of the guys who used to hang out with Herb May over at the pool that was built back in the 1960s."

The Cowan story is typical of the tales of Trump's deal-making that make the rounds in the area. Another from the club's early days recounts Trump's efforts to have the square-dancing ballroom pavilion renovated to provide a venue for weddings, other kinds of dances, and the like. An experienced local contractor was called in, took a look around the facility, and told Trump that what he wanted would cost about $1 million.

"I was thinking more like $500,000," Trump is supposed to have said.

The contractor shook his head. "For what you want, it's a million, fifty percent down to start."

Trump sighed, then reached for his checkbook, handed over $500,000, and the job began. When the work was finished some months later, Trump strolled into the pavilion, glanced at the finished product, and nodded his approval.

"Well done," he said. "I told you it was a $500,000 job."

The contractor might have been expecting it. "You owe me $500,000," he told the developer.

"Well then, sue me," Trump is supposed to have said, walking out.

The contractor is said to have spent a few minutes pondering before he determined his response. Then, instead of going to court, he called his men back in and told them there was a bit more work to be done.

A few weeks later, with the contractor's trailers gone and the site cleaned up, Trump revisited the pavilion, stopping short when he walked inside. There was a line of demarcation extending down the middle of the elegant but compact room. On the left side, all was beautifully redone and resplendent. The right side had been returned to the condition the contractor had found it in originally. There was a note pinned to the doorframe, "Now THIS is what a $500,000 job looks like."

The story elicits a guffaw from Anthony Senecal, who says it is one he's never heard,

"But I can hear him saying, 'I told you it was a $500,000 job,'" Even if wholly apocryphal, it is the sort of story that is likely to be told long after others have assumed the mantle at Mar-a-Lago.

Senecal retired from active duty as a butler in 2009. "I said, 'Donald, fifty years is long enough.' But he said, 'I don't want to lose you.' So I became the unofficial historian of Mar-a-Lago, giving tours and things like that until he got elected and the Secret Service put a stop to tours." Senecal has witnessed a cavalcade of change in those fifty years. The pitch-and-putt golf course is no more, its site now covered with a kind of turf impervious to the hooves of ponies so that annual exhibitions of polo can be staged there each spring. "Mrs. Post used to play golf there first thing every morning, which meant about ten a.m. for her," he says. "But she got frail and it was closed for a long time. And later on, after Mar-a-Lago was a club, that guy who was on TV with that girl for the longest time—Regis Philbin—he liked to go out there and hit shots, but that was about all."

Asked to characterize the difference between the two ownership regimes, Senecal answers quickly. "One was like living in history; the other was pure excitement," he says. "Mrs. Post was from another era and she made it come alive. Trump was a pure dynamo and a lot of the people he had around him were the same way."

His second employer could be exasperating, Senecal admits. "After Mrs. Post had that great dining room table sent to Washington, she had another one made. It was pretty good, but nothing to compare with the first one. Anyways, Trump always liked to tell people the one they were eating at was the original copy. One time he saw me rolling my eyes and after everyone was gone, he says, 'I guess you don't like me telling that story, Tony.' And I said, 'No I don't, because it's not true.' And he says, 'Look, what does it matter? It was a copy itself and everybody who ever ate off the real one is dead now.' So we had a good laugh about that."

Another time, nearing the end of his tenure as the house historian, Senecal recalls standing in the breezeway one Saturday afternoon chatting with the parking valet when they saw a brightly dressed woman wearing a large floppy hat pedaling down the driveway on a bicycle. "I'm looking for Anthony Senecal," the woman announced as she pulled up. "I understand he gives tours of this fabulous place, and I want one." Senecal realized by that point that it was Martha Stewart standing before them. He introduced himself and explained that while he had some things to attend to just then, he would be delighted to show her around on the morrow, at 3:30, say. Their date arranged, Ms. Stewart rode happily off. Later, Senecal bumped into the lord of the manor in the hallway outside his quarters and told him of the incident. Trump nodded. "Great," he said, starting inside. "Show her a good time."

But then he turned back. "Wait a minute. Martha Stewart? What the hell, Tony? Why didn't you drop everything and take her right then?" Before Senecal could respond, Trump was off and running, laying into him for not seizing the moment with such an important personage. His voice had risen to a precipitous level when the door to the Master's Quarters opened and Melania appeared—"she has an unbelievable presence," says Senecal—fixing her husband with a stare. "Donald, I think you need to adjust your tone."

"Trump blinked, looked at her, then at me, and went inside. I went down to the bar and started working on my resignation letter. I was still steaming when Trump showed up. He glances around to make sure nobody's watching, then he grabs my hand and puts a wad of cash in there. 'We don't have to say anything about this, do we?' he says. He pats me on the shoulder and walks off. There was about two grand in the wad. It was about the closest thing I ever got to an apology."

* * *

Since Donald Trump gained the presidency, the attention focused on Mar-a-Lago and on his activities there has burgeoned. He and his family continue to occupy the same Master's Quarters as did Marjorie Merriweather Post, E. F. Hutton, and Deenie. And though security is tightened and a number of rooms are taken up by the staff, club members still have access.

*President Trump and Japanese prime minister Shinzo Abe
speak to the press during their much-discussed
meeting of April 2018 at Mar-a-Lago.*

Certainly the expense to the county's and the nation's taxpayers is significant every time Trump travels to what he fondly calls the Winter White House and, alternatively, the Southern White House. These expenditures also call into question the stipulations of government officials in the 1970s that it would be impossible to provide adequate security for a sitting president if Mrs. Post's bequest were carried out. Difficult and expensive have been proved, but impossible clearly has not.

Likewise, claims that the mansion could never serve as a temporary presidential residence, owing to its place in the flight path of Palm Beach International Airport, have proved to be equally baseless. When the president is in residence at Mar-a-Lago, the FAA declares restrictions on flights within a fifty-five-mile radius, and the Secret Service and the Coast Guard secure approaches to the property both from Lake Worth and from the Atlantic, cordoning off surface streets as well. Taxpayers, residents, and local officials complain about the expense—as much as $3 million per visit—and the inconvenience, but the fact that such measures have become routine suggests that the original protests against accepting Mrs. Post's bequest were based more on the veiled opposition of Mar-a-Lago's neighbors than on concern for any U.S. president's safety.

There has been much discussion of the propriety of allowing those with the means such close access to the president, of the questionable judgment of allowing members awaiting their appetizers in the dining room to observe the president discussing sensitive foreign policy matters with visiting heads of state, and of the owner's profiting by featuring Mar-a-Lago as an adjunct of the presidency. Eyebrows were also raised in 2018, when, at the same time that the president was calling for a zero-tolerance policy on those attempting to circumvent immigration procedures, two separate petitions came from Mar-a-Lago for temporary visas for cooks, servers, and housekeepers on the grounds that no such personnel could be found locally.

Nonetheless, Donald Trump's intuition that he should move heaven and earth to possess the estate that Marjorie Merriweather Post dreamed up nearly a century ago has proved to be one of his most providential impulses. Reports suggest that the value of Mar-a-Lago—protected from alteration but his to sell if he wishes—has risen to the neighborhood of $160 million on an original cash outlay of $2,800 or so and is something of a testament to the enduring appeal of the place.

- 17 -

WHAT REMAINS

There is no predicting what might become of Mar-a-Lago or of Palm Beach in the future. Despite all the covenants of a National Register and in spite of everyone's best intentions, anything could intervene. Sea level rise might turn out to be fact instead of—as some claim—fancy, turning Palm Beach to Atlantis. A hurricane of immense proportions might draw a bead squarely between Hypoluxo and Jupiter Inlet, blasting the island clean. Economic calamity or international strife of an unimaginable scale might put an end to enclaves of luxury as we have always known them, and, for all we know, one postapocalyptic day Palm Beach might once again be a quiet barrier island studded with little but scrub and palmetto.

Impossible, almost surely. But imagine what must have been the thoughts of the natives who glanced out from shore long before there was an island settlement that came to be known as Palm Beach or even an idea of one. Or those of the salty pioneers preceding Henry Flagler, the ones just looking for a quiet place offering a haven from interested authorities. In those early untutored times, who could have envisioned the coming of a Flagler or a Whitehall, of the Stotesburys and the Huttons and the El Mirasols and the Mar-a-Lagos and the Trumps?

Those earlier, unsophisticated inhabitants could have had no concept of what was to come; nor, even had a time-traveler appeared to describe it to them, could they have comprehended it. If asked, they would have had a very simple explanation for their satisfaction with the place. As is explained in Winifred Gallagher's *The Power of Place*, native peoples find in their physical surroundings not only the sources of their material sustenance, but the underpinnings of their factual knowledge and the bases for their emotional satisfaction as well. "To native people, the village isn't just neighbors. It's the spirits of their dead, of trees, animals, and the earth," says psychologist Jerry Mohatt. In practical terms, says zoologist Gordon Orians, this awareness of place leads to such questions as, "Are you where you want to be when it gets dark?"

In his days as a graduate student of psychology this author was once told by his instructor of a group of researchers who wondered what would be the effects of modern technology on a community of African tribespeople so isolated and primitive that they had scarcely seen white men, let alone witnessed anything of modern invention. One night, the researchers gathered the tribe together and set up a movie screen and displayed on it images of ferocious lions bounding across the veldt and seeming to leap straight off the screen toward the audience. The researchers were prepared for the tribespeople to scream and run in terror, much as early filmgoers had done when images of onrushing steam engines were projected onto screens.

But there in remotest Africa, the natives sat impassively as panes of reflected light flashed across their faces. They saw nothing on the screen except puzzling and indecipherable patterns of light and shadow. They had not been conditioned to this excess of invention, and as to whether it was a good or a bad thing they could not say. When the researchers left, the natives went back to their lives and their world, untroubled for a time at least by the phantasms of progress.

But how are we to judge what has become of post-Flagler Palm Beach today? What of its essence has endured? Exactly why has Palm Beach flourished and other enclaves of allure have shimmered into nothing?

Flawless it is not. There has been no dearth of scandal and gossip slipping out from beneath the town skirts since the days of Marjorie and Ned Hutton. Douglas MacArthur's marriage to Eva Stotesbury's daughter Louise quickly dissolved when the general's wife decamped for a tour of Europe—and a number of its handsome young men. In the late 1920s, residents were diverted by the affair of Joe Kennedy—bootlegger and sometime filmmaker—with one of his young starlets, Gloria Swanson. In later years, Joe, Jack, Bobby, and Ted Kennedy were reported to shuffle mistresses with one another at La Querida, where questionable goings-on persisted into the late 1960s.

On Thanksgiving weekend of 1974, town police answered a call to the Palm Beach Towers apartments, where hotel magnates Leona and Harry Helmsley were found bleeding from stab wounds and claiming to be the victims of an unknown assailant. By the time Leona was sent to prison for tax evasion some eighteen years later, that assailant had never been found and most commentators had come to the conclusion that one of the notoriously combative pair had taken out grievances on the other.

In 1976, *Hustler* magazine publisher Larry Flynt leased El Solano (the first Palm Beach home Mizner built for himself) on the oceanfront, where he set up steamy pornographic photo shoots and hosted a number of legendary bacchanals. For a time in 1980, Yoko Ono and John Lennon took up residence at the same El Solano, their always-in-the-papers visits put to an end when Lennon was shot and killed in New York that December. In 1982, the nation was diverted by salacious details emerging from the divorce trial that pitted Roxanne and Peter Pulitzer, the latter the grandson of the newspaper tycoon Joseph Pulitzer and the son of resort wear designer Lilly Pulitzer, against each other. As the testimony contained considerable detail about sexual encounters between the couple and Jacqueline Kimberly, wife of Kleenex heir James Kimberly, media interest was considerable.

Most notorious of all is likely the story that emerged in 1991, when Patricia Bowman, stepdaughter of General Tire's founder William F. O'Neil, accused William Kennedy Smith, grandson of Joe Kennedy and nephew of Jack, Bobby, and Ted, of raping her on a Saturday night in March on the beachfront property of La Querida after a night out. At the trial, news of which consumed the nation and the world, Smith insisted that Bowman had initiated a consensual sexual encounter and suggested that mental imbalance had led her to concoct the rape allegations. In the end, a jury found Smith not guilty, a verdict that caused considerable havoc.

The Bowman-Smith case was probably the most compelling news story to come out of Palm Beach until news of Bernie Madoff's $50 billon Ponzi scheme rocked the nation in 2008. Madoff, former chairman of the NASDAQ stock exchange, was a longtime Palm Beach resident who purchased a home at 401 North Lake Way in 1967 and was also a longtime member of the nearby Palm Beach Country Club. Though the impact of Madoff's swindle was immense in Palm Beach—some 260 of the island's 1,900 or so private homes were said to be on the market in the aftermath of the news—the end result was similar in some ways to that of the Great Depression. As one shopkeeper put it, "Even if your net worth drops from $30 million to $12 million, it's not like you can't afford a new pair of pants." As for the more newly arrived, residents of the ilk of Rush Limbaugh, Jimmy Buffett, Ivana Trump, and Rod Stewart were said to be doing just fine.

One way in which the Madoff scandal had a more lasting impact was within the island's Jewish community, where Madoff had made significant inroads. Even if the portfolios of a number of nonprofit organizations were not invested in Madoff offerings, many individuals on the island were. One director of a major nonprofit undertaking says that the pledges of at least a dozen sizable donors within the Jewish community were cut significantly or eliminated altogether.

* * *

A stroll down Worth Avenue today suggests that since the twenties began to roar relatively little has changed in Palm Beach—on the surface, at least. One can find a Starbucks, but with difficulty; the typical signage of the chain is banned. Also, fashionistas will tell you that Palm Beach remains the nation's only enclave where wearing white is not a misstep between Labor and Memorial Days. Recently, a reporter for the *China Times* summed up a tour of duty there by opining: "If we call *Downton Abbey* a period drama, then Palm Beach is a 'period island' of the Gilded Age."

Indeed, the Gilded Age mansion Whitehall glitters more brightly than ever, though that shine was not easily attained. Jean Matthews in fact saved the structure from the wrecking ball, and Flagler's private railcar was brought down to grace the grounds, but the same daunting costs that frightened away various Mar-a-Lago suitors kept Whitehall in a somewhat comatose state for decades. In 1995, long after Mrs. Matthews's death, the Flagler Museum hired a new director, John Blades, luring him from his post as public affairs chief at Hearst Castle. Though Blades was understandably eager to take the reins at Whitehall, he confessed to some dismay when he arrived in Palm Beach and got the full, behind-the-scenes view of what had become of the nearly century-old palace.

Aerial view of current-day Palm Beach, looking northward from near the island's midpoint. The Breakers is at the upper right, with Whitehall on Lake Worth, opposite.

"I went in as a tourist before I had my interview," Blades said. "I made a list of what I could see needed doing and figured it would probably take twenty years to bring the place back to where it needed to be. But after that first day on the job, after crawling through the attic, basement, and storage areas, I sat down and cried. Not only did I think I couldn't accomplish all that needed to be done, I believed no one could."

Blades's assessment is an object lesson in the practicalities involved in historical preservation, especially where structures of the nature and size of Mar-a-Lago and Whitehall are concerned. The railcar at Whitehall, for instance, had deteriorated to the point where some board members advocated letting it "slip" off its pedestal and sink to the bottom of Lake Worth. Of the once imposing iron fence that had encircled the entire property in the manner befitting any great estate, perhaps the main gate could be salvaged and a hedge planted where the rest was crumbling away, some said.

But Blades recovered from his shock sufficiently to respond that either he would restore Whitehall properly or he would not do it at all. With "one day at a time" as his motto, in eight years Blades had ticked off every item on his tourist-day assessment, including the replacement of some forty thousand roof tiles—"You should have seen all the kiddie pools scattered around the attic to catch the leaks," he says. Even more daunting was the project to bring the electrical system up to modern standards, so that climate control and security systems could be installed.

It took twenty-one years and two dozen capital projects totaling more than $25 million, to bring Whitehall back, including the restoration of a thousand feet of fence at $1,000 per foot and the construction of a $5.5 million Beaux-Arts pavilion where Flagler's meticulously restored personal railcar sits protected from the elements. Though the building was stripped of essentially all furnishings at the time of its conversion to a hotel, most items of importance have since been brought back, and the annual budget has grown from $1.8 million to $6 million, made possible not only by a doubling of the endowment but also by a significant increase in such sources of funding as admissions, retail sales, membership subscriptions, grants, program revenues, and special member events.

"If he could visit, I don't think Flagler would notice much difference," says Blades, who retired in 2016. "It's taken a long time, but we just received agreement on return of the last important suite of furniture [the dining room furniture, from the board room of Old Republic Insurance of Chicago]." Perhaps just as important as restoring the physical premises has been the painstaking task of organizing and gathering documents related to the structure and to Flagler's accomplishments. What once was a warren of storerooms and servants' quarters is now a tight-ship library of photographs, diaries, business records, and letters that document the development of the eastern seaboard of Florida.

* * *

More than a few condominiums ("beehives" is how Tony Senecal refers to them) now dot the Palm Beach townscape, most clustered on the southern fringes of the island and close to downtown. But a drive along Ocean Boulevard northward from Sloan's Curve still presents a matchless array of splendid estates. "I still get a kind of tingly feeling when I round the curve and start passing that string of homes," says Tony Senecal. "And I've been doing it for fifty years. I've never seen any other place like it, and I don't think anybody has."

The names Du Pont and Roosevelt might not be stenciled on the mailboxes, but the holders of those and other such surnames have not fled their digs. A recently published insider's guidebook suggests that perhaps the best way to sample the life of a modern-day Palm Beach plutocrat, if only for a Cinderella-like span, is to buy a ticket to a charity gala. It might not be cheap, but the experience will be as authentic as anyone's, and there will be a worthy repository for those funds.

Or one might opt for a stay, even for a night, at the Breakers, described in a 1928 promotional booklet as "without doubt one of the most magnificent successful examples of a palatial winter resort hotel." Physically, little has changed as regards that magnificence. In the same way that entering the New York Public Library's reading room is to know the essence of "library," strolling through the opulent public rooms of the Breakers is to be enveloped in the sense of "grand hotel."

To maintain that other-era opulence is not an easy task, says Paul Leone, CEO of Flagler System and director of hotel operations. Leone came on board as the company comptroller in 1985 and fell under the same spell that had fascinated the Kenan family. By the mid-1990s Leone was promoted to his present post, having convinced Tom Kenan and Tom's cousin Jim that the company should shed most of its other interests and focus almost exclusively on making the Breakers the leading resort in the world.

"It takes an army to do it," Leone says. There are two thousand employees at the hotel, making for a 3:1 staff-to-guest ratio in an industry where a 2:1 ratio makes for highly attentive service. "And we only hire people who live to make other people happy," Leone says. "We go through fifteen thousand applications to find the six hundred we bring on board every year."

Leone says the hotel is still in the midst of a twenty-five-year, $500 million renovation and modernization project and that an additional $8 million a year is required for maintenance, with the hotel's site on the ocean exacerbating matters. "Every day somebody has to wipe the salt spray off the windows," Leone says. "And I just got off the phone with the company who sold us the last set of playground equipment, warrantied for thirty years. We've had it for three and it already needs to be replaced. I've had a lot of these conversations."

The hotel's very popularity is part of the problem, Leone points out: "We have five hundred thirty-eight rooms, one hundred forty acres of grounds, and average about eighty percent occupancy year-round. On any given day, counting staff, guests, club members, and visitors, there might be five thousand or six thousand people on the property. But I think you'd have a hard time finding so much as a paint chip around here."

A major part of the hotel's appeal has to do with the nature and intricacy of its architecture, the maintenance of the buildings and grounds, and the quality of service accorded its guests, but Leone concedes that sometimes it is just as important to be lucky as it is to be good. "We are able to operate at the level that we do and still stay in business because of where we are located," he says. "People come across the bridge to Palm Beach and they are simply bowled over. They see this palace of a hotel, and all these other magnificent structures like Mar-a-Lago, and Whitehall, and on and on, all of it concentrated together, it's almost unbelievable. It's a tropical island in Florida, the shopping district is world-class and three blocks long, there's an international airport fifteen minutes away, there's never any traffic to speak of, the weather's always good, even in the summer . . . There's just no other place like it."

Many of the elements cited by Leone can be sampled even by those without a stout portfolio or trust fund, of course. But even if the price of a ticket to a gala or an overnight at the Breakers is out of reach, there is one more way to experience the enduring draw of Palm Beach, one that might even be endorsed by the Jeagas or their counterparts on the African veldt:

Begin near dusk and find a place on Ocean Boulevard to leave the car, easy enough with the beach crowd gone. Walk out onto the sand, within sight of the towers of the Breakers if you can manage it, but anywhere up and down the strand will do. Take off the shoes.

There will be a breeze. Stand there in it, wait out the sundown, and count a few stars to the brush of the surf. Imagine yourself a wiry Calusa or a privateer in refuge or Flagler's stonemason or Eva Stotesbury or Ned Hutton. It doesn't really matter who you are. Close your eyes out there and breathe.

Once more.

There.

Are you where you want to be when it gets dark?

ACKNOWLEDGMENTS

I have often told those who ask that the biggest difference I have noticed between the writing of fiction and the writing of history is that when one reaches a point in a fictional narrative when a fact is needed, one can simply make it up. It is fiction, after all. It is not so simple to support a narrative in history, however, and in the writing of this volume, in my continuing effort to find relevance and significance in history's record, I have had quite a bit of help in regard to the harvesting of the necessary facts.

First and foremost, I would like to thank John Blades, former director of the Henry Morrison Flagler Museum in Palm Beach, for his advice, his assistance, and his support—no writer could ask for a more gracious or more valuable resource. I would also like to thank Tracey Kamerer, Chief Archivist at the Flagler Museum; and the Curator of that institution, Kate Bradley, for all their help. I am also indebted to Richard Bernstein of Palm Beach; to Aaron Fuller, Food and Beverage Director at the Mar-a-Lago Club; to William J. Fox, Assistant General Manager of the Bath and Tennis Club; to Leslee Keys, Director of Historic Preservation and Special Initiatives at Flagler College; to Paul Leone, CEO of the Flagler System; and to Anthony Senecal, former personal assistant to both Marjorie Merriweather Post and Donald J. Trump at Mar-a-Lago.

For his assurances that this history of a place was a worthy subject, I am greatly indebted to that inimitable doyen of bookdom and filmdom, Mitchell Kaplan, as I am to my agent nonpareil Kim Witherspoon for convincing George Gibson and Morgan Entrekin, my editor and my publisher at Grove Atlantic, to side with Mitchell. I would also like to acknowledge the mighty aid of Emily Burns, Editorial Assistant at Grove Atlantic, in the intricate process of finding appropriate and available images with which to illustrate this book. Echoing my sentiments above, let me say that no writer could wish for a more supportive and helpful editorial team.

I also thank my dear friend and fellow ink-stained wretch, James W. Hall, for his willingness to watch over my shoulder as I worked through this narrative, and for giving me the tough love and help we all thrive on—only the geniuses are exempt from needing good advice and God bless them every one. Finally, my thanks to my wife, Kimberly, fellow artist and boon companion, for her steady support; and to my daughter Hannah and son Jeremy, whose very presence reminds me why we all continue to try to exceed our reach, each and every day.

NOTES

As this is not a work of traditional scholarship and for the sake of ease for the general reader I have largely forgone the use of typical footnotes and endeavored instead to provide citations and credit for singular sources in the text itself. However, for the benefit of those interested in the basis for the materials in the volume and to aid those interested in further reading and research, I provide the following.

Author's Note

Klepper and Gunther's methodology (see also Gunther, "An Astor Ball for All Time") for their rankings of America's most wealthy produces some interesting results. Their list includes George Washington at no. 59 and Henry Flagler at no. 48 all-time, a few spots behind Warren Buffett, who comes in at no. 39. Sam Walton is listed at no. 14, with Andrew Carnegie at no. 6 and John D. Rockefeller at no. 1.

There is no shortage of web listings touting the nation's largest homes, and the statistics noted in the text follow what is generally proclaimed, but John Blades, former director of the Henry Flagler Museum in Palm Beach (Whitehall) and also former head of the Public Affairs Office at Hearst Castle, suggests that measuring the square footage of the grand mansions may not be an exact science. Blades says, for instance, that the Hearst Castle compound itself contains about 165,000 square feet of living space, about the same as that of the Biltmore Estate—he says that the claim of the Biltmore to be the largest was something of an eye-roller to the Hearst staff. Using methodology comparable to that applied at the Biltmore and at Hearst Castle, Blades says, would place Whitehall's square footage in its seventy-five rooms at 115,000.

Flagrante

The culminating event of the dissolution of the long-troubled marriage between breakfast-foods heiress Marjorie Merriweather Post and noted stockbroker E. F. Hutton is discussed in the two extant Post biographies: William Wright, *Heiress,* 112–15; and Nancy Rubin, *American Empress,* 190–94.

The Mary Baker Eddy quotes are from *Science and Health*: "Human affection," 57; "The nuptial vow," 59.

1. Nouveau Riche

The late-life struggles and demise of cereal tycoon C. W. Post, as well as the disposition of his vast estate, were the stuff of headlines nationwide. Here, as elsewhere in the volume, in-text references to date and title of publication should lead those interested to the original accounts cited. The dissolution of Post's first marriage and its fallout are detailed in Wright, *Heiress* 50–52. Rubin, *American Empress* 60, 66, and 69; and Wright, 53, detail the circumstances of Marjorie's first marriage. Marjorie's description of her father's appendix is from Rubin, *American Empress*, 90, as is the wording of the suicide note, 91. The coroner's declaration is from the *New York Times*, May 10, 1914.

2. Finding Xanadu

Surprisingly enough, no general history of the Lake Worth/Palm Beach region has been compiled, though Palm Beach County in 2009 launched Palm Beach County History Online, a historical journal (the *Tustenegee,* published by the Historical Society of Palm Beach County) and website devoted to the maintenance and sharing of links, photographs, diaries, letters, and other documents meant to make local history "accessible, interesting, and meaningful." There, those interested can find further discussion of materials touched on herein, including "Native Americans," "Pioneer Life," "Flagler Era," "Land Boom & Bust," and other topics.

Notes

On the Jeagas, etc.: Costello, "Boynton's Indian Mounds," *Pages from Boynton Beach History.*

Jonathan Dickinson's observations are taken from *Jonathan Dickinson's Journal*, "The 7th Month, 23; the 4 day of the week."

The wreck of the *Providencia* and the naming of Palm Beach: Eliot Kleinberg, "A Bounty of Sidetracked Coconuts," *Palm Beach Post*, April 18, 2001. The story is also recounted in Tuckwood and Kleinberg, *Pioneers in Paradise*, 21.

Unless otherwise noted, most of the information on Flagler's early career and his relationship with Rockefeller is taken from Les Standiford, *Last Train to Paradise: Henry Flagler and the Spectacular Rise and Fall of the Railroad That Crossed an Ocean*, passim.

Rockefeller's encomiums for Flagler are found in *Random Reminiscences*, 5–6.

On Flagler's introduction to Ida Alice Shourds: Martin, *Henry Flagler*, 73. Thomas Graham, in *Mr. Flagler's St. Augustine*, 39–41, has a lively account of Harry Flagler's dispute with Martin's generally accepted portrait of Ms. Shourds.

Flagler's son's actual name was Henry Harkness Flagler. Former Whitehall director John Blades opines that Flagler, Jr., preferred the use of his nickname in order to escape the long shadow of a father whom he found overbearing.

On early St. Augustine, "St. Augustine Archives," https://bronsondrbronson staughistory.wordpress.com/2011/12/15/dr-bronsons-st-augustine-history/.

Flagler on his reasons for building the Ponce de Leon: Martin, *Henry Flagler*, 91.

Citations regarding Florida populations are drawn from the records of the Florida Census and the U.S. Bureau of the Census.

The tale of Flagler vs. Rockledge has long been the stuff of local legend, with public opinion divided as to the true culprit responsible for the spur's disappearance. However, Brevard County court records detail the final disposition of the matter.

Flagler's proprietary reference to Florida, "My Domain," *Tattler*, 1897.

Dimick's daunting account, part of an interview originally recorded in 1962, is reprinted in *Tustenegee*, 11.

Flagler's interest in the Lake Worth area is detailed in the FEC publication *The Story of a Pioneer*. The reference to the effect on property values is noted on page 18.

Flagler's tactics in acquiring Palm Beach real estate: Martin, *Henry Flagler*, 213–14; and Graham, *Mr. Flagler's*, 290.

Flagler and "palm trees": Lefèvre, quoted in Standiford, *Last Train to Paradise*, 258.

The "one-day plan": Graham, *Mr. Flagler's*, 321.

3. *Madness*
The marriage of Harry Flagler was noted in the *New York Times*, April 26, 1894. Flagler wrote to Dr. Anderson on "a breach between the two that had never healed" on August 19, 1896, Anderson Papers.

Flagler to Anderson on Ida Alice's behavior, August 4, 1885, Anderson Papers.

Much of the drama surrounding Flagler's last years with Ida Alice is documented in the records of the "Divorce Proceedings of the Henry M. Flagler Complainant," 7th Judicial Circuit of Dade County.

"Make the best of it," Flagler to Anderson, November 13, 1896, Anderson Papers.

Dr. Du Jardins's detail of Ida Alice's attack on him is found in the divorce proceedings, as are Dr. MacDonald's accounts of her behavior at the sanatorium.

News of Ida Alice's death and the size of her estate was the stuff of headlines nationwide, including those of the *New York Times*, July 14 and July 17, 1930. In his notes, Martin provides an interesting account of the many dependent relatives of the former Ida Alice Shourds maneuvering for a share in the proceeds of her will, *Henry Flagler*, 213–14.

The real estate records and respective locations of the residences of Mrs. Long and Mr. Salter are noted by Graham, *Mr. Flagler's*, 350.

Significant details of Flagler's early relationship with Mary Lily Kenan are found in Martin, *Henry Flagler*, 150–51; and in Chandler, *The Binghams of Louisville*, 42.

For 1897 as the season when tongues began to wag concerning the true nature of the relationship between Mary Lily and Flagler: Martin, *Henry Flagler*, 150.

4. Buying a Legislature

For colorful accounts of Flagler's manipulation of the Florida legislature: Martin, *Henry Flagler*, 146–47; and Graham, *Mr. Flagler's*, 396–98.

On buying off the legislature, Flagler to Joseph Parrott, May 19, 1903, Flagler Papers.

Notes

Laura Rockefeller's note of August 8, 1901, to her husband John D., regarding Flagler's third marriage, is quoted in Chernow's *Titan*, 346. Some might assume the wealthy Flagler had chosen a "trophy wife" for his third, but an account by contemporary Elizabeth Lehr, one of the social arbiters of Newport, suggests otherwise: "Mary Lily was small and frail. Her little oval face was covered with freckles, her big wistful dark eyes were always rather tired . . . No one ever dreamt of calling her anything but plain," Elizabeth Lehr, *King Lehr*, 158.

The estimation of Mary Lily as a well-suited companion for Flagler comes from an interview with her contemporaries Anna Fremd Hadley and Belle Dimick Enos conducted by Martin, *Henry Flagler*, 153.

For details of Flagler's wedding gifts to Mary Lily: Graham, *Mr. Flagler's*, 371–72.

Characterization of Henry Flagler's generosity toward his third wife in the form of a "marble palace": Martin, *Henry Flagler*, 153.

The final cost of Whitehall was reported by the *New York Herald*, March 30, 1902, and passed along by Martin in the original edition of *Henry Flagler (Florida's Flagler)*, 195. Such figures are open to debate, however. Graham, for instance, notes that newspapers of the day referred to the Hotel Ponce de Leon as a "two million dollar hotel" but categorizes attempts to precisely determine such figures as "an exercise in futility," Graham, *Mr. Flagler's*, 160.

The card game of bridge as a new Palm Beach pastime is noted by Graham, *Mr. Flagler's*, 401.

Frederick Townsend Martin's recollections of Flagler are found in *Things I Remember*, 231–34.

5. End of the Line

Details of Flagler's "city building" at Fort Dallas and his construction of the railroad from Miami to Key West are drawn from Standiford, *Last Train,* passim.

Concise accounts of the building of the Oversea Railway are found in Corliss, "Building the Overseas Railway to Key West"; and Willing, "Florida's Overseas Railroad."

The cost of the Key West extension is often pegged at $28 million, though other estimates are as high as $50 million. One of the difficulties of estimating the costs of Flagler's various undertakings is explained by the fact that he used his own money to pay for most of them. He was under no obligation to divulge details to bankers or stockholders.

The anecdote about Flagler mounting eighteen flights of stairs is from Chandler, *Henry Flagler,* 259.

Another account of Flagler's demise has it that Flagler tripped on an Oriental rug in the grand entrance hall and lay undiscovered by a staff decimated by the master's impending move north for the summer. Other contemporary commentators point out that elderly persons often suffer near-spontaneous hip fractures first, and then fall.

For a summary of the clamor following Flagler's fall: Graham, *Mr. Flagler's,* 483.

6. No Second Acts

The landowner's entreaty to burn unsightly structures is found in the *Tropical Sun,* February 13, 1904.

Columnist Eliot Kleinberg's "Styx Burning Legend Just That," citing Reese and others, appears in the *Palm Beach Post,* February 16, 2000, 28, and is updated, "Pioneer's Photos," on June 30, 2016, 8N. The matter is also recounted in Tuckwood and Kleinberg, *Pioneers in Paradise,* 60–61.

The interview with Styx resident Inez Peppers Lovett: Tuckwood and Kleinberg, 45-46.

For Flagler's justification for building upscale hotels in Florida: "Mr. Flagler Talks," *Jacksonville News-Herald*, June 20, 1887, 6.

For details of the proceeds of Flagler's will: Martin, *Henry Flagler*, 196–97.

One such account of Kenan and Vanderbilt on the *Lusitania* appeared in the *Los Angeles Times*, May 11, 1915, 1.

The account of the bogus Mrs. Flagler's exploits is from the *New York Times*, October 22, 1915, 6.

The context of "Help him out" is found in Chandler, *Binghams of Louisville*, 102.

Kenan's quote of Mary Lily's excitement with Bingham is found in Chandler, *Binghams of Louisville*, 105.

The *Palm Beach Life* announcement of Mary Lily's return was made on February 2, 1916.

Mary Lily vouched for Robert Bingham's character in *New York Evening World*, November 3, 1916, 1.

For Flagler-Bingham wedding, "Mrs. Flagler Weds Ex-Judge Bingham," *New York Times*, November 16, 1916, 11.

Chandler traces the doleful final days of Mary Lily's life in *Binghams of Louisville*, 122–30. Ironically, at the time author Chandler was awaiting word as to whether or not his book on the Binghams would be published, he was also awaiting word on an even more unnerving note: he was himself a victim of heart disease, had been given three to six months to live, and had been placed on a transplant recipients' list. Ultimately he was paired with a donor and received a new heart, with which he would live until his death in 1994.

7. *The Baton Passes*

Flagler is elevated to a place alongside the palm trees and alligators by Derr, *Some Kind of Paradise*, 63.

Nothing real to be found in Florida: Roosevelt, *Florida and the Game Water-Birds of the Atlantic*, 9–10.

On musical beds in Palm Beach: Derr, *Some Kind of Paradise*, 44.

An illustrated purview of other-era Palm Beach homes and buildings is found in Marconi, *Palm Beach: Then and Now*, passim.

Eva Stotesbury as "grande dame": Curl, *Mizner's Florida*, 45.

The Ford quote is passed along in "The Stotesburys," *New York Social Diary*.

Eva Stotesbury's riposte regarding her pearls is from Rubin, *American Empress*, 112. Cleveland Amory tells much the same story, though in his version it is a Mrs. Claude K. Boettcher, named one of the "10 best-dressed women of Denver," who, wearing diamonds in public one morning, got her comeuppance from a grande dame of Palm Beach: "Oh no, my dear, you mustn't. One simply doesn't wear diamonds in the daytime." Replied Mrs. Boettcher, "I thought so too, until I had them," Amory, *Last Resorts*, 7.

Mrs. Stotesbury on her business acumen is from Wright, *Heiress*, 80.

Most commentators agree that Paris Singer was named for the city of his birth, perhaps owing to some particularly inspiring impulse connecting the child and the place. On the other hand, his being child number twenty-two suggests there may have been a more utilitarian reason at work.

The story of Singer's proposed gift of Madison Square Garden to Isadora Duncan is recounted in "Jeoffrey's Birthday Variation," *New York Times,* March 25, 1986, 20.

Paris Singer's auspicious arrival on the scene is detailed in "Paris Singer's Real Estate Plans," *Palm Beach Post,* March 31, 1918.

News of the Everglades Club was announced on the front page of the *Palm Beach Post,* May 3, 1918.

On the club's expansion, *Palm Beach Post,* June 8, 1919.

For a reprise of the toast: McPhee, *Giving Good Weight,* 63.

For more on old money and class distinction in America, see McNamee and Miller, *The Meritocracy Myth,* 63 and passim.

8. Gloria in Excelsis

The quotes from old guard dowagers are from Amory, *Who Killed Society?* 3–4, 11, 13.

See old guard vs. café society in Amory, *Who Killed Society?* 131–33.

Mizner reports his initial encounter with Mrs. Stotesbury in the unpublished second volume of his memoir, 45. Her comment to Mizner is also recounted in Seebohm, *Boca Rococo,* 166.

Descriptions of El Mirasol are drawn from stories in the *Palm Beach Post,* January 27, 1920, and March 31, 1923.

Notes

El Mirasol as the standard for subsequent grand homes: Curl, *Mizner's Florida*, 65.

Architect as doctor: Mizner, *The Many Mizners*, 47–48.

Mizner's substitute for air-conditioning is noted in a sales brochure prepared for the estate in later years, Palm Beach Historical Society.

Curl describes the impact and legacy of El Mirasol in *Mizner's Florida*, 67–68.

The size of Mrs. Stotesbury's allowance is put at $12,000 weekly by Wright, *Heiress*, 78. Amory says $12,500 in *Last Resorts*, 359.

Amory quotes Mrs. Stotesbury on the economic aspects of gold bathroom fixtures in *Last Resorts*, 37.

At the time of this writing the Fields film could be streamed at Stotesbury.com/houses/El Mirasol.

Mizner's pearls of wisdom are from Curl, *Mizner's Florida,* 77.

For her account of the Casa Nana legend, see Seebohm, *Boca Rococo*, 176. She cites the interview with Geisler in Orr, *Addison Mizner: Architect of Dreams and Realities*, 24–25.

The description of a typical Mizner workday is from Curl, *Mizner's Florida,* 77–78.

On Mizner's personal residences, see Curl, *Mizner's Florida,* 70.

For her take on the architectural consistency of Palm Beach, see Seebohm, *Boca Rococo*, 176.

Mizner, "the reverse stand," in *The Many Mizners*, 63.

Curl on Mizner's architecture as the rule for Palm Beach, 133.

Architect Little on Mizner's sensitivity to proportion comes from Bubil, "Mizner the Architect: Villain or Visionary?"

For a deft summary of Mizner's widely told efforts in Boca Raton, his late career, and his demise, see Curl, *Mizner's Florida*, 134–204.

9. The Queen Is Dead—Long Live the Queen

The wedding of Marjorie to E. F. Hutton was widely reported on. The *New York Times* account appeared on July 11, 1920, 22.

For a vivid description of Hutridge and its comings and goings, see Rubin, *American Empress*, 123–27. A *New York Times* piece of November 14, 1985, details the property's later years.

Details of the Fifth Avenue penthouse are drawn from the *New York Times* story of September 2, 1962, and from Lisenbee's biography of Post, "Marjorie Merriweather Post."

Marjorie's impatience with the Everglades Club cottage is from Rubin, *American Empress*, 114.

Marjorie's dealings with Wyeth and her decision to build the home of her dreams are detailed by Mayhew, "Mrs. Post's Mar-a-Lago," and in Johnston and Schezen, *Palm Beach Houses*, 290.

Following the decampment of Ned and Marjorie, Hogarcito was sold to and occupied for some twenty years by Franklyn L. Hutton, Ned's brother, along with Franklyn's second wife, Irene, and his daughter from a previous marriage, Barbara Hutton. The last, who would become a sometime confidante of her illustrious aunt, was known as the embodiment of the "poor little rich girl," the result of various high-profile escapades following her inheritance of the $78 million five-and-dime empire bequeathed to her by her grandfather F. W. Woolworth in 1924, when she was twelve.

Wright details Marjorie's forays with realtor Hull, *Heiress*, 87.

For a summary of the burgeoning fortunes of the Postum Cereal Company, see Rubin, *American Empress*, 132, 136.

Urban's mingling of architectural vision and stagecraft is discussed by Aronson, *Architect of Dreams*, 14–15.

News that Urban had taken over the design of the Huttons' new home was reported by the *Palm Beach Post* on May 7 and May 9, 1925.

Wyeth's disavowal of Mar-a-Lago comes from an interview with the *Palm Beach Daily News*, March 16, 1981.

Mar-a-Lago as "tiny Spanish village," *Palm Beach Post*, May 2, 1925.

Curl characterizes Urban's vision for Mar-a-Lago in "Joseph Urban's Palm Beach Architecture," 442 and passim.

10. *Little Cottage by the Sea*

Marjorie's reasoning for keeping the work at Mar-a-Lago going during the "bust" is quoted in Rubin, *American Empress*, 160–61.

Marjorie's lament over having to sell Postum stock is from a letter to her cousin Dolly Morrow of April 5, 1927, quoted by Rubin, *American Empress*, 161.

Curl summarizes the gestation and completion of the Bath and Tennis Club in "Joseph Urban's Palm Beach Architecture," 454–56.

The term "Urbanesque" may well have begun with the *Daily News* and the laudatory stories of December 20 and 24, 1926.

Griffin's description of "the" table is from Chung, *Living Artfully*, 114.

For details on the size of the original staff at Mar-a-Lago, see Wright, *Heiress*, 91.

There are several similar versions of Hutton's summation of the couple's efforts on Mar-a-Lago. This comes from Rubin, *American Empress*, 161.

The *New York Times*, January 20, 1927, 26, covered the wedding of Marjorie's first daughter by Edward Close, as did many other papers.

On Marjorie's commissioning of a cottage for the newlyweds, Rubin, *American Empress*, 173.

The *Times* piece on Mar-a-Lago's first public event appeared on March 2, 1927, 25. The second event was described in a story on March 14, 1927, 14.

The aside from Eva Stotesbury to Marjorie is from Wright, *Heiress*, 79.

Eleanor's comment regarding the Bulgarian prince, along with the characterization of Marjorie's foray to Buckingham Palace, is from Rubin, *American Empress*, 176.

The tale of Marjorie and the acquisition of Birdseye is rendered by Wright, *Heiress*, 89–91; by Rubin, *American Empress*, 138–44; and by the *New York Times*, October 9, 1956, 35.

11. Hard Times
The impact of the Great Depression on the island of Palm Beach is detailed by Mayhew, "Eye on 1930."

Notes

Plans for Barbara Hutton's coming-out party were suggested in "Gotham Girls Plan Bigger, Better Debuts," *Chicago Tribune*, November 17, 1930, 25. The *New York Times* story describing the event ran on December 23, 1930, 30.

Donahue's death was reported on the front page of the *New York Times*, April 23, 1931.

Barbara Hutton described herself as "Daddy's girl" to *Los Angeles Times* reporters, March 24, 1932, 1.

"It's final," *Chicago Daily Tribune*, January 29, 1933, 11.

Franklyn Hutton denies reports of Barbara's impending marriage, *New York Times*, April 17, 1933, 10.

On Franklyn's voyage to Paris, *New York Times*, May 14, 1933, 21.

Most major papers reported on the Barbara Hutton marriage saga. This account of the squabble between Mdivani and his detractors is from the *Chicago Daily Tribune*, June 1, 1933, 7.

Marjorie's advice to her niece is noted in Rubin, *American Empress*, 182.

The matchless description of Barbara Hutton at her fifth marriage is by Phyllis Battelle in a front-page story for the *Milwaukee Sentinel*, December 31, 1953.

Sturges recalls the conversation in his autobiography, *Preston Sturges*, 255.

News of the 1931 *Register*'s publication and its omissions was noted on page 1 of the *Los Angeles Times*, November 26, 1930.

Eleanor's inheritance from C. W. Post, *Chicago Daily Tribune*, December 8, 1930, 22.

Eleanor's filing for an annulment of her marriage to Sturges was detailed in the *New York Times*, May 25, 1932, 15.

For the account of Sturges claiming to barely remember the marriage to Eleanor, see Wright, *Heiress,* 105–6.

The "baby ribbons" interview is recounted by Rubin, *American Empress*, 184.

12. *Sea Change*
The reference to Hutton and the nation "yachting" itself out of the Depression is from Amory, *Last Resorts*, 384.

On the details of Marjorie's accusations to the court, biographer Wright opines: "Her investigations came to a sudden halt one sunny afternoon at Mar-a-Lago when she caught him hard at it with a chambermaid in the bedroom adjoining her own," *Heiress*, 113. Alternatively, Wright's counterpart Nancy Rubin offers this: "On another occasion the heiress again had silken threads positioned at the entrance to E. F.'s bedroom. This time Marjorie ordered her husband's valet to dust the floor of his bedroom with talcum powder and make up his bed with silk sheets. Legend has it—the court records being sealed—that the threads were found broken and two sets of footprints imprinted in the talcum powder on the floor by the bed . . . At last Marjorie had 'proved' E. F.'s infidelity," *American Empress*, 104.

For details of the Mdivani accident, *New York Times*, December 11, 1935, 11.

The *New York Times* detailed the divorce settlement, September 8, 1935, 7. Additional details come from Rubin, *American Empress,* 198.

Notes

Details of Hutton's resignation were reported in the *New York Times*, December 11, 1935, 11.

The quote from eighty-year-old Marjorie is from Rubin, *American Empress*, 205.

For the story of Marjorie's approach to Mrs. Davies, see Wright, *Heiress*, 122–23.

Details of Marjorie's extravaganzas in the Hutton years in Mayhew, "Mrs. Post's Mar-a-Lago."

On Marjorie's attempts to divest herself of the *Sea Cloud*, Wright, *Heiress*, 204–5. Today, anyone with the wherewithal might book passage on the craft with a few keyboard clicks.

From the time of its opening to the present, any event held at Mar-a-Lago has virtually guaranteed a mention in the society pages, or elsewhere, in the *New York Times*. Events mentioned in this passage were noted in the *Times* on January 9, 1940, 30: February 19, 1940, 22; February 28, 1940, 18; April 2, 1940, 30; December 30, 1940, 14; and April 8, 1941, 31.

The mention of Gloria Vanderbilt overshadowing Mr. and Mrs. Davies is from the *Chicago Daily Tribune*, February 1, 1942, H3.

Though it was long before Ms. Vanderbilt became known for her career as an actress, as a fashion designer of note, and for having given birth to newsman Anderson Cooper, she had already come to prominence with herself (and her multimillion-dollar trust fund) the subject of a sensational custody battle between her mother, a scandal-provoking Vanderbilt; and her aunt, Gertrude Vanderbilt Whitney. (Patriarch John Whitney was one of the nation's Puritan founders, and descendant William Collins Whitney, a Gilded Age financier and railroader, made the Klepper and Gunther list at no. 72.) Gloria Vanderbilt's marriage to

DiCicco lasted only until 1945; later Vanderbilt would say that she took up with DiCicco on the rebound from a fling with Howard Hughes. On her wedding night, she said, she took a long bath and waited for DiCicco to join her in the marital bed. When she woke up early that morning she found him still in the living room, playing cards with Zeppo Marx. Things did not get much better. DiCicco regularly beat her up, Gloria said, often pounding her head against the wall and leaving her bruised and black-eyed. All of this is summarized in Higginbotham, "Last of the Big Spenders."

Mayhew details the wartime fortunes of Mar-a-Lago in "Mrs. Post's Mar-a-Lago."

On the unraveling of Marjorie's marriage to Davies, see *Wright, Heiress,* 189. Marjorie's quote is from *Newsweek*, March 21, 1955.

Post's collecting while she was in Russia has come under some scrutiny. In her unpublished 2016 master's thesis, Lindsay Inge gets to the essence of it: "Post's collecting habits reveal not only details about the Soviet art trade and its role in Soviet-American cultural diplomacy, but also speak to the United States' ambivalent attitude towards the Soviet Union in the 1930s: while embracing artifacts of Russian and Orthodox culture, Post essentially ignored the destructive Soviet policies that made these artifacts available for purchase," "Culture and Diplomacy," 3.

For details of the Red Cross Ball, Chung, *Living Artfully*, 123.

Recounting the demise of Marjorie's marriage to May: Wright, *Heiress*, 208–10.

The comment on the timing of things at Marjorie's square dance gatherings was part of her obituary in the *Miami Herald*, September 13, 1973, 3.

Rose Kennedy is quoted by Mayhew in "Mrs. Post's Mar-a-Lago."

The Dudleys' reminiscences are quoted by Chung, *Living Artfully*, 111.

Marjorie as "housemother," Chung, *Living Artfully*, 120.

All attributions to Anthony Senecal are derived from an interview with the author, October 19, 2018.

Marjorie's intentions for Hillwood were reported in the *New York Times*, May 26, 1966, 52.

Details of the staffing at Mar-a-Lago are from Johnston and Schezen, *Palm Beach Houses*, 103–4.

For her account of Marjorie's dealings with Bryant, see Rubin, *American Empress*, 359.

The alternative account of the state of Florida's interest in Mar-a-Lago is from Cheshire, "The Post Mansion Dilemma."

A certain onus was never to leave La Querida. The beach behind the Kennedy Compound, at 1113 North Ocean Boulevard, was the site where Patricia Bowman alleged that she was raped by Ted Kennedy's nephew William Kennedy Smith on March 30, 1999.

13. A Place in Readiness

Mrs. Stotesbury's allowance and Palm Beach as remarkable island of privilege: Amory, *Last Resorts*, 357, 359.

For the source of the demographic statistics for Palm Beach, Broomell, "Descriptive Name," *New York Times*.

Notes

Teaching rich Americans how to live, Johnston and Schezen, *Palm Beach Houses*, 11.

On Via Mizner: Johnston and Schezen, *Palm Beach Houses*, 16–17; Curl, *Mizner's Florida*, 112–13.

On the Paramount Theater, Nelander, "Theater," *Palm Beach Daily News*, December 15, 2017.

Second generation of Palm Beach architects: Johnston and Schezen, *Palm Beach Houses*, 19–21.

Mayhew dates the construction of Gemini, in "Sotheby's Previews, Wellington's Jumpers, Manalapan's Memories," *Palm Beach Social Diary*, January 31, 2017.

On Whitehall's languishing, "The Bust," *Palm Beach County History Online*.

On Whitehall Hotel's opening, *Palm Beach Post*, December 31, 1926.

Whitehall Hotel a $4 million structure, Federal Writers' Project, *Florida: A Guide*, 232.

Jean Flagler Matthews quoted by Chandler, *Henry Flagler*, 266–67.

On the estimate of Ms. Matthews's fortune, Mayhew, "Oil Swells."

On the establishment of the Henry Morrison Flagler Museum, C. E. W., "Flagler Museum Adds to Gilt," *New York Times*, January 22, 1961.

14. House Without a Home

Cheshire's 1968 story in the *Los Angeles Times* suggested that Palm Beach County officials floated to Marjorie the idea of approaching

Kennedy with the notion of much grander digs on the island. The *Miami Herald* reported the news that Mrs. Johnson had accepted Marjorie's invitation to tour the estate, April 9, 1968, 8.

By this time, the *Miami Herald*, which operated a Palm Beach bureau, had become the virtual paper of record for all things Mar-a-Lago. The rumors were reported in a story of April 16, 1968, 14.

Marjorie's supposed plans for another marriage were reported in the *Miami Herald*'s Suzy Sez column, May 11, 1968, 11.

"empress of Palm Beach": *Miami Herald* April 1, 1969, 28.

Publix and other threats to the island's image of exclusivity were the subject of Hearn, "Growing Pains in Palm Beach," *New York Times*, December 6, 1970.

News of the acceptance bill's introduction came in the *Miami Herald*, January 8, 1972, 26.

Councilman Grace's comments, constituting the first public evidence of local opposition to Marjorie's plans, were reported by the *Herald*, May 2, 1972, 3.

The *Herald* followed the progress of the bill closely: October 14, 1972, 6; and October 25, 1972, 3/4.

Life inside Mar-a-Lago with Mrs. Post at eighty-five was detailed by Van Howe, "The Mansion That Couldn't Be Given Away," passim.

The *Herald* reported on Mrs. Post's hospitalization, February 27, 1973, 4.

The *Herald*'s was a lengthy obituary, September 13, 1973, 3–4. Ms.

Whitmore's comments were included in a story of September 26, 1973, 3-B.

Waindel's comments were reported in the *Miami Herald*, September 18, 1973.

The Nixon-Rebozo trip was reported in the *Miami Herald*, July 8, 1974, 2.

By this time, the *Herald* was devoting detailed attention to the fate of Mar-a-Lago. The interview with Cadieux was included in Fiedler's lengthy piece, "Estate's Too Costly."

Park Service plans to ask Congress to return the property were reported in the *Herald*, March 5, 1975, 4.

Details of the Civic Association letter to President Ford were reported by the *Herald*, March 19, 1975, 3.

"racing through a Rembrandt": *Miami Herald*, February 19, 1979.

Rogers's opposition to the government's involvement in Mar-a-Lago was detailed by the *Herald* in stories of June 10, 1977, 3; September 15, 1977, 3–4; and May 19, 1978, 4.

Details of the cost to maintain the property were reported by the *Herald*, August 1, 1980, 4.

Details regarding the passage of the bill reverting Mar-a-Lago to private ownership were reported in the *Herald*, December 6, 1980, 3.

The sheikh's visit to Palm Beach, *Miami Herald*, February 5, 1981, 3.

Rogers's purchase was reported on by the *Miami Herald*, April 23, 1981, 1.

Word of a possible subdivision of the property was first reported in the *Herald*, June 29, 1981, 30.

News of "three serious contenders" was reported by the *Herald*, January 27, 1983, 1B.

The lament on the demise of the season is from the *Herald*, April 24, 1974, 42.

Plans to identify the whole of the Worth Avenue shopping complex as a historic district were reported by the *Herald*, January 30, 1983, 1B.

Amory is quoted by Skonsky, "Palm Beach: Where Society Still Treads."

On volunteer firemen searching for nickels, Kleinberg, "Royal Poinciana Flagler's 1st Hotel; Breakers Twice Destroyed." The story is also recounted in Tuckwood and Kleinberg, *Pioneers in Paradise*, 58.

On the third incarnation of the Breakers, "New Hotel to Rise on Breakers Site," *New York Times*, March 23, 1925, 19.

The extent of the season noted in the *New York Times*, "Palm Beach Shifts to Year-Round Schedule," November 6, 1960, XX9.

Return of the Breakers to the Kenans, "Breakers Hotel 'Pressure' Denied," *New York Times*, August 15, 1944, 14.

B'nai B'rith charges, "Discrimination Laid to Hotel in Florida," *New York Times*, March 13, 1965, 19.

Pledge from the Breakers: Pearson, "Military to Go Over Johnson's Head," *Los Angeles Times*, February 2, 1966, A6.

Stories on the languishing of Mar-a-Lago ran in the *Miami Herald*, March 1, 1983, 1; and March 17, 1983, 1C.

Frank Kenan's remarks are from Perkins, "Rich Boy Makes Good."

The saga of "Prince" Robert Ewing ran in the *Miami Herald*, September 16, 1983, 1-B.

News of the reputed sale was carried on the front page of the *Miami Herald*, January 8, 1984.

Frederick's comments were reported by the UPI News Track, February 13, 1984.

Stories on the deal's demise ran in the *Miami Herald*, March 26, 1984, 1-C, and May 5, 1984, 8A; and in the UPI News Track, May 5, 1984.

The tax figures were reported in the *Miami Herald* on December 12, 1972, 3; and August 19, 1984, 10D.

The *Miami Herald* reported the Ross deal on August 23, 1984, 8A.

The enduring appeal of the Breakers: *Wall Street Journal*, November 6, 1984, 29.

News of Ross jumping the gun was carried by the *Herald*, January 24, 1985, 21A.

Details of the approval of the Palm Beach Town Council for Ross's deal were reported in the *Miami Herald*, March 12 and March 13, 1985, 2-PB and 6-PB.

The rumors of Ross's change of plan were front-page news in the *Herald*, June 29, 1985; a follow-up story ran on September 11, 1985, 3C.

The *Miami Herald* reported Trump's entry onto the scene on October 11, 1985, 7C.

15. Angel from America

The $10 million figure was reported by the *Miami Herald*, January 3, 1986, 1.

The 2015 version of Trump's attempts to purchase Mar-a-Lago is from Jordan and Helderman, "Inside Trump's Palm Beach Castle."

Trump's characterization of Marjorie Merriweather Post, *Sun-Sentinel*, March 8, 1986, 1B.

The tax assessment figures for 1986 and related details, *Sun-Sentinel*, October 19, 1986, 1B.

Trump's joustings regarding the 1986 tax bill, *Sun-Sentinel*, April 9, 1987, 3B.

Trump's suggestion that the airport might be moved, *Miami Herald*, February 7, 1988, 7B.

Details of the trial on the tax matter, *Sun-Sentinel*, March 30, 1988, 1B.

Details of the judge's verdict, *Miami Herald*, April 9, 1988, 1D.

Tax assessments of Mar-a-Lago for 1987, 1988, *Sun-Sentinel*, September 9, 1988, 1B.

Mortgage with Boston Safe Deposit and Trust, *Miami Herald*, October 2, 1988, 22H.

Trump's out-of-pocket costs for Mar-a-Lago, *Miami Herald*, November 9, 1988, 1A.

Reports on Trump's impending divorce, *Providence Journal*, February 14, 1990, C1.

Plans to dump Mar-a-Lago, *Palm Beach Post*, June 5, 1990, 1A.

Account of Trump's real estate leveraging practices, *Pittsburgh Post-Gazette*, June 22, 1990, D6.

Trump's agreement with his creditors: Harkas, "Mar-a-Lago." *Sun-Sentinel*, July 3, 1990.

Boston Safe's restructuring of its loan: *Palm Beach Post*, September 6, 1990, 6B.

Mar-a-Lago as "best private residence," in Carlson, "Donald Digs Out," *Miami Herald*, November 4, 1990.

Ivana's restraining order was reported by the *Miami Herald*, November 23, 1990, 2A.

Trump's plans to subdivide Mar-a-Lago: Bradbery, "Trump Seeks to Subdivide," *Palm Beach Post*, February 18, 1991.

Casa Apava development and Trump's resolve to hold on, *San Francisco Chronicle*, April 3, 1991, B6.

Curl opposing subdivision, *Palm Beach Post*, August 7, 1991, 1B.

Town landmarks commission rejects subdivision, *Palm Beach Post*, October 9, 1991, 12B.

Zoning commission rejects subdivision, *Palm Beach Post*, December 4, 1991, 1B.

Trump's $50 million suit filed, *Palm Beach Post*, July 7, 1992, 1A.

Trump "in no mood to settle," etc., *Palm Beach Post*, November 6, 1992, 7B.

Trump on the benefits of turning Mar-a-Lago into a club, *Miami Herald*, November 10, 92, 1B.

Rampell's move to settle Trump's $50 million suit against Palm Beach, *Palm Beach Post*, May 14, 1993, 1A.

Town council's agreement on conversion of Mar-a-Lago to a private club, *Palm Beach Post*, June 4, 1993, 1A.

16. *Never Say Ever*
Details of the Grace-Callahan suit, *Palm Beach Post*, October 9, 1993, 2B.

Boston Safe Deposit and Trust's objections to the club concept, *Palm Beach Post*, October 13, 1993, 1B.

Resolution of the Boston Safe Deposit and Trust dispute, *Palm Beach Post*, August 23, 1994, 4B.

Initiation fees and dues announced, *Palm Beach Post*, September 9, 1994, 1D.

Julio Iglesias serenades Marla Maples, *Sun-Sentinel*, October 30, 1994, 2A.

Celebrity member list announced, *Palm Beach Post*, December 12, 1994, 1D.

Notes

Prince Charles and Lady Di as "members," *Palm Beach Post*, December 27, 1994, 1B.

Trump's clarification of the membership "list," *Sun-Sentinel*, January 7, 1995, 2A.

Announcement of the agreement with the National Trust for Historic Preservation, *Miami Herald*, March 28, 1995, 1B.

The *Palm Beach Post* story of 2017 regarding the "preservation easement" was by Stapleton and Mower, December 24, 2017.

The opening of Mar-a-Lago as a club, *Sun-Sentinel*, April 23, 1995, 3B; *Palm Beach Post*, April 24, 1995, 1D.

Trump on a "refund" for Visconti, *Palm Beach Post*, December 9, 1995, 1B.

Initiation fees at $150,000, *Palm Beach Daily News*, August 24, 2003, A1.

Details of the lease for county property for the building of Trump International Golf Club, *Palm Beach Post*, September 4, 1996, 3B.

Improvements to Mar-a-Lago, the "horizontal rhumba," and the flagpole contretemps, *Palm Beach Daily News*, December 27, 2009, 1A.

"I'm a Jew." Interview with the author (subject's name withheld), March 2, 2018, Mar-a-Lago Club.

The "place" of Mar-a-Lago among private clubs is discussed in Grantham, "The Private Clubs of Palm Beach."

The case of the missing hand: Interview with the author (subject's name withheld), March 2, 2018, Mar-a-Lago. Close inspection reveals that there is indeed something off-kilter about the subject's left hand, but exactly what might account for that may ever be shrouded in mystery. Those interested in other accounts might wish to visit the Wiki entry for *The Visionary.*

Cost to taxpayers for a Trump visit to Palm Beach is in Calfas, "Palm Beach Is Sick of Paying for Donald Trump's Visits," *Money.*

Current valuation of Mar-a-Lago is from Peterson-Withorn, "Trump Has Gained More Than $100 Million on Mar-a-Lago," *Forbes.*

17. What Remains
Mohatt and Orians are quoted in Gallagher, *The Power of Place*, 205 and 219 respectively.

A thoroughgoing compendium of Palm Beach scandal, past and present, is found in Weiss and Hoffman, *Palm Beach Babylon*, passim.

Madoff's impact on Palm Beach, Segal, "Poor in Palm Beach," *New York Times,* April 12, 2009.

Madoff's impact on giving, John Blades, interview with the author, October 17, 2018.

Sampling the large life in Palm Beach, Rose, *Palm Beach: The Essential Guide.*

Details of Breakers operations are from an interview with CEO Leone, November 2018.

A visit to Expedia at the time of this book's writing suggested that the cost of a midweek stay at the Breakers in January 2019 began at $1,050 per night.

SELECTED BIBLIOGRAPHY

Books—

Amory, Cleveland. *Who Killed Society?* New York: Harper and Brothers, 1960.

———. *The Last Resorts.* New York: Harper and Brothers, 1952.

Aronson, Arnold. *Architect of Dreams: The Theatrical Vision of Joseph Urban.* New York: Columbia University Libraries, 2000.

Bramson, Seth. *Speedway to Sunshine: The Story of the Florida East Coast Railway.* Erin, Ontario: Boston Mills Press, 2003.

Chandler, David Leon. *The Binghams of Louisville: The Dark History Behind One of America's Great Fortunes.* New York: Crown, 1987.

———. *Henry Flagler: The Astonishing Life and Times of the Visionary Robber Baron Who Founded Florida.* New York: Macmillan, 1986.

Chernow, Ron. *Titan: The Life of John D. Rockefeller, Sr.* New York: Vintage, 1998.

Chung, Estella M. *Living Artfully: At Home with Marjorie Merriweather Post.* London: D. Giles, 2013.

Curl, Donald W. *Mizner's Florida: American Resort Architecture.* New York: Architectural History Foundation; Cambridge, MA, and London, England: MIT Press, 1984.

Derr, Mark. *Some Kind of Paradise: A Chronicle of Man and the Land in Florida*. New York: Morrow, 1989.

Dickinson, Jonathan. *Jonathan Dickinson's Journal or, God's Protecting Providence*. Evangeline Walker Andrews and Charles McLean Andrews, eds. New Haven: Yale, 1945.

Eddy, Mary Baker. *Science and Health with Key to the Scriptures*. Boston: Mary Baker Eddy Foundation, 1986.

Federal Writers' Project. *Florida: A Guide to the Southernmost State*. New York: Oxford University Press, 1939.

Florida East Coast Railway. *The Story of a Pioneer: A Brief History of the Florida East Coast Railway and Its Part in the Remarkable Development of the Florida East Coast*. St. Augustine, FL: Record, 1946.

Gallagher, Winifred. *The Power of Place: How Our Surroundings Shape Our Thoughts, Emotions, and Actions*, New York: Poseidon Press, 1993.

Gannon, Michael. *Florida: A Short History*. Gainesville: University Press of Florida, 1993.

Graham, Thomas. *Mr. Flagler's St. Augustine*. Gainesville: University Press of Florida, 2014.

Graham, Thomas, and Leslee F. Keys. *Hotel Ponce de Leon: The Architecture and Decoration*. St. Augustine, FL: Flagler College, 2013.

Johnston, Shirley (text), and Roberto Schezen (photos). *Palm Beach Houses*. Secaucus, NJ: Rizzoli, 1991.

Kessler, Ronald. *The Season: Inside Palm Beach and America's Richest Society*. New York: HarperCollins, 1999.

Klepper, Michael, and Robert Gunther. *The Wealthy 100: From Benjamin Franklin to Bill Gates—A Ranking of the Richest Americans, Past and Present*. Secaucus, NJ: Carroll, 1996.

Lehr, Elizabeth Drexel. *King Lehr and the Gilded Age*. Philadelphia: Lippincott, 1935.

Marconi, Richard A. *Palm Beach: Then and Now*. Charleston, SC: Arcadia, 2013.

Martin, Frederick Townsend. *Things I Remember*. London: Eveleigh Nash, 1913.

Martin, Sidney Walter. *Henry Flagler: Visionary of the Gilded Age*. Lake Buena Vista, FL: Tailored Tour Publications, 1998.

———. *Florida's Flagler*. Athens: University of Georgia, 1949.

McNamee, Stephan J., and Robert K. Miller. *The Meritocracy Myth*. Lanham, MD: Rowman and Littlefield, 2004.

McPhee, John. *Giving Good Weight*. New York: Farrar, Straus and Giroux, 1979.

Mizner, Addison. *The Many Mizners*. New York: Sears Publishing, 1932.

Orr, Christina. *Addison Mizner: Architect of Dreams and Realities (1872–1933)*. Palm Beach: Norton Gallery and School of Art, 1977.

Rockefeller, John D. *Random Reminiscences of Men and Events*. New York: Doubleday, 1909.

Roosevelt, Robert Barnwell. *Florida and the Game Water-Birds of the Atlantic Coast and the Lakes of the United States*. New York: Orange Judd, 1884.

Rose, Rick. *Palm Beach: The Essential Guide to America's Legendary Resort Town*. Guilford, CT: Globe Pequot, 2017.

Rubin, Nancy. *American Empress: The Life and Times of Marjorie Merriweather Post*. Lincoln, NE: iUniverse Star, 2004.

Seebohm, Caroline. *Boca Rococo: How Addison Mizner Invented Florida's Gold Coast*. New York: Clarkson Potter, 2001.

Standiford, Les. *Last Train to Paradise: Henry Flagler and the Spectacular Rise and Fall of the Railroad That Crossed an Ocean*. New York: Crown, 2002.

Sturges, Preston. *Preston Sturges by Preston Sturges: His Life in Words*. Sandy Sturges, ed. New York: Simon and Schuster, 1990.

Tuckwood, Jan, and Eliot Kleinberg. *Pioneers in Paradise: West Palm Beach the First 110 Years*. Athens, GA: Longstreet, 1994.

Weiss, Murray, and Bill Hoffman. *Palm Beach Babylon: Sins, Scams and Scandals*. New York: Birch Lane Press, 1992.

Wright, William. *Heiress: The Rich Life of Marjorie Merriweather Post*. Washington, DC: New Republic Books, 1978.

Articles—

Bailey, James A., and Thomas K. Resk. "The Mysterious Death of America's Richest Woman in 1917, Mary Lil' (RIP)," *Forensic Science, Medicine, and Pathology* 4 (2008), 55–59.

Battelle, Phyllis. "Dazed Bride Wears Black, Carries Soda and Scotch at Spanish Ceremony," *Milwaukee Sentinel*, December 31, 1953.

Bradbery, Angela. "Trump Seeks to Subdivide Mar-a-Lago," *Palm Beach Post*, February 18, 1991.

Broomell, Sally. "Descriptive Name: Palm Beach Acquired Its by Accident, Just the Way It Got Its Trees," *New York Times*, November 13, 1960.

Browne, Jefferson B. "Across the Gulf by Rail to Key West," *National Geographic* 7 (1896): 203–7.

Bubil, Harold. "Mizner the Architect: Villain or Visionary?" *Sarasota Herald Tribune*, January 27, 2008.

C. E. W. "Flagler Museum Adds to Gilt of Palm Beach," *New York Times*, January 22, 1961.

Calfas, Jennifer. "Palm Beach Is Sick of Paying for Donald Trump's Weekend Visits to Mar-a-Lago," *Money*, March 16, 2017.

Caputo, Marc. "Trump Dubs Mar-a-Lago the New 'Winter White House,'" *Politico/PoliticoFlorida*, January 18, 2017.

Carlson, Gus. "Donald Digs Out," *Miami Herald*, November 4, 1990.

Cheshire, Maxine. "The Post Mansion Dilemma," *Los Angeles Times*, October 16, 1968.

Corliss, Carlton J. "Building the Overseas Railway to Key West," *Tequesta* 13 (1953): 3–21.

Costello, David J. "Boynton's Indian Mounds," *Pages from Boynton Beach History*, www.boyntonbeach.com/history/indians.

Curl, Donald W. "Joseph Urban's Palm Beach Architecture," *Florida Historical Quarterly* 71, no. 4 (April 1993): 436–57.

Dangremond, Sam. "A History of Mar-a-Lago, Donald Trump's American Castle," *Town and Country*, December 22, 2017.

Dimick, Ella J. "Transportation from 1876 to 1896: Reprinted from the *Lake Worth Historian*, 1896," *Tustenegee* 5, no. 12 (August 31, 2014): 10–13.

Fiedler, Tom. "Estate's Too Costly, Dangerous for Use," *Miami Herald*, July 14, 1974.

Flagler, Henry. "My Domain," *Tattler* 6, no. 4 (February 6, 1897): 2.

Glover, F. H. "The Greatest Men of Florida," *Suniland: The Magazine of Florida* 1, no. 5 (February 1925): 36–39.

Grantham, Loretta. "The Private Clubs of Palm Beach," *Palm Beach Post*, June 5, 1999.

Gunther, Robert. "An Astor Ball for All Time: How We Chose the Richest Americans," *American Heritage* 49, no. 6 (1998).

Harkas, Margo. "Mar-a-Lago on $450,000 a Month," *Sun-Sentinel*, July 3, 1990.

Hearn, George L. "Growing Pains in Palm Beach," *New York Times*, December 6, 1970.

Higginbotham, Adam. "Last of the Big Spenders," *Telegraph*, November 23, 2004.

Jordan, Mary, and Rosalind S. Helderman. "Inside Trump's Palm Beach Castle and His 30-Year Fight to Win Over the Locals," *Washington Post*, November 14, 2015.

Kleinberg, Eliot. "Pioneer's Photos Give Glimpse of Palm Beach's Mysterious Styx," *Palm Beach Post*, June 30, 2016.

———. "A Bounty of Sidetracked Coconuts at the Root of Palm Beach's Name," *Palm Beach Post*, April 18, 2001.

———. "Royal Poinciana Flagler's 1st Hotel: Breakers Twice Destroyed," *Palm Beach Post*, March 22, 2000.

———. "Styx Burning Legend Just That," *Palm Beach Post*, February 16, 2000.

Major, Howard. "Small Buildings: A Theory Relating to Spanish and Italian Houses in Florida," *Architectural Forum* 45 (August 1926): 97–104.

Marchman, Watt P. "The Ingraham Everglades Exploring Expedition, 1892," *Tequesta* 7 (1947): 3–43.

Mayhew, Augustus. "Mrs. Post's Mar-a-Lago," *New York Social Diary*, February 7, 2017.

———. "Sotheby's Previews, Wellington's Jumpers, Manalapan's Memories," *Palm Beach Social Diary*, January 31, 2017.

———. "Eye on 1930: Palm Beach 'Enjoying One of Its Largest Seasons,'" *Palm Beach Daily News*, February 20, 2011.

———. "Oil Swells: The Standard Oil Crowd in Palm Beach," *New York Social Diary*, November 30, 2010.

Nelander, John. "Theater Once Drew Giants in Entertainment," *Palm Beach Daily News*, December 15, 2017.

"Palm Beach, a Period Island in Florida," *China Daily*, April 10, 2017.

Pearson, Drew. "Military to Go Over Johnson's Head," *Los Angeles Times*, February 2, 1966.

Perkins, David. "Rich Boy Makes Good," *Business, North Carolina: Charlotte* 10, no. 4 (April 1990): 44.

Peterson-Withorn, Chase. "Donald Trump Has Gained More Than $100 Million on Mar-a-Lago," *Forbes*, April 23, 2018.

Segal, David. "Poor in Palm Beach. It's Relative," *New York Times*, April 12, 2009.

Skonsky, Steve. "Palm Beach: Where Society Still Treads," *Miami Herald*, January 2, 1977.

Stapleton, Christine, and Lawrence Mower. "Mar-a-Lago Tax Deal Veiled from IRS Review," *Palm Beach Post*, December 24, 2017.

"The Stotesburys," *New York Social Diary*, January 27, 2010.

Van Howe, Tom, "The Mansion That Couldn't Be Given Away," *Miami Tropic*, November 19, 1972, 26–44.

Willing, David L. "Florida's Overseas Railroad," *Florida Historical Quarterly* 35, no. 4 (April 1957): 287–302.

Newspapers and Magazines—

Associated Press	*Norfolk Virginian-Pilot*
China Daily (US)	*Palm Beach Daily News*
Chicago Daily News	*Palm Beach Post*
Chicago Tribune	*Pittsburgh Post-Gazette*
Kansas City Star	*Providence Journal*
Los Angeles Times	*San Francisco Chronicle*
Miami Herald	*Sarasota Herald-Tribune*
Milwaukee Sentinel	*South Florida/Ft. Lauderdale Sun-Sentinel*
New York Evening World	
New York Times	*Wall Street Journal*
Newsweek	*Washington Post*

Interviews—

Bernstein, Richard. Palm Beach, March 2018.

Blades, John. Palm Beach, various, March 2018, October 2018.

Fox, William J. Bath and Tennis Club, March 2018.

Leone, Paul. CEO-Flagler System, November 2018.

Name withheld. Mar-a-Lago Club, March 2018.

Senecal, Anthony. Palm Beach, October 2018.

Other—

Anderson, Andrew. Papers, St. Augustine Historical Society, St. Augustine, FL.

Brevard County Records, 7th Circuit Court, March 30, 1909, no. 70, bk. 2, 403.

Divorce Proceedings of the Henry M. Flagler Complainant vs. Ida A. Flagler Defendant, Divorce Case. Circuit Court, 7th Judicial Circuit of Florida, in and for Dade County.

Dr. Bronson's St. Augustine History, https://bronsondrbronsonstaughistory.wordpress.com/2011/12/15/dr-bronsons-st-augustine-history/.

El Mirasol Sales Brochure, n.d. Mizner Collection, Historical Society of Palm Beach County.

Flagler, Henry M. Papers, Henry Morrison Flagler Museum, Palm Beach, FL.

Florida Census Records.

Inge, Lindsay T. "Culture and Diplomacy: Marjorie Merriweather Post and Soviet-American Relations, 1933–1939," unpublished master's thesis, University of Maryland, 2016.

Lisenbee, Kenneth. "Marjorie Merriweather Post: A Biography," www.PaulBowles.org//marjoriemerriweatherpost.html.

Mizner, Addison. Unpublished memoir typescript, Mizner Collection, Historical Society of Palm Beach County.

Palm Beach County History Online.

www.Stotesbury.com.

United States Historical Census.

INDEX

Index

Index

IMAGE CREDITS

Image credits for the insert section are as follows: Image 1.1: Library of Congress, Geography and Map Division. Image 1.2: University of Michigan Library Digital Collections, Bentley Image Bank, Bentley Historical Library. Item number HS13908. Image 1.3: Courtesy of Sea Cloud Cruises GmbH. Images 2.1 and 2.2: Courtesy of the Flagler Museum Archives, Palm Beach, Florida. Image 3.1: Beinecke Rare Book and Manuscript Library, Yale University, via Wikimedia Commons. Image 3.2: Historic American Buildings Survey (HABS) FLA, 50-PALM, 11--3. Library of Congress Prints and Photographs Division. Image 4.1: Courtesy of the Florida Historical Society, Library of Florida History, Photographic Collection, Palm Beach County, Box 1, Folder 6. Image 4.2: Courtesy of the State Archives of Florida. Image 5.1: Historic American Buildings Survey (HABS) FLA, 50-PALM, 12--10. Library of Congress Prints and Photographs Division. Image 5.2: Courtesy of Boca Raton Historical Society & Museum. Image 6.1: Joseph Urban Collection, Box 29 Folder 8, Rare Book and Manuscript Library, Columbia University. Image 6.2: Historic American Buildings Survey. Library of Congress Prints and Photographs Division. Image 7.1: C.M. Stieglitz for the New York World-Telegram. Library of Congress Prints and Photographs Division. Image 7.2: University of Michigan Library Digital Collections, Bentley Image Bank, Bentley Historical Library. Item Number HS15428. Image 8.1: © Christopher Ziemnowicz, via Wikimedia Commons. Image 8.2: Courtesy of Anthony Senecal. Image 8.3: © Christopher Ziemnowicz, via Wikimedia Commons.

Credits for the images running throughout the text are as follows. Frontispiece: Historical American Buildings Survey (HABS) FLA, 50-PALM, 1-39. Library of Congress, Prints and Photographs Division. Page 23: University of Michigan Library Digital Collections. Bentley Image Bank, Bentley Historical Library. Item number BL000127. Page 37: State Library and Archives of Florida. Page 48: State Library and Archives of Florida. Page 54: State Library and Archives of Florida. Page 58: Florida Park Service Collection. Series 236, Box 4, FF52. State Library and Archives of Florida. Page 71: Courtesy of the Flagler College Archives, Proctor Library, Flagler College, St. Augustine, FL. Copyright Flagler College, St. Augustine, Florida. Page 74: Courtesy of the Flagler College Archives, Proctor Library, Flagler College, St. Augustine, FL. Copyright Flagler College, St. Augustine, Florida. Page 95: Library of Congress, Prints & Photographs Division, photograph by Harris & Ewing, LC-DIG-hec-23289. Page 108a: Library of Congress, Prints & Photographs Division, George Grantham Bain Collection, LC-B2- 4879-9. Page 108b: Library of Congress, Prints & Photographs Division, George Grantham Bain Collection, LC-B2- 737-1. Page 111: State Library and Archives of Florida. Page 122: State Library and Archives of Florida. Page 133: University of Michigan Library Digital Collections. Bentley Image Bank, Bentley Historical Library. Item number HS14330. Page 145: Library of Congress, Prints & Photographs Division, George Grantham Bain Collection, LC-B2- 3821-1. Page 154: Library of Congress, Prints & Photographs Division, HABS [or HAER or HALS], HABS FLA, 50-PALM,1--28. Page 159: Wikimedia Commons. Page 181: State Library and Archives of Florida. Page 201: State Library and Archives of Florida. Page 249: Photographed by Shealah Craighead. Official White House Photo via Wikimedia Commons. Page 256: Photo by Michael Kagdis for Proper Media Group via Wikimedia Commons.